2006 SUPPLEMENT TO

THE LAW OF BIOETHICS: INDIVIDUAL AUTONOMY AND SOCIAL REGULATION

By

Marsha Garrison
Professor of Law
Brooklyn Law School

Carl E. Schneider
Chauncey Stillman Professor of Law and
Professor of Internal Medicine
University of Michigan

AMERICAN CASEBOOK SERIES®

Mat #40391351

Thomson/West have created this publication to provide you with accurate and authoritative information concerning the subject matter covered. However, this publication was not necessarily prepared by persons licensed to practice law in a particular jurisdiction. Thomson/West are not engaged in rendering legal or other professional advice, and this publication is not a substitute for the advice of an attorney. If you require legal or other expert advice, you should seek the services of a competent attorney or other professional.

American Casebook Series and West Group are trademarks registered in the U.S. Patent and Trademark Office.

© 2006 Thomson/West
      610 Opperman Drive
      P.O. Box 64526
      St. Paul, MN 55164–0526
      1–800–328–9352

Printed in the United States of America

ISBN–13: 978–0–314–16255–7
ISBN–10: 0–314–16255–0

TABLE OF CONTENTS

Page

Chapter 1. The Principle of Autonomy: The Example of Informed Consent 1
1. The Doctrine of Informed Consent 1
   - C. Mandated Disclosure in Informed Consent 10
     1. Mandated Disclosure as a Method of Legal Regulation 10
     2. Informed Consent for Lawyers: Why the Difference? 15
2. Vindicating Patients' Autonomy 19
3. Patients' Autonomy and Patients' Health 21
4. Is Informed Consent Effective? Regulating Medical Practice 24
6. Doctor and Patient in Context: The Problem of Confidentiality 25
   - A. Confidentiality as Privilege and Duty: Testimonial Privileges 26
     - *Jaffee v. Redmond* 26
     - Notes on Privacy 40
     - Notes on Private Remedies for Breaches of Confidentiality 43
     - Notes and Questions on Jaffee, Privacy, and Privilege 46
   - B. Confidentiality as Privilege and Duty: The Duty to Warn 51
     - *Tarasoff v. Regents of the University of California* . 51
     - *A Note on the Subsequent History of Tarasoff* 57
     - Notes and Questions on the Rationale of Tarasoff . 58
     - Notes and Questions on Tarasoff as Precedent ... 64
     - Notes and Questions on Confidentiality and Lawyers 74
   - C. The National Administrative Regulation of Privacy: HIPAA 80
     - *HHS Regulations Issued on the Authority of the Health Insurance Portability and Accountability Act* 80
     - *42 U.S.C. § 1320(d)(5)* 102
     - *42 U.S.C. § 1320(d)(6)* 103

    Northwestern Memorial Hospital v. Ashcroft 104
    Notes and Questions on Life After HIPAA 113
    A Modest HIPAA Problem 115
  D. Confidentiality and the Innocent Bystander 120

Chapter 2. The Principle of Autonomy: Law at the End of Life 127
2. Stopping 127
    The Case of Harold Shipman 127

Chapter 3. Killing 136
1. An Introductory Problem: The Case of Diane 136
3. Assisted Suicide as a Right 136
    3. The Pain of Death and the Death of Pain 136
    Hoover v. Agency for Health Care Administration . 141
    Amy J. Dilcher, Damned If They Do, Damned If They Don't 148
    2. The Institutional Question Revisited: Drugs, Death, and Federalism 152
    Conant v. Walters 155
    Pearson v. McCaffrey 160
    Notes and Questions on Conant and Pearson . . . 162
    Gonzales v. Raich 165
    Notes and Questions on Gonzales v. Raich 179
    Oregon v. Ashcroft 179
    Notes and Questions on Gonzales v. Oregon 196

Chapter 4. Deciding for Others: Autonomy or Beneficence? 197
2. Formerly Competent Patients: Who Should Decide? What Standards Should Govern? 197
    In Re Schiavo 197
    Notes and Questions 202
  D. Treatment for Mental Illness: A Special Case? . . . 206
3. Patients with Future Competence: Making Medical Decisions for Children 209
  B. Parents' Rights and Children's Interests 209
  D. The Newborn 210
    John M. Freeman, On Learning Humility, A Thirty-Year Journey 210
5. The Participation of Mentally Incapacitated Patients In

　　　　Medical Research 214

Chapter 5.　The Body as Commodity **216**
2.　My Body, My Property? 216
3.　Transferring the Body 218
　　B.　Transfers After Death 218
4.　Increasing the Supply of Organs for Transplantation 223
　　A.　Transplantable Organs: The Imbalance Between
　　　　Supply and Demand 223

Chapter 6.　Reproduction and Birth **226**
1.　Maternal-Fetal Conflict 226
2.　Choosing Our Children 228
3.　Technological Conception 230
　　A.　The Status of the Preembryo 230
　　　　In re Marriage of Witten 230
　　B.　Parental Rights and Obligations 242
　　　　K.M. v. E.G. 242

Chapter 7.　Autonomy in a Bureaucratic World **258**
1.　Allocating Medical Resources: Who Should Decide? What
　　Criteria Should We Use? 258
　　C.　The Allocation Problem in Microcosm: The Case of
　　　　Organ Transplants 258
2.　The Patient in the Bureaucracy 261
　　B.　Medical Ethics in the Age of Bureaucracy 261
　　　　1. Stating the Problem: Conflicts of Interest 261
　　　　Aetna Health, Inc. v. Davila 261

Chapter 1

THE PRINCIPLE OF AUTONOMY: THE EXAMPLE OF INFORMED CONSENT

SECTION 1. THE DOCTRINE OF INFORMED CONSENT

39. *This continues question 2.b.ii.*

Recall the famous case of *Jacobson v. Massachusetts*, 197 US 11 (1905), which held that the state may require citizens to submit to smallpox vaccination:

> The defendant insists that his liberty is invaded when the state subjects him to fine or imprisonment for neglecting or refusing to submit to vaccination; that a compulsory vaccination law is unreasonable, arbitrary, and oppressive, and, therefore, hostile to the inherent right of every freeman to care for his own body and health in such way as to him seems best; and that the execution of such a law against one who objects to vaccination, no matter for what reason, is nothing short of an assault upon his person. But the liberty secured by the Constitution . . . does not import an absolute right in each person to be, at all times and in all circumstances, wholly freed from restraint. There are manifold restraints to which every person is necessarily subject for the common good. Society based on the rule that each one is a law unto himself would soon be confronted with disorder and anarchy. Real liberty for all could not exist under the operation of a principle which recognizes the right of each individual person to use his own, whether in respect of his person or his property, regardless of the injury that may be done to others. . . . Even liberty itself . . . is only freedom from restraint under conditions essential to the equal enjoyment of the same right by others. . . .
>
> [I]f we are to attach, any value whatever to the knowledge . . . touching smallpox and the methods most usually employed to eradicate that disease, it cannot be adjudged that the present regulation of the board of health was not necessary in order to protect the public health . . . . Smallpox being prevalent and increasing at Cambridge, the court would usurp the functions of another branch of government if it adjudged, as matter of law, that

the mode adopted under the sanction of the state, to protect the people at large was arbitrary, and not justified by the necessities of the case. . . . every well-ordered society charged with the duty of conserving the safety of its members the rights of the individual in respect of his liberty may at times, under the pressure of great dangers, be subjected to such restraint, to be enforced by reasonable regulations. . . .

Jacobson "arose from a 1902 outbreak of smallpox." The Rev. Mr. Henning Jacobson was a Swedish immigrant who helped "found the Augustana Lutheran Church in Cambridge." He was "a charismatic preacher and a community leader" who "practiced a form of pietism in which spirituality was infused into everyday life." Mr. Jacobson was represented by a Harvard-trained lawyer who "was associated with the Anti-Vaccination League and lived a few blocks from one of its leaders . . . who had become infamous . . . when he contracted smallpox after viisiting Boston's smallpox hospital on a dare from the director of the Boston Board of Health." Wendy E. Parmet et al, *Individual Rights Versus the Public's Health – 100 Years After* Jacobson v. Massachusetts, 352 NEJM 652 (2005).

The last smallpox case in the US was in 1949, and the disease was declared eradicated in 1980, but there are fears that it might be spread by terrorists. A survey found 73% of of emergency room personnel willing to be vaccinated under a voluntary federal program, and a telephone survey found about 60% of adults would want to be vaccinated if vaccinations were offered. The vaccine's side effects can include fever and swollen lymph nodes and, rarely, encephalitis. Over 100,000 military personnel have been vaccinated "with four reported cases of suspected vaccine-related serious adverse events." Worth W. Everett et al, *Smallpox Vaccination: A National Survey of Emergency Health Care Providers*, 10 Academic Emergency Medicine 606 (2003).

Insert on page 49 directly before (b) The Exceptions.

Canterbury says that "all risks potentially affecting the decision must be unmasked" and that a risk is "'material when a reasonable person . . . would be likely to attach significance to the risk or cluster of risks in deciding whether or not to forego the proposed therapy.'" So how much information do patients think is material to their decision? In one large-scale study, "[m]ost subjects (76.2%)

responded that they would want to hear of any adverse effects, no matter how rare. A greater percentage, 83.1%, responded that they would want to hear of any serious adverse effect, no matter how rare." Dewey K. Ziegler et al, *How Much Information About Adverse Effects of Medication Do Patients Want from Physicians?*, 161 Archives of Internal Medicine 706, 708 (2001). In that study, "[a]lthough more than 50% of respondents at all educational levels asked to hear about all adverse effects, there was a significant difference between the different educational groups with increasing desire to know all adverse effects in the less well-educated group . . . ." How scrupulously should these preferences be honored by doctors and juries?

51. *Add before subsection 2.*

Does your view of these cases change in light of the following information from Kathleen M. Boozang, *The Therapeutic Placebo: The Case for Patient Deception*, 54 Florida L Rev 687 (2002)? Placebo research suggests "that pretreatment emphasis on success improves positive outcomes. . . . [P]lacebos also produce a negative, or 'nocebo effect.' Thus, it should be medically contraindicated for physicians and pharmaceutical companies to disclose to patients the potential adverse effects of a drug . . . . [U]sing patient conditioning, . . . physicians could intersperse placebos with analgesics, thereby allowing smaller doses of drugs . . . ." In addition, "[n]umerous studies have shown that a significant percentage of patients experience a substantial (at least half) reduction of severe clinical pain with the introduction of an inert substance or drug."

58. *This replaces the present Question 1.*

1. The physicians in *A Hidden Agenda* thought their patient had AIDS, but he adamantly declined to be tested. The physicians could easily have tested him without his consent, since they were drawing blood for many other tests. Should they have been inhibited by their patient's refusal? One doctor, Joel Howell, *What is the Difference Between an HIV and a CBC: Commentary*, 18 HCR 18 (Aug/Sept 1988), observes, "Hospitalized patients have their blood drawn regularly. Physicians do not ask their consent to check a blood count, to monitor antibiotic levels, to assess thyroid status, or to do other 'routine' tests. In the interest of efficiency, we do not ask specific consent for each laboratory examination." Another doctor writes, "Except for tests for heritable genetic disorders, HIV is the only

laboratory, radiographic, or pathologic test for which specific consent is broadly required. For all other tests, there is widespread belief that either implicit consent, or a general consent to medical care, is adequate to protect autonomous choice." Scott D. Halpern, *HIV Testing Without Consent in Critically Ill Patients*, 284 JAMA 745 (2005). Dr. Halpern reports that "[s]pecific consent for HIV testing is required in all 53 US states and territories."

Should consent always be required? Dr. Howell thinks so, because an HIV test

> places the patient at greater risk for adverse consequences than other blood tests. First, there is the risk of a false-positive test result, the magnitude of which depends on the pretest probability that a patient has been infected with the HIV virus. . . . A false-positive test should be detected by additional testing, but in the interim the patient would suffer. Graver risks would come from true-positive test results: risks to [the patient's] relationships (both sexual and social if test results were inappropriately disclosed), to her treatment by medical personnel, to her insurability, to schooling, to housing, and were she employed, to job security.

Dr. Howell was writing almost twenty years ago. Dr. Halpern suggests that

> although HIV infection retains unique features, the need to consider it an exceptional illness requiring exceptional policies has been weakened. HIV exceptionalism facilitated the understanding of a new, terrifying illness during its first decade, but in retrospect, HIV has much more in common with earlier epidemics, such as tuberculosis and syphilis, than was initially appreciated. Indeed, maintaining exceptional policies for HIV may perpetuate stigmatization by reinforcing the belief that patients with HIV are "different." Requiring consent for HIV testing risks perpetuating stigmatization while simultaneously limiting the quality of care that at-risk persons may receive. The disenfranchised group is thus doubly harmed.

Is requiring informed consent for HIV tests effective? A *Hidden Agenda* provoked this from Bernardino Roca & Enrique Simon, 338 NEJM 1544 (1998):

If the law requires informed consent for HIV testing, why not . . . for . . T-lymphocyte subgroups? Why not for differential white-cell counts (in an appropriate clinical setting, a very low lymphocyte count strongly suggests HIV infection)? Why not for an inspection of the tongue (hairy leukoplakia is virtually diagnostic of HIV infection)? . . . [R]equiring informed consent only for HIV testing not only provokes absurd diagnostic difficulties, but also contributes to the psychological burden and stigma associated with HIV infection.

Did the patient in *A Hidden Agenda* have any kind of moral obligation to be tested? An obligation to himself? To his wife? To the doctors, nurses, and technicians who encountered him? Would knowing he was infected lead them to behave more cautiously and thus lessen their risk of infection?

In August 1987, CDC published a document entitled "Recommendations for Prevention of HIV Transmission in Health-Care Settings." . . . [It] recommended that blood and body fluid precautions be consistently used for all patients regardless of their bloodborne infection status. This extension of blood and body fluid precautions to all patients is referred to as "Universal Blood and Body Fluid Precautions" or "Universal Precautions." Under universal precautions, blood and certain body fluids of all patients are considered potentially infectious for human immunodeficiency virus (HIV), hepatitis B virus (HBV), and other bloodborne pathogens.

Universal precautions are intended to prevent parenteral, mucous membrane, and nonintact skin exposures of health-care workers to bloodborne pathogens. In addition, immunization with HBV [hepatitis B] vaccine is recommended as an important adjunct to universal precautions for health-care workers who have exposures to blood.

Kristi J. Ferguson et al, *Critical Incidents of Nonadherence with Standard Precautions Guidelines Among Community Hospital-Based Health Care Workers*, 19 J General Internal Medicine 726 (2004), summarize recent research:

Although universal precautions guidelines have been in place since 1987, suboptimal adherence has been documented extensively despite evidence that failure to use barrier precautions increases the risk of mucocutaneous blood and body fluid exposure and adherence decreases risk. . . .that [N]onadherence among physicians and nurses is associated with inadequate knowledge, forgetfulness, workload, workplace safety climate, and the perception that colleagues also failed to adhere, while adherence is associated with seeing precautions as a way to avoid injury or exposure and with concern about protecting colleagues. Even the most effective intervention studies, however, have concluded that more work needs to be done to reduce exposures to blood-borne pathogens.

In the Ferguson study,

> Nonadherence to routine glove use (routine glove use defined as 100% of the time) was higher among those respondents who believed that adherence interfered with their ability to provide care (61% did not wear gloves all of the time compared to the overall rate of 44%) and among those who believed that the patient did not pose a risk (56% did not wear gloves all of the time). On the other hand, the proportion of those who did not use gloves routinely was lower among those who said a break in precautions occurred because equipment was not effective (22% did not wear gloves all of the time) and among those who forgot (30% did not wear gloves all of the time).

Is there any social interest in discovering whether someone like the patient in *A Hidden Agenda* is HIV-positive? Could much of the (considerable) amount spent diagnosing him have been saved by an HIV test? If the patient is HIV-positive, do the people with whom he has had sexual relations have an interest in being informed? Do the following data from CDC, MMWR, *HIV Prevalence, Unrecognized Infection, and HIV Testing Among Men Who Have Sex With Men – Five U.S. Cities, June 2004 - April 2005*, reprinted in 294 JAMA 674 (2005) affect your view?: "Studies of HIV infection among young men who have sex with men (MSM) in the mid to late 1990s revealed high rates of HIV prevalence, incidence, and unrecognized infection . . . . [In the present study,] of MSM surveyed, 25% were infected with HIV, and 48% of those infected were unaware of their infection."

Do patients understand that they are *not* being checked for HIV infection when they visit the hospital? E.J. Sobo, *Choosing Unsafe Sex: AIDS-Risk Denial Among Disadvantaged Women* (U Penn Press, 1995), learned that many poor women

> assumed that any blood drawn by a clinician was checked for all pathogens, HIV included . . . . Some thought that testing was mandatory. Others thought that they were tested for HIV when in the

> hospital for surgical or other invasive procedures . . . . I asked several white middle-class women about their experience with HIV tests; the same pattern of assumption emerged . . . . [I]t was assumed that a gynecological check-up would include an HIV test . . . .

59. Replace Question 2 with the following:

2. What should doctors tell patients about HIV testing when seeking consent? Larry Gostin, *Hospitals, Health Care Professionals, and AIDS: The "Right to Know" the Health Status of Professionals and Patients*, 48 Md L Rev 12 (1989), writes, "Unless HCPs [healthcare providers] tell their patients about the powerful emotional and psychological impact of HIV-positive test results, the HCPs have not provided them with all the information a reasonable patient would find relevant . . . ." Professor Gostin apparently believes that patients should be told of the danger of false positives; that "[s]ome patients bear an intolerable psychological burden when informed that they are HIV-positive"; that "suicide can result from news of a positive test result"; that confidentiality cannot be guaranteed; and that disclosure "can cause ostracism among family and friends, and can result in the loss of a job, a home, a place in school, insurance, or other benefits." Is such disclosure legally required? Ethically?

3. A number of state "have enacted limited expansions of informed consent duties, generally in response to focused advocacy by patient groups." William M. Sage, *Regulating Through Information Disclosure Laws and American Health Care,* 99 Columbia L Rev 1701 (1999). For example, more than a third of the states have statutes provoked by the sense that doctors were not describing the full range of choices for treating breast cancer.

> The majority of these statutes provide for the creation of standardized informational summaries by an independent medical body, to be distributed to patients who are diagnosed with or considered to be at high risk for developing breast cancer. For example, California requires the development of a "standardized written summary in layman's language and in a language understood by the patient," to be developed with recommendations from a Cancer Advisory Council, and printed and made available to physicians and surgeons by the Medical Board of California.

Many of these statutes "make failure to comply one of the grounds for discipline against the physician--either independently, or by explicit inclusion in the definition of 'unprofessional conduct.'" Joan H. Krause, *Reconceptualizing Informed Consent in an Era of Health Care Cost Containment*, 85 Iowa L Rev 261 (1999).

Do these statutes work? According to Ann Butler Nattinger et al, *The Effect of Legislative Requirements on the Use of Breast-Conserving Surgery*, 335 NEJM 1035 (1996), the laws were

> temporally associated with slight increases (6 to 13 percent) in the use of breast-conserving surgery in the states with the most directive laws. The increases were transient, however, lasting from 3 to 12 months, after which the use of breast-conserving surgery reverted to the level expected on the basis of the trend in states without specific legislation.
>
> Why was the apparent effect of these laws so small? The assumption underlying these statutes was that women with breast cancer were not being fully informed of their choices and that measures to increase the discussion of alternative treatments would lead to increases in the use of breast-conserving surgery. However, a major determinant of the choice of therapy appears to be the recommendation of the surgeon, which would not be expected to be affected by the legislation. Also, research by Nayfield et al suggests that only a minority of patients with cancer pursue a decision-making process that is enhanced by additional information; for some patients such information may complicate the process.

Abortion has been another spark for such statutes. *Planned Parenthood of Eastern Pennsylvania v. Casey*, 505 US 833 (1992), found 18 Pa. Cons.Stat. § 3205 (1990) constitutional. The Court said the statute required

> that at least 24 hours before performing an abortion a physician inform the woman of the nature of the procedure, the health risks of the abortion and of childbirth, and the "probable gestational age of the unborn child." The physician . . . must inform the woman of the availability of printed materials published by the State describing the fetus and providing information about medical assistance for childbirth, information about child support from the father, and a list of agencies which provide adoption and other services as alternatives to abortion. An abortion may not be performed unless the woman certifies in writing that she has been informed of the

availability of these printed materials and has been provided them if she chooses to view them. . . .

In attempting to ensure that a woman apprehend the full consequences of her decision, the State furthers the legitimate purpose of reducing the risk that a woman may elect an abortion, only to discover later, with devastating psychological consequences, that her decision was not fully informed. . . .

A [similar] requirement . . . was described in *Thornburgh [v. American College of Obstetricians and Gynecologists*, 476 U.S. 747] as "an outright attempt to wedge the Commonwealth's message discouraging abortion into the privacy of the informed-consent dialogue between the woman and her physician." . . . [W]e depart from the holdings of *Akron* [*v. Akron Center for Reproductive Health, Inc.*, 462 U.S. 416,] and *Thornburgh* to the extent that we permit a State to further its legitimate goal of protecting the life of the unborn by enacting legislation aimed at ensuring a decision that is mature and informed, even when in so doing the State expresses a preference for childbirth over abortion. [A]n informed choice need not be defined in such narrow terms that all considerations of the effect on the fetus are made irrelevant. . . . [R]equiring that the woman be informed of the availability of information relating to fetal development and the assistance available should she decide to carry the pregnancy to full term is a reasonable measure to ensure an informed choice, one which might cause the woman to choose childbirth over abortion.

60. *Insert after first (incomplete) paragraph.*

Would Professor Gostin's approach discourage people from being tested? Is his information accurate? In a study by Jeffrey M. Moulton et al, *Results of a One Year Longitudinal Study of HIV Antibody Test Notification from the San Francisco General Hospital Cohort*, 4 J Acquired Immune Deficiency Syndromes 787 (1991), the "most striking finding was the lack of any significant increase in levels of distress in close proximity to notification among seropositives." Elaine M. Sieff et al, *Anticipated Versus Actual Reaction to HIV Test Results*, 112 Am J Psychology 298-311 (1999), reports that

> knowledge of one's disease status in the asymptomatic state does not generally result in distress, depression, or suicide. Although there may be initial reactions of distress and shock upon learning that the test result is positive, these effects

appear to dissipate rapidly over time. In fact, based on the psychological measures used in these studies, those who received an informative test result (negative or positive) showed less psychopathology than those who declined notification of their test results or those who could not receive more informative test results. It appears that asymptomatic people cope well with the news that they are HIV or HD positive.

This study's "most striking finding was the lack of any significant increase in levels of distress in close proximity to notification among seropositives." the study's "results suggest that the anticipated response to an HIV test result is more extreme – more distress if positive and much less distress if negative – than experienced." Sieff et al worry that the "overestimation of distress following a positive HIV test result may prevent some people from seeking testing."

63. *Replace the current section C with the following:*

C. Mandated Disclosure in Informed Consent and in the Law

1. Mandated Disclosure as a Method of Legal Regulation

It is easy to forget but crucial to remember that when lawmakers regulate an activity, they must select a method. The law of bioethics particularly favors one method – requiring disclosure of information. The doctrine of informed consent obliges doctors to tell patients their treatment choices. As we will see the administrative law of research ethics embodies the principle that researchers must warn subjects of the risks of experiments. The Patient Self-Determination Act compels medical institutions to remind patients about advance directives. The federal government's new privacy regime instructs medical institutions to describe their privacy rules to patients. Some states have tried to specify information women seeking abortions must be given about fetal life and alternatives to abortion.

Not just the law of bioethics, but health law in general repeatedly imposes disclosure requirements. For example, they are central to the recurring proposals for patients' bills of rights. Likewise, "[v]irtually every bill . . . to regulate managed care devotes major portions to information disclosure and dissemination . . . ." William M. Sage, *Regulating Through Information: Disclosure Laws and*

American Health Care, 99 Columbia L Rev 1701 (1999). And now proposals for "consumer-directed health care" tantalize us with the dream that well-informed patients can make health care markets work effectively.

If disclosure requirements are popular, surely they are effective. Isn't it obvious that people making decisions need information, want it, and will use it? Doesn't an irresistible array of arguments justify disclosure requirements? The *moral* rationale for disclosure is that it liberates people from the servitude to other people which ignorance creates. The *prophylaxis* rationale assumes that people can be deterred from abusing each other by requiring predators to warn the prey. The *market* rationale holds that the production and allocation of goods is best regulated through markets and that markets work best when purchasers know most. And the *welfare* rationale suggests that one way to enhance people's well-being is to give them the information they need to protect themselves.

Perversely, there is good reason to doubt that disclosure requirements in health law work as intended. But can they be fixed? One way to assess disclosure rules in health law is to ask whether they succeed in the many other areas of law that require them: Are people buying worthless stocks? Securities laws say, "Disclose!" Are people borrowing money at usurious rates? Consumer protection laws say, "Disclose!" Are people injured by things they buy? Products-liability law says, "Disclose!" Are police bullying criminal suspects into waiving their rights? *Miranda* says, "Disclose!" Are people signing disadvantageous marital agreements? Family law says, "Disclose!"

Do such disclosure requirements work? Well, what is "success"? Presumably, the goal is to improve the decisions recipients of information make. The baseline for evaluation, then, is the quality of the decisions people would make were there no disclosure laws. Crudely defined, success means improving decisions enough to justify the costs of the disclosure requirement to the government, the disclosers, the recipients, and the rest of us.

Obviously, this standard of assessment is heroically challenging to apply, but there is reason to doubt that it is often met. If disclosure requirements prosper anywhere, it should be in securities markets, since they are dominated by institutions which have incentives and resources to assimilate and apply the information companies disclose. But even there, scholars cannot agree that companies would disclose less were there no securities laws (since companies have economic reasons to disclose information to investors) or that the disclosures that are made improve investors' decisions or the markets' efficiency.

Nor is it clear that other disclosure regimes justify their costs. Take *Miranda* warnings: They "'have little or no effect on a suspect's propensity to talk . . . . Next to the warning label on cigarette packs, *Miranda* is the most widely ignored piece of official advice in our society.' . . . Not only has *Miranda* largely failed to achieve its stated and implicit goals, but police have transformed *Miranda* into a tool of law enforcement . . . ." Richard A. Leo, *Questioning the Relevance of* Miranda *in the Twenty-First Century*, 99 Mich L Rev 1000 (2001). And while the evidence of failure is hardly uniform, "the efforts of researchers to prove by scientific means that on-product warnings are indeed effective to modify safety-related behavior in actual or simulated real-world applications have generally yielded disappointing results." Hildy Bowbeer & David S. Killoran, Liriano v. Hobart Corp: *Obvious Dangers, The Duty to Warn of Safer Alternatives, and the Heeding Presumption*, 65 Brooklyn L Rev 717 (1999).

Why don't disclosure requirements work better? Principally, disclosure succeeds only if *many* often onerous conditions are all met. Let us briskly review eight of them.

First, information must actually be provided. However, disclosers may have reasons to withhold it. Disclosures cost money and can compromise disclosers' interest. Disclosers can respond by following the letter of the law and not the spirit, by obscuring and even suppressing information, by presenting information misleadingly, and by dressing disclosures prettily. Furthermore, disclosure requirements are hard to enforce: They usually affect so many transactions that the law cannot supervise them well administratively, and people from whom information is withheld rarely are injured or aggressive enough to make suits economically sensible.

Second, the information disclosed must be the right information – germane, accurate, and complete. However, even a willing discloser will often not know what to disclose. Some safety warnings apparently make people less cautious, not more. Cigarette warnings seem to have helped convince Americans that the dangers of smoking are *greater* than they actually are. However, the young start smoking partly because they misunderstand people's ability to stop. Yet you can't tell people *everything*, because that swamps them in more information than they can manage.

Third, the audience must receive the information. But often the information is, and even must be, inconspicuous. Furthermore, 40 to 44 million Americans, or approximately one quarter of the US population, are functionally illiterate, another 50 million have marginal literacy skills, and many of the rest have trouble comprehending even modestly complex verbal and numerical data.

Fourth, recipients must attend to the information they perceive. But recipients commonly fail to recognize the relevance and significance of information or think they already know all they need to, and so they are easily convinced that the effort of heeding information will not be repaid. For example, one "of the most consistent findings in the literature . . . is that a consumer's responsiveness to warnings is strongly affected by perceived hazardousness." Those perceptions are influenced by many things, including "the overall appearance of a product, . . . perceived controllability of the hazard and its harmful consequences, . . . a person's ability to imagine various ways in which an injury might occur while using a product, . . . familiarity with the product, . . . level of education or a person's abilities of processing information, . . . and the presence, . . . salience, . . . and content of warnings." Sadly, "[m]ost of these factors are difficult to influence." Monica Trommelen, *Effectiveness of Explicit Warnings*, 25 Safety Science 79 (1997).

Fifth, people must understand the information. This requires the kind of analytic effort most of us resist. Resistance is often reasonable, for as Alfred North Whitehead said, "It is a profoundly erroneous truism, repeated by copy-books and by eminent people when they are making speeches, that we should cultivate the habit of thinking about what we are doing. . . . . Civilization advances by extending the number of important operations which we can perform without thinking about them. Operations of thought are like cavalry charges in a battle -- they are strictly limited in number, they require fresh horses, and must only be made at decisive moments." But even when we recognize that cavalry charges are necessary we don't always bring out the fresh horses.

Sixth, recipients must believe what they are told. But people are skeptical. They scout information that does not fit their view of the world. Furthermore, recipients often have reasons (good and bad) to fear that disclosers are shaping information to serve their own interests and not the recipients'. (How many suspects believe what the police tell them?) Such attitudes make recipients all too prone to spurn even reliable information.

Seventh, people must decide to use the information. But people dislike incorporating new information into decisions, if only because that demands still more work. They must therefore be convinced that the information will be worth that effort. Sometimes it isn't, but how can they know until they have tried?

Eighth, recipients must use the information intelligently. The woeful infrequency of this even where you would expect it most often is suggested by the need for books with titles like *Why Smart People Make Big Money Mistakes and How to Correct Them.* Even experienced investors overvalue their own judgment, are sooner swayed by vivid than dry data, imagine that new evidence confirms their earlier opinions, and suffer from the squadrons of systematic faults in reasoning that besiege us all. And so, "[d]uring the Internet frenzy, firms that announced that they were changing their name to include 'dot.com' experienced abnormal returns, regardless of whether the announcement coincided with a change in business plan." Stephen J. Choi & A.C. Pritchard, *Behavioral Economics and the SEC,* 56 Stanford L Rev 1 (2003). To put this crucial point differently, people's decisions do not always change, much less improve, with more information.

But why do lawmakers so often choose disclosure requirements when evidence for their success is at best so elusive and at worst so damning? One answer is that the structure of most law-making does little to encourage assessments of disclosure rules. Those rules are generally inspired by indignation over genuine problems, indignation inflamed by anecdote. Attention is directed to what is wrong and the imperative of change, not to the effectiveness of the law's means. Anyway, it seems obvious that disclosure works, and there is no easy way to test its effectiveness in advance. And law is made by just the people – the well-educated and well-situated – best able to take advantage of disclosures.

Furthermore, disclosure may be the only kind of regulation available to the law-making agency. For example, courts can create a cause of action against doctors who do not disclose information to patients, but courts cannot establish an administrative apparatus to supervise disclosure. And not least, disclosure requirements cost lawmakers little, since they shift the costs of regulation to the entities being regulated. For example, the Patient Self-Determination Act added pennies to the federal budget, but it cost hospitals over $100,000,000 just to set up compliance programs. Finally, once disclosure rules have been implemented, courts have no resources for or — it must be said — interest in reviewing their effectiveness, and Congress moves on to other issues.

When the law selects ineffective means, problems remain unsolved. Foolish means can make problems worse and engender new ones. And even bootless means divert resources from worthier uses.

2. Informed Consent for Lawyers: Why the Difference?

Law has with some asperity imposed a duty of informed consent on physicians. Law has imposed a much lighter burden on itself. Why?

Sometimes the law talks a good game:

> Counsel's function is to assist the defendant, and hence counsel owes the client a duty of loyalty, a duty to avoid conflicts of interest. . . . From counsel's function as assistant to the defendant derive the overarching duty to advocate the defendant's cause and the more particular duties to consult with the defendant on important decisions and to keep the defendant informed of important developments in the course of the prosecution.

Strickland v. Washington, 466 U.S. 668 (1984). But if we look more closely, a different picture emerges. Consider the ABA Model Rules of Professional Conduct:

> Rule 1.2 (a) A lawyer shall abide by a client's decisions concerning the objectives of representation, subject to paragraphs (c), (d) and (e), and shall consult with the client as to the means by which they are to be pursued. A lawyer shall abide by a client's decision whether to accept an offer of settlement of a matter. In a criminal

case, the lawyer shall abide by the client's decision, after consultation with the lawyer, as to a plea to be entered, whether to waive jury trial and whether the client will testify. [The exceptions in paragraphs (c), (d) and (e) have to do with limiting the objectives of representation after consultation, not promoting crime or fraud, and consultation where the client expects improper assistance.]

Rule 1.2(a) distinguishes "objectives" and "means." The Comment says, "In questions of means, the lawyer should assume responsibility for technical and legal tactical issues, but should defer to the client regarding such questions as the expense to be incurred and concern for third persons who might be adversely affected." The Legal Background commentary explains, "Historically, lawyers have been deemed to be the master of procedural and tactical aspects of litigation. This inherent authority is derived from the lawyer's expertise in legal strategy and procedure. Thus, even over the objection of the client, lawyers have been permitted to present or refuse to present certain witnesses; stipulate to the use of testimony from a prior trial; withdraw or refuse to submit a defense as a matter of trial expediency or tactics; and decline cross examination." The Commentary also notes, however, that "some courts have found that in the event of a disagreement the client's judgment should prevail even in matters of tactics, procedure, or the drafting of documents."

The Comment sees that a "clear distinction between objectives and means sometimes cannot be drawn." The Legal Background commentary suggests the distinction "is often expressed as the difference between decisions that are procedural or tactical in nature and decisions that directly affect the ultimate resolution of the case or the substantive rights of the client." That commentary summarizes the Comment as saying "that when a clear distinction cannot be made between 'objectives' and 'means,' a joint undertaking is appropriate" and suggests "it is this 'joint' nature of the lawyer-client relationship that is most instrumental in determining how specific decisions are made." Does medical informed consent recognize the same distinction between ends and means? Should it?

Rule 1.4 (a) A lawyer shall keep a client reasonably informed about the status of a matter and promptly comply with reasonable requests for information. (b) A lawyer shall explain a matter to the extent reasonably necessary to permit the client to make informed decisions regarding the representation.

The Comment to Rule 1.4 states: "The client should have sufficient information to participate intelligently in decisions concerning the objectives of the representation and the means by which they are to be pursued, to the extent the client is willing and able to do so." The Comment thinks "[a]dequacy of communication depends in part on the kind of advice or assistance involved." The "guiding principle is that the lawyer should fulfill reasonable client expectations for information consistent with the duty to act in the client's best interests, and the client's overall requirements as to the character of representation." Thus "in negotiations where there is time to explain a proposal the lawyer should review all important provisions with the client . . . ." And in litigation "a lawyer should explain the general strategy and prospects of success and ordinarily should consult the client on tactics that might injure or coerce others." Still, "a lawyer ordinarily cannot be expected to describe trial or negotiation strategy in detail."

The Comment avers that "a lawyer may be justified in delaying transmission of information when the client would be likely to react imprudently to an immediate communication. Thus a lawyer might withhold a psychiatric diagnosis of a client when the examining psychiatrist indicates that disclosure would harm the client." The Legal Background comment, however, says "this delay is specifically limited to rare circumstances like psychiatric diagnoses and 'should not be taken to mean that a lawyer may withhold information simply because he fears his client will make an imprudent legal judgment, such as accepting an inadequate settlement offer.'"

There is essentially no law of informed consent applied to lawyers. But "in reviewing a claim of ineffective assistance of counsel, courts have had to decide whether defense counsel's failure to involve a defendant in making, or failure to defer to the client's wishes regarding, a particular strategic decision constitutes deficient or inadequate representation." In "the vast majority of cases" courts "routinely hold that defense counsel's representation was constitutionally adequate because counsel exercised reasonable professional judgment when she made the particular strategic or tactical decision at issue. Moreover, the defendant is deemed to be bound by counsel's strategic and tactical judgment calls even though he may not have been consulted or may have disagreed with counsel's strategy." In short, "appellate opinions generally promote the traditional lawyer-centered approach to decisionmaking" and give lawyers "almost unchallengeable authority to make strategic and tactical decisions." Rodney J. Uphoff & Peter B. Wood, *The Allocation of Decisionmaking Between Defense Counsel and Criminal Defendant: An Empirical Study of Attorney-Client Decisionmaking*, 47 U of Kansas L Rev 1 (1998).

In still other contexts case law reflects a similar view of the lawyer's authority over the client's case. "[W]hen a defendant chooses to have a lawyer manage and present his case, law and tradition may allocate to the counsel the power to make binding decisions of trial strategy in many areas. This allocation can only be justified . . . by the defendant's consent, at the outset, to accept counsel as his representative." *United States v. Faretta*, 422 US 806, 820 - 821 (1975). On the other hand, in *Burton v. Alabama*, 651 So2d 641, 656 (Ala Crim App 1993), the appellant was challenging

> the penalty phase of the proceedings. The appellant initially argues that the trial court interfered with his attorney-client relationship by calling two of his codefendants to the stand after his attorney had told the court that they could add nothing that would help the appellant in mitigation.
>
> The record clearly shows that it was the appellant's wish to call these two witnesses. The court had a lengthy colloquy with the appellant concerning his desire to have his two codefendants testify at the penalty phase of the proceedings. The court, after talking with the appellant, complied with his wishes.
>
> An attorney represents a criminal defendant and is obliged by Rule 1.2, Alabama Rules of Professional Conduct, to "abide by a client's decisions concerning the objectives of representation····" An attorney can only make recommendations to a client as to how to conduct his defense; the ultimate decision, however, lies with the client. There was no interference with the attorney-client relationship here, when the trial court was honoring the appellant's wishes.

Commentators rarely discuss the ethical and legal obligation of lawyers to obtain their clients informed consent to the lawyer's "treatment," and when they do the results are mixed. A leading legal-ethics casebook, for example, thinks the idea that lawyers and clients should share legal decisions is difficult to reconcile with several considerations. First, the lawyer usually knows more about the legal aspects of the problem than the client, and more than the client practically can be told. Second, the lawyer typically is inured to the emotional distress of conflict and can therefore deal with it more steadily . . . . Third, the decisions in carrying out a legal matter often require unabashed assertiveness . . . . Lawyers are used to taking such measures, while ordinary people are not. Also, some clients expect the lawyer to take responsibility for a difficult choice: "What should I do?"

Geoffrey C. Hazard, Jr., et al, *The Law and Ethics of Lawyering* 473 (Foundation 1999). What would we say if doctors made arguments like this?

So, Uphoff and Wood believe, "[g]iven the mixed guidance provided by legal commentators, case law, and professional standards regarding the proper division of decisionmaking responsibility, lawyers are relatively free to decide for themselves whether they will share decisionmaking power with their clients." How do lawyers respond to this freedom? In Uphoff and Wood's survey of public defenders, "38% of respondents agreed, at least to some extent, with the statement that lawyers should allow their clients to make all important decisions." This figure obscures some complexity, since "the commitment of our responding lawyers to sharing decisionmaking responsibility with their clients varies significantly from issue to issue."

And how do lawyers account for their reluctance to give clients the authority doctors are supposed to give lawyers? "[T]he client's general low intelligence and a concern that the client would make a poor, hurtful decision were identified by the highest percentage of respondents as the two factors that almost always or most of the time limit the client's participation in decisionmaking."

SECTION 2. VINDICATING PATIENTS' AUTONOMY

78. *Add at the bottom of the page.*

After Dr. Benson's death, his widow sued the Board, the Department and Richard Danila (the author of the NEJM article) claiming the article "violated the decedent's statutory privacy rights, and caused the decedent to suffer emotional and physical devastation, and professional humiliation and ostracism." The court held the "alleged violations are . . . personal to the decedent, not violations of the estate's property interests" and that the cause of action did not survive Dr. Benson. *Estate of Benson v. Minnesota Board of Medicine*, 526 NW2d 634 (MinnApp 1995).

According to Mitchell H. Katz, *The AIDS Pandemic: Complacency, Injustice, and Unfulfilled Expectations*, 350 NEJM 2108 (2004), "Exhaustive investigations of the patients of HIV-infected physicians, including those who perform invasive procedures, have not detected a single additional infection."

95. Insert in question 4, in its second line, after the sentence "Do they?"

One scholar says doctors "lie to obtain insurance coverage for their patients, they lie to protect their patients from family discord or humiliation; they conceal medical errors from patients and their families; they hide medication in mentally disabled patients' food; they lie to each other; they withhold information about research; they conceal from terminally ill patients that they are going to die; and they give placebos to patients." Kathleen M. Boozang, *The Therapeutic Placebo: The Case for Patient Deception*, 54 Florida L Rev 687 (2002).

95. Insert after the first paragraph of question 4..

Professor Boozang suggests that doctors "can instigate the placebo effect by putting the most positive spin on prognostic information. . . . In the words of a stroke patient's treating physician: 'Having reviewed the data and examined him, I know he is unlikely to recover much use of his arm. I couch my answer carefully, full of caveats and uncertainty that I do not completely feel.'" Are these doctors "lying"? Dr. Ubel's colleagues "were reluctant to provide *specific* predictions to patients Their reluctance is based not on a desire to withhold information from patients but on uncertainty about their predicting abilities." Peter A. Ubel, *Truth in the Most Optimistic Way*, 134 Annals of Internal Medicine 1142 (2001). Dr. Ubel guesses "that many physicians base their communication on the way patients react to their prognoses. When patients are 'too pessimistic' about their illnesses, physicians emphasize hope in order to lift their spirits.

When patients are 'too optimistic,' physicians make sure patients understand the gravity of their situations."

99. Insert after the quotation from Signorile.

More systematically: "Mildly but unrealistically positive beliefs can improve outcomes in patients with chronic or terminal diseases. For example, a late-1980s study of patients with AIDS found that those who stated that they 'refused to believe that this problem has happened' lived 9 months longer than those who indicated that they 'tried to accept what might happen.' Moreover, unrealistically optimistic views have been shown to improve quality of life." Peter A. Ubel, *Truth in the Most Optimistic Way*, 134 Annals of Internal Medicine 1142 (2001).

SECTION 3. PATIENTS' AUTONOMY AND PATIENTS' HEALTH

115. Insert at end of page.

Now cast your mind back to *Canterbury v. Spence*. What could and should Dr. Spence have done and said to give Mr. Canterbury enough information to decide whether to have surgery? Consider one study of 106 patients facing "routine neurosurgical procedures." David A. Herz et al, *Informed Consent: Is It a Myth?*, 30 Neurosurgery 453 (1992). Twenty-two of these patients "underwent anterior cervical disectomy and interbody spinal fusion procedures, and 84 underwent lumbar laminectomies." Patients were educated in three stages (that were apparently developed "in collaboration with a doctoral level lay educator"). First, the physician explained "the spinal anatomy and physiology, the procedure, the "reasons for considering surgery," the surgical techniques (in detail), the non-surgical alternatives to the procedure, and the "[o]perative goals and aspects of postoperative care." The surgeon used "printed materials and anatomical models" to make his points more clearly, he invited questions, and he asked patients to repeat in their own words what they had learned.

Second, patients and their families and friends were invited to an "education conference, performed by a Master's level nurse educator, covering the same topics." Like the surgeon, the nurse used visual aids, solicited questions, and tried to test patients' understanding orally. Third, patients spoke again with the surgeon.

"There was further opportunity to ask questions and receive information regarding any perceived gaps in knowledge."

Directly after meeting with the nurse, patients were tested on what they learned. When given multiple-choice questions, patients answered 53.1% of the questions correctly. Asked open-ended questions, patients scores sunk to 34%. Scores improved with patients' education, but even patients "with graduate education" scored only 64.8% and 36.5% (multiple choice and open-ended, respectively). More particularly, scores on questions about the nature of the illness and details of the proposed surgery were 67% and 52%. Scores on questions about the risks of the surgery were 50% and 22.8%. Scores on questions about post-operative care were 26.7% and 43%. And scores on questions about the goals and benefits of the surgery were 35% and 26%.

Patients were best at describing their diagnosis and the surgical procedure, but they did not equivalently understand the goals and benefits of the surgery. They were less successful at identifying the risks of the procedure, even though a large part of the law of informed consent is about just that topic. What is more, patients did comparatively badly at what we might hope they would do best – understanding how they needed to care for themselves after the surgery.

Another study so forcefully describes the failures of doctors' attempts to give patients the information they need to make decisions about living wills that it deserves to be described in some detail. Physicians with a mean age of 37 years and a mean of 11 years experience were asked to "discuss 'advance directives'" with some of their own patients (whom they had known for an average of two and a half years) who were either at least 65 years old or suffering from a serious illness.

Only 70% of these conversations mentioned CPR. What is particularly discouraging is that "the patients who had these discussions greatly overestimated their chances of survival after an in-hospital cardiopulmonary arrest." Their "median estimate of the probability of survival to hospital discharge was 70%, compared with a 20% median probability of survival stated by their physicians." There were "no significant differences in responses between patients" who had discussed CPR and those who had not when they were asked whether patients usually need a ventilator after CPR.

The bad news continues: "Patients whose discussions included mechanical ventilation had a poor understanding of what this procedure entails, and a significant number harbored important misconceptions. . . . No subject who discussed ventilators had a good understanding of what they involved, and 50% had a poor understanding . . . ." So what is "fair understanding" (which is a step up from a "poor understanding")? This:

> *Interviewer:* Do you know how it [ventilation] works to make you breathe?
> *Patient:* No. . . .
> *Interviewer:* What do you think it would be like to be on one?
> *Patient:* Oh, I don't want to be on one.
> *Interviewer:* OK. Do you have any idea what it might be like to be one?
> *Patient:* I don't know.

Almost a quarter of the patients in the study already had an advance directive. One might hope that they would already be well-informed about the relevant medical facts, or at least that they would have specially benefitted from the conversation required by the study. But "[p]articipants who had previously written ADs did not have better knowledge of CPR or mechanical ventilation on any of these measures. In fact, those who had ADs were more likely to express the [false] view that ventilators directly kept the heart beating . . . ."

In sum, Fischer et al conclude that "patients left the conversations with serious misunderstandings about CPR and mechanical ventilation." One might hope that patients might perceive the unreliability of their knowledge and draw conclusions from it cautiously. But Fischer et al comment that one "of the most disconcerting findings of this study was that patients expressed strong preferences about treatments that they did not understand" (like the patient I quoted a moment ago). Gary S. Fischer et al, *Patient Knowledge and Physician Predictions of Treatment Preferences After Discussion of Advance Directives*, 13 J General Internal Med 447 (1998).

Can consent can ever be truly informed? We can imagine an ideal world in which patients often attain some satisfactory level of comprehension. But it is at least fair to say that sincere and energetic attempts to inform patients regularly fail, even when time and resources have been lavished that the ordinary patient and physician will never have.

116. Insert at the end of the last full paragraph..

It is surely awkward to say that someone else's decision is wrong But we can ask whether the decisions people make are the decisions they would have made had they realized what they were doing. Consider one study, in which people were asked given a choice between a cancer treatment which resulted in death 10% of the time (along with some side-effects of the treatment) and watchful waiting which resulted in death 5% of the time. When the treatment was a pill, 38% of the sample chose it. When the treatment was surgery, 65% of the people chose it. Angela Fagerlin et al, *Cure Me Even If It Kills Me: Preferences for Invasive Cancer Treatment* (forthcoming).

SECTION 4. IS INFORMED CONSENT EFFECTIVE? REGULATING MEDICAL PRACTICE

133. Insert after Note 5.

6. Suppose Dr. Spence told you that the operation on Mr. Canterbury failed because Dr. Spence made an error while performing the surgery. What legal advice would you give him? Dr. Spence might well be liable in a malpractice action, but would he also be liable if he failed to reveal the error to Mr. Canterbury? Should he be?

"'Ethical and professional guidelines make clear that physicians have a responsibility to disclose medical errors, and recent standards link disclosure of unexpected outcomes to hospital accreditation.'" Kathleen M. Mazor et al, *Communicating With Patients About Medical Errors: A Review of the Literature*, 164 ArIM 1690 (2004). "In a survey of US physicians, 77% responded that physicians should be required to tell patients when errors are made in their care." Patients and family members overwhelmingly want to be told about errors. However,

[s]tudies using retrospective self-report by physicians and trainees suggest that disclosure often does not occur. During interviews about how mistakes were handled, trainees mentioned the patient or family in 6% of the cases. When queried about their most significant medical mistake in the last year, 24% of trainees had discussed the error with the patient or family, and a similar rate (21%) was found in a later study of physicians. [In a] survey of hospital risk managers . . . 65% of managers indicated that hospital practice was always to disclose death or serious injury, and 37% indicated that their practice was always to disclose serious short-term harm.

In a national study, hospital risk managers "reported that the most common elements of the disclosure process were explanations (92%), an undertaking to investigate the incident (98%), an apology (68%), and an acknowledgment of harm (66%). Less frequently reported were offering to share the results of the investigation (41%) and assuming responsibility for harm (33%). Eight-two percent of risk managers reported that hospitals offered to pay the costs of associated care."

In one study, 91% of the people bringing malpractice actions "reported that desire for an explanation was a reason for their pursuing legal action. When asked whether anything could have been done once the incident occurred that would have prevented the need for legal action, 41% responded affirmatively; many suggested explanation and apology (39%)." One VA facility instituted a policy of "extreme honesty" about medical errors. "[A]lthough the number of claims against [that] facility was high (only 5 facilities had more claims), the total amount of payments was low (only 7 facilities reported lower payments)."

150. Substitute this material for pages 150 - 189.

SECTION 6. DOCTOR AND PATIENT IN CONTEXT: THE PROBLEM OF CONFIDENTIALITY

Whatever in connection with my professional practice or not in connection with it I see or hear in the life of men which ought not to be spoken abroad I will not divulge . . . .

Hippocratic Oath

So far, we have examined the principle of autonomy by assessing the doctrine of informed consent. In particular, we have asked how far that principle is normatively desirable and empirically practical. We now turn to another problem in the relations between doctor and patient that arises from our ideas about the autonomy and authority of the patient and that raises questions about the costs and benefits of promoting that autonomy and authority.

A. Confidentiality as Privilege and Duty: Testimonial Privileges

It is certain that the patients would never have spoken if it had occurred to them that their admissions might possibly be put to scientific uses, and it is equally certain that to ask themselves for leave to publish their case would be quite unavailing.

Sigmund Freud, *Fragment of an Analysis of a Case of Hysteria*

As the quotation above from the Hippocratic Oath suggests, doctors have long owed patients a duty of confidentiality. This ethical duty has become the subject of law in several contexts. We will begin with two: First, when may a patient prevent a doctor from testifying in court about the patient's confidences by invoking the patient's "privilege"? Second, when may or must a doctor reveal some kind of threat a patient may pose?

JAFFEE v. REDMOND
518 US 1 (1996)

STEVENS, J.

After a traumatic incident in which she shot and killed a man, a police officer received extensive counseling from a licensed clinical social worker. The question we address is whether statements the officer made to her therapist during the counseling sessions are protected from compelled disclosure in a federal civil action brought by the family of the deceased. Stated otherwise, the question is whether it is appropriate for federal courts to recognize a "psychotherapist privilege" under Rule 501 of the Federal Rules of Evidence. . . .

II

Rule 501 of the Federal Rules of Evidence authorizes federal courts to define new privileges by interpreting "common law principles ... in the light of reason and experience." . . . The Senate Report accompanying the 1975 adoption of the Rules indicates that Rule 501 "should be understood as reflecting the view that the recognition of a privilege based on a confidential relationship ... should be determined on a case-by-case basis." The Rule thus . . . directed federal courts to "continue the evolutionary development of testimonial privileges."

The common-law principles underlying the recognition of testimonial privileges can be stated simply. " 'For more than three centuries it has now been recognized as a fundamental maxim that the public ... has a right to every man's evidence. When we come to examine the various claims of exemption, we start with the primary assumption that there is a general duty to give what testimony one is capable of giving, and that any exemptions which may exist are distinctly exceptional, being so many derogations from a positive general rule.' " . . . Exceptions from the general rule disfavoring testimonial privileges may be justified, however, by a " 'public good transcending the normally predominant principle of utilizing all rational means for ascertaining truth.' " . . .

III . . . .

Like the spousal and attorney-client privileges, the psychotherapist-patient privilege is "rooted in the imperative need for confidence and trust." Treatment by a physician for physical ailments can often proceed successfully on the basis of a physical examination, objective information supplied by the patient, and the results of diagnostic tests. Effective psychotherapy, by contrast, depends upon an atmosphere of confidence and trust in which the patient is willing to make a frank and complete disclosure of facts, emotions, memories, and fears. . . . [D]isclosure of confidential communications made during counseling sessions may cause embarrassment or disgrace. For this reason, the mere possibility of disclosure may impede development of the confidential relationship necessary for successful treatment. . . . By protecting confidential communications between a psychotherapist and her patient from involuntary disclosure, the proposed privilege thus serves important private interests.

Our cases make clear that an asserted privilege must also "serv[e] public ends." Thus, the purpose of the attorney-client privilege is to "encourage full and frank communication between attorneys and their clients and thereby promote broader public interests in the observance of law and administration of justice." And the spousal privilege . . . is justified because it "furthers the important public interest in marital harmony." The psychotherapist privilege serves the public interest by facilitating the provision of appropriate treatment for individuals suffering the effects of a mental or emotional problem. The mental health of our citizenry, no less than its physical health, is a public good of transcendent importance. . . .

The likely evidentiary benefit that would result from the denial of the privilege is modest. If the privilege were rejected, confidential conversations between psychotherapists and their patients would surely be chilled, particularly when it is obvious that the circumstances that give rise to the need for treatment will probably result in litigation. Without a privilege, much of the desirable evidence to which litigants such as petitioner seek access--for example, admissions against interest by a party--is unlikely to come into being. This unspoken "evidence" will therefore serve no greater truth-seeking function than if it had been spoken and privileged.

That it is appropriate for the federal courts to recognize a psychotherapist privilege under Rule 501 is confirmed by the fact that all 50 States and the District of Columbia have enacted into law some form of psychotherapist privilege. . . . Because state legislatures are fully aware of the need to protect the integrity of the factfinding functions of their courts, the existence of a consensus among the States indicates that "reason and experience" support recognition of the privilege. In addition, given the importance of the patient's understanding that her communications with her therapist will not be publicly disclosed, any State's promise of confidentiality would have little value if the patient were aware that the privilege would not be honored in a federal court.[12] Denial of the federal privilege therefore would frustrate the purposes of the state legislation that was enacted to foster these confidential communications.

It is of no consequence that recognition of the privilege in the vast majority of States is the product of legislative action rather than judicial decision. Although common-law rulings may once have been the primary source of new developments in federal privilege law, that is no longer the case. In *Funk v. United States*, 290 U.S. 371 (1933), we recognized that it is appropriate to treat a consistent body of policy determinations by state legislatures as reflecting both "reason" and "experience." That rule is properly respectful of the States and at the same time reflects the fact that once a state legislature has enacted a privilege there is no longer an opportunity for common-law creation of the protection. The history of the psychotherapist privilege illustrates the latter point. In 1972 the members of the Judicial Conference Advisory Committee noted that the common law "had indicated a disposition to recognize a psychotherapist-patient privilege when legislatures began moving into the field." The present unanimous acceptance of the privilege shows that the state lawmakers moved quickly. That the privilege may have developed faster legislatively than it would have in the courts demonstrates only that the States rapidly recognized the wisdom of the rule as the field of psychotherapy developed.[13]

The uniform judgment of the States is reinforced by the fact that a psychotherapist privilege was among the nine specific privileges recommended by the Advisory Committee in its proposed privilege rules. . . . In rejecting the proposed draft that had specifically identified each privilege rule and substituting the present more open-ended Rule 501, the Senate Judiciary Committee explicitly stated that its action

---

[12]. At the outset of their relationship, the ethical therapist must disclose to the patient "the relevant limits on confidentiality." See American Psychological Association, Ethical Principles of Psychologists and Code of Conduct, Standard 5.01 (Dec. 1992). . . .

[13]. Petitioner . . . discounts the relevance of the state privilege statutes by pointing to divergence among the States concerning the types of therapy relationships protected and the exceptions recognized. . . . These variations in the scope of the protection are too limited to undermine the force of the States' unanimous judgment that some form of psychotherapist privilege is appropriate.

"should not be understood as disapproving any recognition of a psychiatrist-patient ... privileg[e] contained in the [proposed] rules." . . .

IV

All agree that a psychotherapist privilege covers confidential communications made to licensed psychiatrists and psychologists. We have no hesitation in concluding in this case that the federal privilege should also extend to confidential communications made to licensed social workers in the course of psychotherapy. The reasons for recognizing a privilege for treatment by psychiatrists and psychologists apply with equal force to treatment by a clinical social worker such as Karen Beyer. Today, social workers provide a significant amount of mental health treatment. Their clients often include the poor and those of modest means who could not afford the assistance of a psychiatrist or psychologist, but whose counseling sessions serve the same public goals. Perhaps in recognition of these circumstances, the vast majority of States explicitly extend a testimonial privilege to licensed social workers. . . .

We part company with the Court of Appeals on a separate point. We reject the balancing component of the privilege implemented by that court and a small number of States. Making the promise of confidentiality contingent upon a trial judge's later evaluation of the relative importance of the patient's interest in privacy and the evidentiary need for disclosure would eviscerate the effectiveness of the privilege. . . . [I]f the purpose of the privilege is to be served, the participants in the confidential conversation "must be able to predict with some degree of certainty whether particular discussions will be protected. An uncertain privilege, or one which purports to be certain but results in widely varying applications by the courts, is little better than no privilege at all."

These considerations are all that is necessary for decision of this case. A rule that authorizes the recognition of new privileges on a case-by-case basis makes it appropriate to define the details of new privileges in a like manner. Because this is the first case in which we have recognized a psychotherapist privilege, it is neither necessary nor feasible to delineate its full contours in a way that would "govern all conceivable future questions in this area." . . .

SCALIA, J., with whom THE CHIEF JUSTICE joins as to Part III, dissenting.

The Court has discussed at some length the benefit that will be purchased by creation of the evidentiary privilege in this case: the encouragement of psychoanalytic counseling. It has not mentioned the purchase price: occasional injustice. That is the cost of every rule which excludes reliable and probative evidence--or at least every one categorical enough to achieve its announced policy objective. In the case of some of these rules, such as the one excluding confessions that have not been properly "Mirandized," the victim of the injustice is always the impersonal State or the faceless "public at large." For the rule proposed here, the victim is more likely to be some individual who is prevented from proving a valid claim--or (worse still) prevented from establishing a valid defense. The latter is particularly unpalatable for those who love justice, because it causes the courts of law not merely to let stand a wrong, but to become themselves the instruments of wrong.

In the past, this Court has well understood that the particular value the courts are distinctively charged with preserving--justice--is severely harmed by contravention of "the fundamental principle that ' "the public ... has a right to every man's evidence." ' " Testimonial privileges, it has said, "*are not lightly created nor expansively construed,* for they are in derogation of the search for truth." Adherence to that principle has caused us, in the Rule 501 cases we have considered to date, to reject new privileges, see *University of Pennsylvania v. EEOC,* 493 U.S. 182 (1990) (privilege against disclosure of academic peer review materials); *United States v. Gillock,* 445 U.S. 360 (1980) (privilege against disclosure of "legislative acts" by member of state legislature), and even to construe narrowly the scope of existing privileges, see, *e.g., United States v. Zolin,* 491 U.S. 554, 568-570 (1989) (permitting *in camera* review of documents alleged to come within crime-fraud exception to attorney-client privilege); development of testimonial privileges." *Trammel v. United States,* 445 U.S. 40 (1980) (holding that voluntary testimony by spouse is not covered by husband-wife privilege). The Court today ignores this traditional judicial preference for the truth, and ends up creating a privilege that is new, vast, and ill defined. . . .

I

The . . . Court makes its task deceptively simple by the manner in which it proceeds. It begins by characterizing the issue as "whether it is appropriate for federal courts to recognize a 'psychotherapist privilege,' " and devotes almost all of its opinion to that question. Having answered that question (to its satisfaction) in the affirmative, it then devotes *less than a page of text* to answering in the affirmative the small remaining question whether "the federal privilege should also extend to confidential communications made to licensed social workers in the course of psychotherapy."

Of course the prototypical evidentiary privilege analogous to the one asserted here--the lawyer-client privilege--is not identified by the broad area of advice giving practiced by the person to whom the privileged communication is given, but rather by the *professional status* of that person. Hence, it seems a long step from a lawyer-client privilege to a tax advisor-client or accountant-client privilege. But if one recharacterizes it as a "legal advisor" privilege, the extension seems like the most natural thing in the world. That is the illusion the Court has produced here: It first frames an overly general question ("Should there be a psychotherapist privilege?") that can be answered in the negative only by excluding from protection office consultations with professional psychiatrists (*i.e.,* doctors) and clinical psychologists. And then, having answered that in the affirmative, it comes to the *only* question that the facts of this case present ("Should there be a social worker-client privilege with regard to psychotherapeutic counseling?") with the answer seemingly a foregone conclusion. At that point, to conclude against the privilege one must subscribe to the difficult proposition, "Yes, there is a psychotherapist privilege, but not if the psychotherapist is a social worker."

Relegating the question actually posed by this case to an afterthought makes the impossible possible in a number of wonderful ways. For example, it enables the Court to treat the Proposed Federal Rules of Evidence developed in 1972 by the Judicial Conference Advisory Committee as strong support for its holding, whereas they in fact counsel clearly and directly against it. The Committee did indeed recommend a "psychotherapist privilege" of sorts; but more precisely, and more relevantly, it recommended a privilege for psychotherapy conducted by "a person authorized to practice medicine" or "a person licensed or certified as a psychologist," which is to say that *it recommended against the privilege at issue here. . . .* The Proposed Rule figures prominently in the Court's explanation of why that privilege deserves recognition and is ignored in the single page devoted to the sideshow which happens to be the issue presented for decision. . . .

II . . . .

Effective psychotherapy undoubtedly is beneficial to individuals with mental problems, and surely serves some larger social interest in maintaining a mentally stable society. But merely mentioning these values does not answer the critical question: Are they of such importance, and is the contribution of psychotherapy to them so distinctive, and is the application of normal evidentiary rules so destructive to psychotherapy, as to justify making our federal courts occasional instruments of injustice? On that central question I find the Court's analysis insufficiently convincing to satisfy the high standard we have set for rules that "are in derogation of the search for truth."

When is it, one must wonder, that *the psychotherapist* came to play such an indispensable role in the maintenance of the citizenry's mental health? For most of history, men and women have worked out their difficulties by talking to, *inter alios,* parents, siblings, best friends, and bartenders--none of whom was awarded a privilege against testifying in court. Ask the average citizen: Would your mental health be more significantly impaired by preventing you from seeing a psychotherapist, or by preventing you from getting advice from your mom? I have little doubt what the answer would be. Yet there is no mother-child privilege.

How likely is it that a person will be deterred from seeking psychological counseling, or from being completely truthful in the course of such counseling, because of fear of later disclosure in litigation? . . . what extent will the evidentiary privilege reduce that deterrent? The Court does not try to answer the first of these questions; and it *cannot possibly have any notion* of what the answer is to the second, since that depends entirely upon the scope of the privilege, which the Court amazingly finds it "neither necessary nor feasible to delineate." If, for example, the psychotherapist can give the patient no more assurance than "A court will not be able to make me disclose what you tell me, unless you tell me about a harmful act," I doubt whether there would be much benefit from the privilege at all. That is not a fanciful example, at least with respect to extension of the psychotherapist privilege to social workers. See Del.Code Ann., Tit. 24, § 3913(2) (1987) . . . .

Even where it is certain that absence of the psychotherapist privilege will inhibit disclosure of the information, it is not clear to me that that is an unacceptable state of affairs. Let us assume the very worst in the circumstances of the present case: that to be truthful about what was troubling her, the police officer who sought counseling would have to confess that she shot without reason, and wounded an innocent man. If (again to assume the worst) such an act constituted the crime of negligent wounding under Illinois law, the officer would of course have the absolute right not to admit that she shot without reason in criminal court. But I see no reason why she should be enabled *both* not to admit it in criminal court (as a good citizen should), *and* to get the benefits of psychotherapy by admitting it to a therapist who cannot tell anyone else. And even less reason why she should be enabled to *deny* her guilt in the criminal trial--or in a civil trial for negligence--while yet obtaining the benefits of psychotherapy by confessing guilt to a social worker who cannot testify. It seems to me entirely fair to say that if she wishes the benefits of telling the truth she must also accept the adverse consequences. To be sure, in most cases the statements to the psychotherapist will be only marginally relevant, and one of the purposes of the privilege (though not one relied upon by the Court) may be simply to spare patients needless intrusion upon their privacy . . . But surely this can be achieved by means short of excluding even evidence that is of the most direct and conclusive effect.

The Court confidently asserts that not much truth-finding capacity would be destroyed by the privilege anyway, since "[w]ithout a privilege, much of the desirable evidence to which litigants such as petitioner seek access ... is unlikely to come into being." If that is so, how come psychotherapy got to be a thriving practice before the "psychotherapist privilege" was invented? Were the patients paying money to lie to their analysts all those years? Of course the evidence-generating effect of the privilege (if any) depends entirely upon its scope, which the Court steadfastly declines to consider. And even if one assumes that scope to be the broadest possible, is it really true that most, or even many, of those who seek psychological counseling have the worry of litigation in the back of their minds? I doubt that, and the Court provides no evidence to support it.

The Court suggests one last policy justification: since psychotherapist privilege statutes exist in all the States, the failure to recognize a privilege in federal courts "would frustrate the purposes of the state legislation that was enacted to foster these confidential communications." This is a novel argument indeed. A sort of inverse pre-emption: The truth-seeking functions of *federal* courts must be adjusted so as not to conflict with the policies *of the States*. . . . Moreover, since state policies regarding the psychotherapist privilege vary considerably from State to State, *no* uniform federal policy can possibly honor most of them. . . .

The Court's failure to put forward a convincing justification of its own could perhaps be excused if it were relying upon the unanimous conclusion of state courts in the reasoned development of their common law. It cannot do that, since *no* State has such a privilege apart from legislation.[1] What it relies upon, instead, is "the fact that all

---

[1]. The Court observes: "In 1972 the members of the Judicial Conference Advisory Committee noted that the common law 'had indicated a disposition to recognize a psychotherapist-patient privilege when legislatures began moving into the field.' Proposed Rules, 56 F.R.D., at 242 (citation omitted)." The sole support the Committee invoked was a student Note . . . . That source, in turn, cites (and discusses) a single case recognizing a common-law psychotherapist privilege: the unpublished opinion of a judge of the Circuit Court of Cook County, Illinois, . . . which, in turn, cites no other cases.

I doubt whether the Court's failure to provide more substantial support for its assertion stems from want of trying. Respondents and all of their *amici* pointed us to only four other state-court decisions supposedly adopting a common-law psychotherapist privilege. . . . It is not surprising that the Court thinks it not worth the trouble to cite them: (1) In *In re "B,"* 394 A.2d 419 (1978), the opinions of four of the seven justices *explicitly rejected* a nonstatutory privilege; and the two justices who did recognize one recognized, not a common-law privilege, but rather (*mirabile dictu*) a privilege "constitutionally based," "emanat[ing] from the penumbras of the various guarantees of the Bill of Rights, ... as well as from the guarantees of the Constitution of this Commonwealth. (2) *Allred v. State*, 554 P.2d 411 (Alaska 1976), held that no privilege was available in the case before the court, so what it says about the existence of a common-law privilege is the purest dictum. (3) *Falcon v. Alaska Pub. Offices Comm'n*, 570 P.2d 469 (1977), a later Alaska Supreme Court case, proves the last statement. It *rejected* the claim by a physician that he did not have to disclose the names of his patients, even though some of the physician's practice consisted of psychotherapy . . . . And finally, (4) *State v. Evans*, 454 P.2d 976 (1969), created a limited privilege, applicable to court-ordered examinations to determine competency to stand trial, *which tracked a privilege that had been*

50 States and the District of Columbia have [1] *enacted into law* [2] *some form* of psychotherapist privilege." Let us consider both the verb and its object: The fact [1] that all 50 States have *enacted* this privilege argues not *for,* but *against,* our adopting the privilege judicially. At best it suggests that the matter has been found not to lend itself to judicial treatment . . . . At worst it suggests that the privilege commends itself only to decisionmaking bodies in which reason is tempered, so to speak, by political pressure from organized interest groups (such as psychologists and social workers), and decisionmaking bodies that are not overwhelmingly concerned (as courts of law are and should be) with justice.

And the phrase [2] "some form of psychotherapist privilege" covers a multitude of difficulties. The Court concedes that there is "divergence among the States concerning the types of therapy relationships protected and the exceptions recognized." To rest a newly announced federal common-law psychotherapist privilege upon "the States' *unanimous judgment* that some form of psychotherapist privilege is appropriate," is rather like announcing a new, immediately applicable, federal common law of torts, based upon the States' "unanimous judgment" that *some* form of tort law is appropriate. In the one case as in the other, the state laws vary to such a degree that the parties and lower federal judges confronted by the new "common law" have barely a clue as to what its content might be.

III . . . .

The Court . . . has "no hesitation in concluding . . . that the federal privilege should also extend" to social workers – and goes on to prove that by polishing off the reasoned analysis with a topic sentence and two sentences of discussion . . . . So much for the rule that privileges are to be narrowly construed.

---

legislatively created after the defendant's examination.

In light of this dearth of case support--from all the courts of 50 States, down to the county-court level--it seems to me the Court's assertion should be revised to read: "The common law had indicated *scant* disposition to recognize a psychotherapist-patient privilege when (*or even after*) legislatures began moving into the field."

Of course this brief analysis . . . contains no explanation of why the psychotherapy provided by social workers is a public good of such transcendent importance as to be purchased at the price of occasional injustice. Moreover, it considers only the respects in which social workers providing therapeutic services are *similar* to licensed psychiatrists and psychologists; not a word about the respects in which they are different. A licensed psychiatrist or psychologist is an expert in psychotherapy--and that may suffice (though I think it not so clear that this Court should make the judgment) to justify the use of extraordinary means to encourage counseling with him, as opposed to counseling with one's rabbi, minister, family, or friends. One must presume that a social worker does *not* bring this greatly heightened degree of skill to bear, which is alone a reason for not encouraging that consultation as generously. Does a social worker bring to bear at least a significantly heightened degree of skill--more than a minister or rabbi, for example? I have no idea, and neither does the Court. The social worker in the present case, Karen Beyer, was a "licensed clinical social worker" in Illinois, a job title whose training requirements consist of a "master's degree in social work from an approved program," and "3,000 hours of satisfactory, supervised clinical professional experience." It is not clear that the degree in social work requires *any* training in psychotherapy. The "clinical professional experience" apparently will impart some such training, but only of the vaguest sort, judging from the Illinois Code's definition of "[c]linical social work practice," viz., "the providing of mental health services for the evaluation, treatment, and prevention of mental and emotional disorders in individuals, families and groups based on knowledge and theory of psychosocial development, behavior, psychopathology, unconscious motivation, interpersonal relationships, and environmental stress." . . . With due respect, it does not seem to me that any of this training is comparable in its rigor (or indeed in the precision of its subject) to the training of the other experts (lawyers) to whom this Court has accorded a privilege, or even of the experts (psychiatrists and psychologists) to whom the Advisory Committee and this Court proposed extension of a privilege in 1972. Of course these are only *Illinois'* requirements for "social workers." Those of other States, for all we know, may be even less demanding. Indeed, I am not even sure there is a nationally accepted definition of "social worker," as there is of psychiatrist and psychologist. It seems to me quite irresponsible to extend the so-called "psychotherapist privilege" to all licensed social workers, nationwide, without exploring these issues.

Another critical distinction between psychiatrists and psychologists, on the one hand, and social workers, on the other, is that the former professionals, in their consultations with patients, *do nothing but psychotherapy.* Social workers, on the other hand, interview people for a multitude of reasons. . . . Thus . . . it will be necessary to determine whether the information provided to the social worker was provided to him *in his capacity as a psychotherapist,* or in his capacity as an administrator of social welfare, a community organizer, etc. Worse still, if the privilege is to have its desired effect (and is not to mislead the client), it will presumably be necessary for the social caseworker to advise, as the conversation with his welfare client proceeds, which portions are privileged and which are not.

Having concluded its three sentences of reasoned analysis, the Court then invokes . . . the "experience" of the States . . . . It says that "the vast majority of States explicitly extend a testimonial privilege to licensed social workers." There are two elements of this impressive statistic, however, that the Court does not reveal.

First--and utterly conclusive of the irrelevance of this supposed consensus to the question before us--the majority of the States that accord a privilege to social workers do *not* do so as a subpart of a "psychotherapist" privilege. The privilege applies to *all* confidences imparted to social workers, and not just those provided in the course of psychotherapy. . . .

Thus, in Oklahoma, as in most other States having a social-worker privilege, it is not a subpart or even a derivative of the psychotherapist privilege, but rather a piece of special legislation similar to that achieved by many other groups, from accountants, to private detectives. These social-worker statutes give no support, therefore, to the theory (importance of psychotherapy) upon which the Court rests its disposition.

Second, the Court does not reveal the enormous degree of disagreement among the States as to the scope of the privilege. . . .

[T]urning to those States that do have an appreciable privilege of some sort, the diversity is vast. In Illinois and Wisconsin, the social-worker privilege does not apply when the confidential information pertains to homicide, and in the District of Columbia when it pertains to any crime "inflicting injuries" upon persons. In Missouri, the privilege is suspended as to information that pertains to a criminal act, and in Texas when the information is sought in any criminal prosecution. In Kansas and Oklahoma, the privilege yields when the information pertains to "violations of any law," in Indiana, when it reveals a "serious harmful act," and in Delaware and Idaho, when it pertains to any "harmful act." In Oregon, a state-employed social worker like Karen Beyer loses the privilege where her supervisor determines that her testimony "is necessary in the performance of the duty of the social worker as a public employee." In South Carolina, a social worker is forced to disclose confidences "when required by statutory law or by court order for good cause shown to the extent that the patient's care and treatment or the nature and extent of his mental illness or emotional condition are reasonably at issue in a proceeding." The majority of social-worker-privilege States declare the privilege inapplicable to information relating to child abuse. And the States that do not fall into any of the above categories provide exceptions for commitment proceedings, for proceedings in which the patient relies on his mental or emotional condition as an element of his claim or defense, or for communications made in the course of a court-ordered examination of the mental or emotional condition of the patient. . . .

No State has adopted the privilege without restriction; the nature of the restrictions varies enormously from jurisdiction to jurisdiction; and 10 States . . . effectively reject the privilege entirely. It is fair to say that there is scant national consensus even as to the propriety of a social-worker psychotherapist privilege, and none whatever as to its appropriate scope. In other words, the state laws to which the Court appeals for support demonstrate most convincingly that adoption of a social-worker psychotherapist privilege is a job for Congress.

* * *

The question before us today is not whether there should be an evidentiary privilege for social workers providing therapeutic services. Perhaps there should. But the question before us is whether (1) the need for that privilege is so clear, and (2) the desirable contours of that privilege are so evident, that it is appropriate for this Court to craft it in common-law fashion, under Rule 501. Even if we were writing on a clean slate, I think the answer to that question would be clear. But given our extensive precedent to the effect that new privileges "in derogation of the search for truth" "are not lightly created," *United*

States v. Nixon, 418 U.S. 683, 710 (1974). the answer the Court gives today is inexplicable.

In its consideration of this case, the Court was the beneficiary of no fewer than 14 *amicus* briefs supporting respondents, most of which came from such organizations as the American Psychiatric Association, the American Psychoanalytic Association, the American Association of State Social Work Boards, the Employee Assistance Professionals Association, Inc., the American Counseling Association, and the National Association of Social Workers. Not a single *amicus* brief was filed in support of petitioner. That is no surprise. There is no self-interested organization out there devoted to pursuit of the truth in the federal courts. The expectation is, however, that this Court will have that interest prominently--indeed, primarily--in mind. Today we have failed that expectation, and that responsibility. . . .

Notes on Privacy

"Privacy" is the best of words, it is the worst of words. It is the word of wisdom, it is the word of foolishness, it means everything, it means nothing. In short, some of the noisiest authorities insist on its being received, for good or for evil, in the superlative degree of comparison only. Who could object to privacy? Who knows what it means? Who actually wants?

People who believe that "privacy" really means something important generally use two arguments, as Ferdinand Shoeman, *Privacy: Philosophical Dimensions*, 21 Am Phil Q 1999 (1984), explains:

> 1. Arguments designed to show that respect for privacy is a key component in the more general regard for human dignity. The appeal here is to such conditions as moral integrity, individuality, consciousness of oneself as a being with moral character and worth, and consciousness of oneself as a being with a point of view, searching for meaning in life.

> 2. Arguments designed to show that respect for privacy is integral to our understanding of ourselves as social beings with varying kinds of relationships, each in its way important to a meaningful life. Both of these approaches attempt to demonstrate a connection between respect for privacy and certain individual, social and political ideals.

Morally skeptical treatments of privacy have generally adopted one of two approaches:

1. Some suggest that the kinds of interests protected by privacy are not really distinctive or morally illuminating, and hence do not constitute an independent moral category.

2. Others argue that protecting privacy and recognition of institutions of privacy may be harmful to the individual in making him psychologically vulnerable, and detrimental to the society through the encouragement of a-social or anti-social attitudes.

Legally, the confusion and debate are at least as great. Dean Prosser noted long ago (William L. Prosser, *Privacy*, 48 Calif L Rev 383, 389 (1960)) that tort provides remedies against four kinds of invasion of privacy:

1. Intrusion upon the plaintiff's seclusion or solitude, or into his private affairs.

2. Public disclosure of embarrassing private facts about the plaintiff.

3. Publicity which places the plaintiff in a false light in the public eye.

4. Appropriation, for the defendant's advantage, of the plaintiff's name or likeness.

Since Dean Prosser wrote, the Supreme Court has greatly confused matters by categorizing some kinds of constitutional rights under the rubric of privacy.

Is privacy really important? Carl E. Schneider & Margaret F. Brinig, *An Invitation to Family Law* (West, 2001), ask:

> Isn't privacy culturally determined and hence arbitrary? For most of . . . history, for example, houses were small and had relatively few rooms; servants, apprentices, and boarders lived with the family; and several people might sleep in a single bed. Today, such living arrangements would commonly be regarded as giving people too little privacy. If the things we think of as private are simply culturally determined, cannot they be changed by a cultural decision . . . ? And might it not be desirable to take the opportunity to narrow the scope of privacy? Consider the following arguments.

To begin with, privacy may be simply unnecessary. Why should people want to keep private things of which there is no reason to be ashamed? Why should people be able to keep private things of which they are ashamed? Is it honest to live one life in public and another in private? Is it healthy? . . .

Isn't privacy actively harmful? . . . First, privacy can . . . [make] people feel isolated and unhappy. People are social animals. They do not like to feel separated from the rest of society, or even that they are radically different from other people. But if some important subjects are barred from conversation or public knowledge, people may not know that there are other people who are like them. They may thus be deprived of the comfort that comes from knowing that they are not alone and from getting to know people who share their characteristics. . . .

Second, and relatedly, isn't "privacy" in fact simply another mechanism of social control, a means of keeping people from knowing what others are doing and learning that they are not alone? . . .

Third, there is an association in our minds between privacy and shameful subjects. This can mean that subjects that come within the scope of privacy can easily come to be thought of as subjects for embarrassment. This can have deplorable consequences. For instance, people might be deterred from seeking psychotherapy they need by the embarrassment that can be associated with it. . . .

Fourth, and more broadly, Richard Wasserstrom writes, "We have made ourselves vulnerable — or at least far more vulnerable than we need be — by accepting the notion that there are thoughts and actions concerning which we ought to feel ashamed or embarrassed. When we realize that everyone has fantasies, desires, worries about all sorts of supposedly terrible, wicked, and shameful things, we ought to see that they really are not things to be ashamed of at all."

Fifth, Wasserstrom makes another standard argument against privacy: "[F]orthrightness, honesty, and candor are, for the most part, virtues, while hypocrisy and deceit are not. Yet this emphasis upon the maintenance of a private side to life tends to encourage hypocritical and deceitful ways of behavior. Individuals tend to see themselves as leading dual lives – public ones and private ones. . . . This way of living is hypocritical because it is, in essence, a life devoted to camouflaging the real, private self from public scrutiny. It is a dualistic, unintegrated life that renders the individuals who live it needlessly vulnerable, shame ridden, and lacking in a clear sense of self."

>Sixth is another standard attack on privacy . . . . Proponents of this criticism are afraid that private life may become so central to people that public life will be injured. Public life is . . . considered important because it is thought of as the means by which people take responsibility for the state of the society in which they live and the people with whom they share society. Private life is the life led thinking about oneself, one's family, and one's close friends. These critics . . . worry that people will become concerned about these things to the exclusion of the larger welfare of the society or of people who are strangers to them.

As you read these materials on confidentiality, you should ask yourself exactly what any given rule is protecting. Something called "privacy"? Something more specific, if less grand?

Notes on Private Remedies for Breaches of Confidentiality

Jaffee speaks of various state remedies for breaches of medical confidentiality. The state remedies vary enormously, but here is a brief sampling of some common approaches. In *McCormick v. England*, 494 SE2d 431 (Ct App S Car 1997), the defendant, Dr. England, was the McCormick family physician when the McCormicks', divorce action raised issues about the custody of the McCormick children. Mr. McCormick

>submitted two letters to the family court regarding Mrs. McCormick's emotional status. One . . . was prepared by Dr. England and was addressed "To Whom It May Concern." . . . Dr. England diagnosed McCormick as suffering from "major depression and alcoholism, acute and chronic." Further, Dr. England stated the children had experienced school difficulties due to the family discord caused by McCormick's drinking. He stated it was his medical opinion that McCormick was "a danger to herself and to her family with her substance abuse and major depressive symptoms," and concluded that she required hospitalization.

Mrs. McCormick sued for negligence, libel, invasion of privacy, outrage, breach of confidence, and civil conspiracy. The court observed that South Carolina had no physician-patient testimonial privilege. However, as the South Carolina Supreme Court had noted in "*South Carolina State Board of Medical Examiners v. Hedgepath,* 480 S.E.2d 724 (1997): 'The terms "privilege" and "confidences" are not synonymous, and a professional's duty to maintain his client's confidences is independent of the issue whether he can be legally compelled to reveal some or all of those confidences, that is, whether those communications are privileged.'"

In *Hedgepath*, the State Board of Medical Examiners had disciplined a doctor for breaching 26 S.C.Code Ann. Regs. 81-60(D) (Supp.1996): "A physician shall respect the rights of patients . . . and shall safeguard patient confidence within the constraints of the law." The *McCormick* court said that in

> the absence of express legislation, courts have found the basis for a right of action for wrongful disclosure in four main sources: (1) state physician licensing statutes, (2) evidentiary rules and privileged communication statutes which prohibit a physician from testifying in judicial proceedings, (3) common law principles of trust, and (4) the Hippocratic Oath and principles of medical ethics which proscribe the revelation of patient confidences. The jurisdictions that recognize the duty of confidentiality have relied on various theories . . . , including invasion of privacy, breach of implied contract, medical malpractice, and breach of a fiduciary duty or a duty of confidentiality.

The *McCormick* court concluded that South Carolina "has a public policy in favor of maintaining the confidentiality of physician-patient relationships." The court cited not only *Hedgepath* and the statutes it invoked, but also *Hodge v. Shea*, 168 SE2d 82 (1969), in which the South Carolina Supreme Court "stated that the physician-patient relationship is a confidential relationship." The McCormick court thought "the reasoning of the cases from other jurisdictions persuasive on this issue" and held "that an actionable tort lies for a physician's breach of the duty to maintain the confidences of his or her patient in the absence of a compelling public interest or other justification for the disclosure."

The court decided that the "existence of a cause of action for invasion of privacy should not preclude our recognition of an independent tort for a physician's breach of confidence because the actions are distinguishable." It said,

Invasion of privacy consists of the public disclosure of private facts about the plaintiff, and the gravamen of the tort is publicity as opposed to mere publication. The defendant must intentionally reveal facts which are of no legitimate public interest . . . . In addition, the disclosure must be such as would be highly offensive and likely to cause serious mental injury to a person of ordinary sensibilities.

Thus, an invasion of privacy claim narrowly proscribes the conduct to that which is "highly offensive" and "likely to cause serious mental injury." This standard is not consistent with the duty attaching to a confidential relationship because it focuses on the content, rather than the source of the information. The unauthorized revelation of confidential medical information should be protected without regard to the degree of its offensiveness. The privacy standard would not protect information that happens to be very distressing to a particular patient, even though the individual would likely not have revealed it without the expectation of confidentiality.

Further, the requirement of "publicity" . . . would preclude many cases involving a breach of confidentiality. Publicity involves disclosure to the public, not just an individual or a small group. However, where the information disclosed is received in confidence, "one can imagine many cases where the greatest injury results from disclosure to a single person, such as a spouse, or to a small group, such as an insurance company resisting a claim."

Did Mrs. McCormick have an action for breach of contract? Consider *Doe v. Roe*, 400 NYS2d 668 (1977):

Dr. Joan Roe is a physician who has practiced psychiatry for more than fifty years. Her husband, Peter Poe, has been a psychologist for some 25 years. The plaintiff and her late, former husband were each patients of Dr. Roe for many years. The defendants, eight years after the termination of treatment, published a book which reported verbatim and extensively the patients' thoughts, feelings, and emotions, their sexual and other fantasies and biographies, their most intimate personal relationships and the disintegration of their marriage. Interspersed among the footnotes are Roe's diagnoses of what purport to be the illnesses suffered by the patients and one of their children.

The court held "that a physician, who enters into an agreement with a patient to provide medical attention, impliedly covenants to keep in confidence all disclosures made by the patient concerning the patient's physical or mental condition as well as all matters discovered by the physician in the course of examination or treatment." The court said:

> Mr. Poe's liability is equally clear. True, he and the plaintiff were not involved in a physician-patient relationship and he certainly had no contractual relationship to her. But . . . Poe, like anyone else with access to the book, knew that its source was the patient's production in psychoanalysis. He knew as well as, and perhaps better than Roe, of the absence of consent, of the failure to disguise. If anyone was the actor in seeing to it that the work was written, that it was manufactured, advertised and circulated, it was Poe. He is a co-author of the and a willing, indeed avid, co-violator of the patient's rights and is therefore equally liable.

Are you convinced by this reasoning? Does it matter whether a patient's remedy for a breach of the ethical duty of confidentiality is in tort or in contract?

Notes and Questions on *Jaffee*, Privacy, and Privilege

1. "At the second trial, Jaffee sought $100,000 in damages on her § 1983 claim and $2,000,000 in damages on her state-law wrongful death claim. Jaffee again prevailed on her civil rights claim; the jury awarded her the full $100,000. Unlike in the first trial, however, the jury this time found for the defendants on Jaffee's state-law claim." *Jaffee v. Redmond*, 142 F3d 409 (7th Cir 1998).

2. *US v. Stevens*, 1999 WL 453948 (AF CtCrimApp):

> A court-martial is a search for the truth. However, the truth is often as elusive as a cat. Normally, once an accused makes an admission that suggests an allegation against him is true, it's out of the bag forever. However, a privilege allows an accused to put the cat back in the bag. Only a rule-maker, for good and sufficient policy reasons, can grant an accused the privilege to use the bag again. The President is our rule-maker. Article 36, UCMJ, 10 U.S.C. § 836. He has provided us with the following rule about privileges, "Notwithstanding any other provision of these rules, information not otherwise privileged does not become privileged on the basis that it was acquired by a medical officer or civilian physician in a professional capacity." Mil. R. Evid. 501(d). As a result, it is clear

that the Mil. R. Evid. does not recognize a doctor-patient privilege. Further, it also includes treatment that falls within the medical specialties of psychiatry and psychology.

3. A key witness in *United States v. Mazzola*, 217 FRD 84 (2003), was the brother of two tax-fraud defendants and the son of another. The defendants sought access to psychotherapeutic records relating to the witness's "mental instability" and his relations with his family. The magistrate granted them that access:

> Unlike the circumstance at issue in *Jaffee*, this case is a criminal prosecution involving the medical records of a key government witness. The evidentiary benefit of allowing access to such medical records to defense counsel in order to effectively prepare and cross examine Joseph Mazzola is great. Although the societal interest in guarding the confidentiality of communications between a therapist and his or her client is significant, it does not outweigh the need for effective cross examination of this key government witness at the criminal trial. Reason and experience caution against recognizing a blanket federal common law privilege for therapist records of an important government witness regarding therapy sessions temporally proximate to the criminal charges.
>
> Because a federal common law privilege does not apply, it becomes necessary to address whether Joseph Mazzola has a privacy privilege rooted in the Constitution protecting the medical records at issue. The right of privacy founded in the Fourteenth Amendment's concept of personal liberty protects the right of an individual such as Joseph Mazzola to avoid disclosing personal and private matters. See *Whalen v. Roe*, 429 U.S. 589 (1977). At best, however, the Constitution "provides *qualified* protection for medical records." The individual's right to privacy in avoiding disclosure of medical records as well as the federal policy of protecting the privacy of a patient's medical records are therefore balanced against the defendant's interest in examining the medical records of a key government witness and the concomitant right to cross examine that witness. . . .
>
> Defendants have a Sixth Amendment right to confront the witnesses testifying against them. . . .

Mental disorders such as an addiction to drugs are highly probative of credibility and may materially effect the accuracy of a witness' testimony. The scope and depth of Joseph Mazzola's drug use during the time period covered by the Indictment, as evidenced by the medical records, may impact his ability to perceive the events in question. . . . Medication prescribed to Joseph Mazzola, primarily for back pain, sinusitis, gastroesophageal reflux disease and kidney stones, is material to assess the depth, degree and ongoing nature of Joseph Mazzola's drug problem. Severe psychological issues coupled with the magnitude of the continued use of prescription medication after the time period covered by the Indictment impacts Joseph Mazzola's acuity and ability to testify accurately at trial. . . .

Likewise, information in the medical records about the perceived abuse from his father, a co-defendant, as well as from familial co-defendants . . . will assist the jury in evaluating Joseph Mazzola's credibility and motivations for testifying. Defendant Stephen J. Mazzola also has an interest in obtaining information in the medical records relative to Joseph Mazzola's financial difficulties in order to support the defense that Joseph Mazzola was embezzling the under-reported funds. References in the medical records to Joseph Mazzola's fragility, mental instability and anxiety are material to his perception of events during the time period charged in the Indictment and his ability to recall and testify to such events at trial.

4. Who is a therapist? When is a therapist a therapist? In Massachusetts, a sexual assault counsellor is "a person who is employed by or is a volunteer in a rape crisis center, has undergone thirty-five hours of training, who reports to and is under the direct control and supervision of a licensed social worker, nurse, psychiatrist, psychologist or psychotherapist and whose primary purpose is the rendering of advice, counselling or assistance to victims of sexual assault." Mass.G.L. ch. 233, § 20J. Why might there be no privilege? Why did *US v. Lowe*, 948 FSupp 97 (D Mass 1006), hold that there was?

5. Is there a "peer review" privilege in federal law? That issue arose in *Nilavar v. Mercy Health System - Western Ohio*, 210 FRD 597 (2002). The court defined peer review as

the system by which groups or committees of physicians review the work of their colleagues to evaluate the soundness of the colleague's medical decisions in any given situation. The practice . . . helps root out incompetence in the medical profession, which, in turn, leads to a higher overall level of health care for patients. . . . While the practice is invaluable to the profession of medicine, reviewing physicians have an obvious interest in maintaining the confidentiality of their reviews, particularly so as not to become implicated in any civil suit which may arise out of the treating physician's negligence. The import of Defendants' assertion of privilege in objecting to Plaintiff's various discovery requests is easily recognized: privileged matter is not discoverable.

The *Nilavar* court acknowledged that if

Jaffee were the only source of authority for the Court's decision in this case, Defendants' argument that a physician peer review privilege should be recognized would pose a close question indeed. As with the psychotherapist-patient privilege recognized in *Jaffee,* the states are substantially, if not completely, in harmony in recognizing a physician peer review privilege. However, the great weight of the *federal* cases, many of them decided after *Jaffee,* counsel that such a privilege does not exist in the federal common law . . . .

Nilavar reviewed seven "federal court cases in support of the proposition that a physician peer review privilege exists." One, *Cohn v. Wilkes General Hosp*, 127 FRD 117 (WDNC 1989), an antitrust case,

found that a policy favoring a physician peer review privilege was demonstrated by the passage of the Health Care Quality Improvement Act of 1986, 42 U.S.C. § 11101, *et seq.* ("HCQIA"), wherein Congress noted the need to protect the confidentiality of physician peer review materials so as not to discourage physicians from engaging in such practice out of fear of liability under other federal laws. . . . Congress specifically found that physicians' fears of treble damage liability under the Sherman Act "unreasonably discourages physicians from participating in effective professional peer review.". . .

The HCQIA was enacted in the interest of both reducing medical incompetence and protecting physicians who take part in the peer review process, which ultimately exposes such medical incompetence. In return for requiring "professional review bodies," defined as groups of health care professionals who review the work of their colleagues, to report to the Secretary of Health and Human Services, among other things, any action taken which adversely affects a physician's clinical privileges, the statute guarantees that all such information "reported under this subchapter [shall be] considered confidential and shall not be disclosed," except under certain circumstances not relevant herein. Far from creating a broad privilege, Congress, in enacting the HCQIA, carefully crafted a very specific privilege, applicable to peer review material *submitted to the Secretary* pursuant to the dictates of the mandatory reporting provisions of that statute. . . .

Without the comforting guarantee of absolute confidentiality, it is unlikely that, . . . in the attorney-client context, the truth in both civil and criminal matters would be anything more than an illusory ideal; or that, in the psychotherapist-patient context, emotionally distraught individuals would seek professional consultation for their illnesses. Defendants have not convinced this Court that the need for confidentiality in the peer review process, as implicated in this particular case, rises to the highest level of importance as it does in those other contexts, or that the process will not function properly in the absence of a federal evidentiary privilege. . . .

Is *Nilavar* consistent with *Jaffee*? *Jaffee* critically relied on the pattern of privilege laws in the states. Is the pattern in *Nilavar* significantly different from the pattern in *Jaffee*? Is the "peer-review" privilege significantly less important than the psychotherapist-patient privilege? Professions have historically been accorded a large measure of autonomy on the theory that only professionals can evaluate other professionals. And desire for the esteem of one's colleagues is a large part of drives professionals to do their work well:

The intramural competition that professions cultivate is far from foolproof as a means of sustaining high levels of proficiency and ethical conduct among practitioners, but our reliance upon it is far-reaching and by no means misplaced; competition does constrain individual conduct in useful ways. In effect, professions are markets in which competing practitioners try to acquire not only income and assets, but also a good reputation—a stock of favorable impressions of one's self and one's work in the minds of others, especially fellow practitioners, who are better equipped than anyone else to pass judgment. . . . Trust can best be elicited collectively by requiring all practitioners systematically to submit to the critical appraisal of their peers. The result is an occupational subculture that tends to be acutely status conscious, but which also tolerates greater candor and higher levels of criticism and conflict than would be thought acceptable in most human communities.

Thomas L. Haskell, *The New Aristocracy,* The New York Review of Books 47, 52 (Dec. 4, 1997).

Medicine has a robust tradition of frank self-criticism. Not least, the mortality and morbidity conference has traditionally brought the doctors in a unit together to discuss cases "where expectations are positive and outcomes are negative." Charles L. Bosk, *Forgive and Remember: Managing Medical Failure* (U Chicago Press, 1979). At this meeting, "failure is accounted for professionally." It is, for example, "the only occasion in surgical training that exists for public and open criticism of attending surgeons." In the conference, "[a]ttending surgeons [sometimes] publicly abase themselves before an audience of their colleagues and subordinates. They publicly claim that they made mistakes in the handling of the case." This "[p]utting on the hair shirt is the major and most striking activity of formalized retrospective peer review. By this practice surgeons excuse their mistakes by admitting them. The major punishment of the practice is the embarrassment of a public confessional and the pain the outcome itself actually causes the surgeon's conscience. As a form of social control, this admission of error rests on the self-surveillance and self-reports of the individuals involved."

B. Confidentiality as Privilege and Duty: The Duty to Warn

TARASOFF v. REGENTS OF THE UNIVERSITY OF CALIFORNIA
Supreme Court of California (Cal 1976)

TOBRINER, JUSTICE.

On October 27, 1969, Prosenjit Poddar killed Tatiana Tarasoff. Plaintiffs, Tatiana's parents, allege that . . . Poddar confided his intention to kill Tatiana to Dr. Lawrence Moore, a psychologist employed by the Cowell Memorial Hospital at the University of California at Berkeley. . . . No one warned plaintiffs of Tatiana's peril.

Concluding that these facts set forth causes of action against neither therapists and policemen involved, nor against the Regents of the University of California as their employer, the superior court sustained defendants' demurrers to plaintiffs' second amended complaints without leave to amend. . . .

1. *Plaintiffs' complaints.* . . .

Plaintiffs' first cause of action, entitled "Failure to Detain a Dangerous Patient," alleges that on August 20, 1969, Poddar was a voluntary outpatient receiving therapy at Cowell Memorial Hospital. Poddar informed Moore, his therapist, that he was going to kill an unnamed girl, readily identifiable as Tatiana, when she returned home from spending the summer in Brazil. Moore, with the concurrence of Dr. Gold, who had initially examined Poddar, and Dr. Yandell, Assistant to the director of the department of psychiatry, decided that Poddar should be committed for observation in a mental hospital. Moore orally notified Officers Atkinson and Teel of the campus police that he would request commitment. He then sent a letter to Police Chief William Beall requesting the assistance of the police department in securing Poddar's confinement.

Officers Atkinson, Brownrigg, and Halleran took Poddar into custody, but, satisfied that Poddar was rational, released him on his promise to stay away from Tatiana. Powelson, director of the department of psychiatry at Cowell Memorial Hospital, then asked the police to return Moore's letter, directed that all copies of the letter and notes that Moore had taken as therapist be destroyed, and "ordered no action to place Prosenjit Poddar in 72-hour treatment and evaluation facility."

Plaintiffs' second cause of action, entitled "Failure to Warn On a Dangerous Patient," incorporates the allegations of the first cause of action, but adds the assertion that defendants negligently permitted Poddar to be released from police custody without "notifying the parents of Tatiana Tarasoff that their daughter was in grave danger from Posenjit Poddar." Poddar persuaded Tatiana's brother to share an apartment with him near Tatiana's residence; shortly after her return from Brazil, Poddar went to her residence and killed her. . . .

2. *Plaintiffs can state a cause of action against defendant therapists for negligent failure to protect Tatiana.*

[The court held that the first cause of action was "barred by governmental immunity."] The second cause of action can be amended to allege that Tatiana's death proximately resulted from defendants' negligent failure to warn Tatiana or others likely to apprise her of her danger. . . .

[L]iability should be imposed "for an injury occasioned to another by his want of ordinary care or skill" as expressed in section 1714 of the Civil Code. Thus, "whenever one person is by circumstances placed in such a position with regard to another . . . that if he did not use ordinary care and skill in his own conduct . . . he would cause danger of injury to the person or property of the other, a duty arises to use ordinary care and skill to avoid such danger."

We depart from "this fundamental principle" only upon the "balancing of a number of considerations"; major ones "are the foreseeability of harm to the plaintiff, the degree of certainty that the plaintiff suffered injury, the closeness of the connection between the defendant's conduct and the injury suffered, the moral blame attached to the defendant's conduct, the policy of preventing future harm, the extent of the burden to the defendant and consequences to the community of imposing a duty to exercise care with resulting liability for breach, and the availability, cost and prevalence of insurance for the risk involved."

The most important of these considerations in establishing duty is foreseeability. As a general principle, a "defendant owes a duty of care to all persons who are foreseeably endangered by his conduct, with respect to all risks which make the conduct unreasonably dangerous." . . .

Although, . . . under the common law, . . . one person owed no duty to control the conduct of another nor to warn those endangered by such conduct, the courts have carved out an exception . . . in cases in which the defendant stands in some special relationship to either the person whose conduct needs to be controlled or . . . to the foreseeable victim of that conduct. . . . [A] relationship of defendant therapists to either Tatiana or Poddar will suffice to establish a duty of care; as explained in section 315 of the Restatement Second of Torts, a duty of care may arise from either "(a) a special relation . . . between the actor and the third person which imposes a duty upon the actor to control the third person's conduct, or (b) a special relation . . . between

the actor and the other which gives to the other a right of protection."
. . .

[P]laintiffs' pleadings . . . establish as between Poddar and defendant therapists the special relation that arises between a patient and his doctor or psychotherapist. Such a relationship may support affirmative duties for the benefit of third persons. Thus, for example, a hospital must exercise reasonable care to control the behavior of a patient which may endanger other persons. A doctor must also warn a patient if the patient's condition or medication renders certain conduct, such as driving a car, dangerous to others.

Although the California decisions that recognize this duty have involved cases in which the defendant stood in a special relationship *both* to the victim and to the person whose conduct created the danger, we do not think that the duty should logically be constricted to such situations. Decisions of other jurisdictions hold that the single relationship of a doctor to his patient is sufficient to support the duty to exercise reasonable care to protect others against dangers emanating from the patient's illness. The courts hold that a doctor is liable to persons infected by his patient if he negligently fails to diagnose a contagious disease or, having diagnosed the illness, fails to warn members of the patient's family. . . .

Defendants contend, however, that imposition of a duty to exercise reasonable care to protect third persons is unworkable because therapists cannot accurately predict whether or not a patient will resort to violence. In support of this argument amicus representing the American Psychiatric Association and other professional societies cites numerous articles which indicate that therapists, in the present state of the art, are unable reliably to predict violent acts; their forecasts, amicus claims, tend consistently to overpredict violence, and indeed are more often wrong than right. . . .

Obviously we do not require that the therapist . . . render a perfect performance; the therapist need only exercise "that reasonable degree of skill, knowledge, and care ordinarily possessed and exercised by members of (that professional specialty) under similar circumstances." . . .

In the instant case, however, the pleadings . . . allege that defendant therapists did in fact predict that Poddar would kill, but were negligent in failing to warn. . . .

[O]nce a therapist does in fact determine, or . . . should have determined, that a patient poses a serious danger of violence to others, he bears a duty to exercise reasonable care to protect the foreseeable victim of that danger. . . .

Defendants further argue that free and open communication is essential to psychotherapy; that "Unless a patient . . . is assured that . . . information (revealed by him) can and will be held in utmost confidence, he will be reluctant to make the full disclosure upon which diagnosis and treatment . . . depends." The giving of a warning, defendants contend, constitutes a breach of trust which entails the revelation of confidential communications. . . .

Against this interest, however, we must weigh the public interest in safety from violent assault. The Legislature has undertaken the difficult task of balancing the countervailing concerns. In evidence Code section 1014, it established a broad rule of privilege to protect confidential communications between patient and psychotherapist. In Evidence Code section 1024, the Legislature created a specific and limited exception to the psychotherapist-patient privilege: "There is no privilege . . . if the psychotherapist has reasonable cause to believe that the patient is in such mental or emotional condition as to be dangerous to himself or to the person or property of another and that disclosure of the communication is necessary to prevent the threatened danger."

We realize that the open and confidential character of psychotherapeutic dialogue encourages patients to express threats of violence, few of which are ever executed. Certainly a therapist should not be encouraged routinely to reveal such threats; such disclosures could seriously disrupt the patient's relationship with his therapist and with the persons threatened. To the contrary, the therapist's obligations to his patient require that he not disclose a confidence unless such disclosure is necessary to avert danger to others, and even then that he do so discreetly, and in a fashion that would preserve the privacy of his patient to the fullest extent compatible with the prevention of the threatened danger.

The revelation of a communication under the above circumstances is not a breach of trust or a violation of professional ethics; as stated in the Principles of Medical Ethics of the American Medical Association (1957), section 9: "A physician may not reveal the confidence entrusted to him in the course of medical attendance . . . *unless he is required to do so by law or unless it becomes necessary in order to protect the welfare of the individual or of the community.*" (Emphasis added.) . . .

[The concurring and dissenting opinion of Justice Mosk is omitted.]

CLARK, Justice (dissenting). . . .

Overwhelming policy considerations weigh against imposing a duty on psychotherapists to warn a potential victim against harm. While offering virtually no benefit to society, such a duty will frustrate psychiatric treatment, invade fundamental patient rights and increase violence. . . .

DETERRENCE FROM TREATMENT

First, without substantial assurance of confidentiality, those requiring treatment will be deterred from seeking assistance. . . . Apprehension of . . . stigma – apparently increased by the propensity of people considering treatment to see themselves in the worst possible light – creates a well-recognized reluctance to seek aid. This reluctance is alleviated by the psychiatrist's assurance of confidentiality.

FULL DISCLOSURE

Second, the guarantee of confidentiality is essential in eliciting the full disclosure necessary for effective treatment. . . . Until a patient can trust his psychiatrist not to violate their confidential relationship, "the unconscious psychological control mechanism of repression will prevent the recall of past experiences."

SUCCESSFUL TREATMENT

Third, even if the patient fully discloses his thoughts, assurance that the confidential relationship will not be breached is necessary to maintain his trust in his psychiatrist — the very means by which treatment is effected.

A Note on the Subsequent History of Tarasoff

We know from *People v. Poddar*, 518 P2d 342 (Cal 1974), that Poddar

> was born into the Harijan ("untouchable") caste in Bengal, India. He came to the University of California campus at Berkeley as a graduate student in September 1967 and resided at the International House. In the fall of 1968 he attended folk dancing classes at the International House, and it was there he met Tanya. They saw each other weekly throughout the fall, and on New Year's Eve she kissed defendant. He interpreted the act to be a recognition of the existence of a serious relationship. This view was not shared by Tanya who, upon learning of his feelings, told him that she was involved with other men and otherwise indicated that she was not interested in entering into an intimate relationship with him.
>
> As a result of this rebuff defendant underwent a severe emotional crisis. He became depressed and neglected his appearance, his studies and his health. He remained by himself, speaking disjointedly and often weeping. This condition persisted, with steady deterioration . . . . Defendant [Poddar] did have occasional meetings with Tanya during this period and tape recorded various of their conversations in an attempt to ascertain why she did not love him.
>
> During the summer of 1969 Tanya went to South America. After her departure defendant began to improve and at the suggestion of a friend sought psychological assistance. In October, after Tanya had returned, defendant stopped seeing his psychologist. The latter then wrote to the campus police alerting them that, in his opinion, defendant was suffering from paranoid schizophrenia, acute and severe. The psychologist recommended that defendant be civilly committed.
>
> On October 27, 1969, defendant went to Tanya's home to speak with her. She was not at home, and her mother told him to leave. Defendant returned later, armed with a pellet gun and a kitchen knife, and found Tanya alone. She refused to speak with him, and when he persisted, she screamed. At this point defendant shot her with the pellet gun. She ran from the house, was pursued,

caught and repeatedly and fatally stabbed by defendant. He then returned to Tanya's home and called the police.

Poddar was eventually convicted, but the conviction was reversed. "Rather than go through another lengthy trial (the first was over three weeks), more than five years after the fact, the state released Poddar on condition he immediately leave for India and not reenter the United States. He returned to India and, according to one commentator, is happily married to an attorney." Fillmore Buckner & Marvin Firestone, *"Where the Public Peril Begins": 25 Years After Tarasoff*, 21 J Legal Med 187 (2000).

Notes and Questions on the Rationale of Tarasoff

When *Tarasoff* was decided, "a myriad of commentators in the area of mental health decried the decision as undermining the practice of psychotherapy by destroying the tenets of confidentiality." Buckner & Firestone, *supra*. The following notes and questions explore the criticisms (many of them made in Justice Clark's dissent) that sparked that reaction.

1. Is the dissent convincing when it argues that, "without substantial assurance of confidentiality, those requiring treatment will be deterred from seeking assistance"?

    a. What evidence does the dissent adduce? Is it persuasive?

    b. What logic does the dissent adduce? Is it persuasive?

    c. The most recent survey of evidence on the subject reports that "[t]here is just no evidence thus far that patients have been discouraged from coming to therapy . . . ." Buckner & Firestone, *supra*. Is this empirical evidence consistent with Justice Clark's empirical evidence? If you believed Justice Clark's logic was convincing, how would you now explain the evidence that patients have not been deterred from seeking help?

2. Is it true, as the dissent believes, that "the guarantee of confidentiality is essential in eliciting the full disclosure necessary for effective treatment . . ."?

    a. What evidence does the dissent adduce? Is it persuasive?

    b. What logic does the dissent adduce? Is it persuasive?

    c. The most recent survey of evidence on the subject reports that "[t]here is just no evidence thus far that patients have been discouraged from speaking freely . . . ." Buckner & Firestone, *supra*. Is this empirical evidence consistent with Justice Clark's empirical evidence? If you believed Justice Clark's logic was convincing, how would you now explain the evidence that patients have not been deterred from seeking help?

3. Is it a problem, as the dissent suggests, that, "even if the patient fully discloses his thoughts, assurance that the confidential relationship will not be breached is necessary to maintain his trust in his psychiatrist — the very means by which treatment is effected"?

    a. What evidence does the dissent adduce? Is it persuasive?

    b. What logic does the dissent adduce? Is it persuasive?

    c. Consider the following case report and observations from Lawson R. Wulsin, et al, *Unexpected Clinical Features of the* Tarasoff *Decision: The Therapeutic Alliance and the "Duty to Warn,"* 140 Am J Psychiatry 601 (1983):

> Mr. A, a 20-year-old single man, was admitted to the day hospital at the Massachusetts Mental Health Center 18 months after stabbing a stranger in the neck. He had attempted assaults on his mother and on numerous hospital staff members, demonstrating a range of behaviors consistent with the *DSM-III* diagnoses of alcoholism and antisocial personality disorder. He often heard the voice of his deceased father saying, "Kill, kill!" and "Die, die!";

specifically, the voice commanded him to kill his mother. He refused to allow his family to be contacted or involved in his treatment, but he asked for help with the voices. He had no other sign of psychosis, and antipsychotic medication brought him little detectable relief. When Mr. A's hallucinations took the form of commands to kill his mother, we . . . became concerned about a possible duty to third parties. . . .

The treatment staff concluded that, in an "open ward" setting, a duty to warn did exist; transfer to a closed unit was rejected as too regressive. In keeping with the principle of maintaining the therapeutic alliance whenever possible, especially in legal matters, we elected to involve the patient maximally . . . . [W]e proposed a draft of a letter that would inform Mr. A's mother of the danger to her and that would also serve to document our response to her son's threats. In keeping with an alliance-seeking approach, Mr A's therapist went over the letter and the attendant rationale with him. The letter stated that the patient "feared he might harm [his mother]." Mr. A agreed with the content of the letter and insisted on talking to his mother before we mailed the letter, fearing the letter would cause his mother to wish never to speak to him again. His mother first responded to the letter by saying that he should be "locked up with the key thrown away." During the ensuing conversation, however, she stated openly, "I love you"' Mr. A responded, "I love you, too," and both began to cry.

Thereafter, Mr. A abided by a temporary agreement with the therapist not to see his mother outside the treatment setting; but he continued telephoning her and the family every day. Although his mother volunteered information to us by telephone, she otherwise refused to participate actively in her son's treatment. No civil commitment or further intervention was necessary for Mr. A.

The clinical context that gives rise to the issue of a *Tarasoff* duty contains an inherent paradox; the patient seems to act to thwart his own wishes. That is, the patient who intends harm informs the therapist, who has – in theory at least – some power to prevent that harm. The paradox of informing the therapist reflects the patient's fear of his own aggressive wishes and his ambivalence toward actually harming the victim. . . . [I}nforming the victim forces a graphic labeling of affects and moves them, as it were, back into the interpersonal context where they developed; more importantly, the patient talks to the intended victim instead of acting. If the warning is performed with explicit recognition of the patient's ambivalence about the intended harm, it allows the therapist to ally with the healthy part of the patient's ego that fears the assault.

First, the patient's relationship with the victim is brought to center stage in the therapy; the warning process . . . serves to pull the potential victim actively into the therapy (though only marginally and briefly in our case). Second, the patient can identify with the therapist's deliberate (verbal) approach to negotiating with the intended victim. In support of this view, our patient has, in fact, been able to interact verbally in other aggression-producing situations. Finally, the approach described may permit use of a "less restrictive therapeutic setting," where the alliance functions in place of an elaborate panoply of constraints and warnings to promote the patient's ability to work therapeutically with people, including particularly the intended victim.

4. Is *Tarasoff* inherently unfair to psychotherapists on the grounds that they cannot accurately predict dangerousness? In rejecting the *Tarasoff* principle, *Boynton v. Burglass*, 590 S2d 446 (1991), says:

"Psychiatry is not . . . an exact science, and psychiatrists disagree widely and frequently on what constitutes mental illness, on the appropriate diagnosis to be attached to given behavior and symptoms, on cure and treatment, and on the likelihood of future dangerousness." *Ake v. Oklahoma*, 470 U.S. 68, 81 (1985). Although . . . a physician owes a duty to warn members of a patient's immediate family of the existence and dangers of a communicable disease, "[u]nlike a physician's diagnosis, which can be verified by x-ray, surgery, etc., the psychiatrist cannot verify his diagnosis, treatment or predicted prognosis except by long-term follow-up and reporting."

The outward manifestations of infectious diseases lend themselves to accurate and reliable diagnoses. However, the internal workings of the human mind remain largely mysterious. The "near-impossibility of accurately or reliably predicting dangerousness has been well-documented."

a. How would the majority in *Tarasoff* respond to this criticism? Does the criticism apply well to *Tarasoff*'s facts? To its reasoning?

b. Do you always need to be a psychiatrist to predict dangerousness?

5. The criticisms of *Tarasoff* seem to assume that, before the case was decided, the standard of practice was not to warn. Is that true?

a. Recall first that we are told in the opinion that the then-current AMA Principles of Medical Ethics obviated confidentiality where necessary to protect "the individual or the community."

b. Even before *Tarasoff* many psychiatrists felt the duty of confidentiality did not bar them from trying to keep patients from harming other people.

> [T]wo decades before *Tarasoff*, a study of the issue of confidentiality by Little and Strecker revealed that, when the possibility of imminent violence on the part of the patient existed, 32% of psychiatrists said they would report this to the police, and 18% said they would hospitalize the patient. Thus, 50% were willing to breach confidentiality in the face of imminent violence to third parties even before *Tarasoff*. Also, well before *Tarasoff*, prominent psychiatrists . . . had expressed the belief that to reveal confidential information under circumstances where violence was imminent was neither a breach of trust nor unethical.

Buckner & Firestone, *supra*. A *Stanford Law Review* student note says almost half the therapists surveyed had warned victims *before Tarasoff*. Another study found that at least 60% of the therapists polled thought the *Tarasoff* obligation was mandated by their professional ethics, and at least 75 % considered it mandated by their personal ethics. Daniel J. Givelber, et al, Tarasoff, *Myth and Reality: An Empirical Study of Private Law in Action*, 1984 Wisc L Rev 443.

c. Long before *Tarasoff*, psychiatrists could commit potentially violent patients. A study by "McNiel and Binder noted that, between 1973 and 1983, there was a large increase in the use of dangerousness as grounds for civil commitment. They attributed this increase to professional sensitivity to the issue of potential violence due to the *Tarasoff* case. They intimated that psychiatrists also may have used involuntary hospitalization as a way of protecting themselves from future lawsuits." Buckner & Firestone, *supra*

d. The law has long obliged doctors to report some medical conditions: They ordinarily must tell the police when patients have gunshot wounds. Doctors commonly must to report venereal disease to the public health authorities, and those authorities may do contact tracing, which "has been a major prevention strategy within the context of sexually transmitted disease limitation programs for quite a number of years." David P.T. Price, *Between Scylla and Charybdis: Charting a Course to Reconcile the Duty of Confidentiality and the Duty to Warn in the AIDS Context*, 94 Dickinson L Rev 435 (1990).

6. The abstract of R.L. Binder & D.E. McNiel, *Application of the* Tarasoff *Ruling and its Effect on the Victim and the Therapeutic Relationship*, 47 Psychiatric Services 1212 (1996), reports:

> Almost half of the residents (N = 22) [who were contacted] reported having issued a *Tarasoff* warning. Most warnings were issued for patients seen in inpatient units and emergency rooms. In almost half of the cases, the resident was unable to contact the intended victim but did report the threat to a law enforcement agency. In almost three-fourths of the cases in which the intended victim was contacted, the individual already knew of the threat. The most common reaction among those warned was anxiety mixed with thankfulness; most expressed an intent to modify their behavior to increase safety. The second most common reaction was denial that the patient would ever hurt them. Clinicians reported that in most cases issuing the warning had a minimal or a positive effect on the psychotherapeutic relationship.

More generally, one survey concludes "that the concerns about the potential loss of confidentiality have not had the adverse impact on psychiatric practice that the amici curiae and Justice Clark's strong dissent in *Tarasoff* predicted." Buckner & Firestone, *supra*. In part, psychiatrists "have learned to live with *Tarasoff*, recognizing that good common sense, sound clinical practice, careful documentation, and a genuine concern for the patients are almost always sufficient to fulfill their legal obligations." Paul Applebaum, et al, *Statutory Approaches to Limiting Psychiatrists' Liability for Their Patients' Violent Acts*, 146 Am J Psychiatry 821 (1989). *Tarasoff* may even have produced a net gain for psychiatrists and their patients: "Ultimately, *Tarasoff* has stimulated greater awareness of the violent patient's potential for acting out such behavior, encouraging closer scrutiny and better documentation of the therapist's examination of this issue. Buckner & Firestone, *supra*.

7. If the criticisms of *Tarasoff* are convincing is it wrongly decided? The dispute between the majority and the dissent is a classic policy debate in which each alternative has costs and benefits. How well does the court analyze those elements of the debate? This is a dispute about the effects the proposed rule of liability would have on therapy, a dispute as to which empirical evidence could be crucial. What evidence does the majority cite? The dissent?

Notes and Questions on *Tarasoff* as Precedent

1. Buckner & Firestone, *supra*, say that many people thought *Tarasoff* an aberration "not likely to be followed elsewhere and likely to be severely modified by California courts." But it has been adopted by courts and legislatures in many jurisdictions and "expanded to include a wide variety of health care practitioners."

> There has been a continuum of cases based on its precedent that have promulgated a broad duty for health care practitioners to protect the general public from foreseeable harm. These cases have clustered around two central issues — the practitioner's duty to protect the public from a patient who presents a danger while driving a motor vehicle and the practitioner's failure to protect the public from a patient who may transmit an infectious disease. More recently, a third danger has appeared as a likely nidus for future cases — the practitioner's failure to protect the public from a patient who may transmit a genetically based disease.

However, *Tarasoff* has been restricted in some respects: "Many states . . . enacted laws limiting a therapist's liability so long as certain specific actions are taken by the therapist when a patient threatens violence. California enacted a statute in 1985 wherein the therapist may gain immunity from liability if reasonable efforts are made to warn the potential victim and the local police are contacted." Generally, these restrictive statutes "require an actual threat toward an identifiable victim."

On the other hand is *Kolbe v. Iowa*, 661 NW2d 142 (2003): Justin Allen Schulte suffered from an inherited juvenile macular degeneration called Stargardt's Disease. He could not see straight-on and had to rely on his peripheral vision. Defendants were Schulte's ophthalmologists, who were state employees. On several occasions they advised the Iowa Department of Transportation that Schulte could see well enough to drive. Their recommendations were reviewed by the IDOT Medical Advisory Board, and Schulte was several times given a driver's license, although always with some restrictions.

> Almost three months after Schulte passed his last road test renewing his driving privileges, he struck a bicyclist causing serious injuries. Charles and Susan Kolbe were riding bicycles on a two-lane, paved road. They were moving east in the eastbound lane "well to the right of the center line of the roadway." Schulte was driving between forty-five and fifty miles per hour eastbound on the same road. Using his peripheral vision, Schulte first saw Susan when he was about 150 to 200 feet behind her. As Schulte passed Susan, he slowed down to about ten miles per hour and nearly hit her. Schulte, not seeing Charles, continued driving in a straight line and increased his speed to forty-five to fifty miles per hour. Schulte hit Charles driving in excess of his speed restriction. Charles was thrown into the air over the front of Schulte's car, hit the left side of the windshield and roof, and then landed on the ground beyond the car. Charles was severely injured.
>
> The central issue in this appeal is whether . . . physicians owe a duty to unknown third parties when rendering an opinion to the Iowa Department of Transportation regarding a patient's competency to drive. . . .
>
> [T]here is no more of a special relationship between Shulte's physicians and Kolbes than there is between the physicians and the entire driving public. No relation exists between the physicians and Kolbes that is sufficiently close and direct to support a legal claim against the physicians for Charles's injuries. . . .

The physicians were not responsible for issuing the operator's permit. That decision was made by the IDOT. The Iowa Department of Transportation has authority, under appropriate circumstances, to issue an operator's license to a person with Stargardt's Disease. The recommendation of Schulte's physicians was but one factor considered by the IDOT in its decision to issue Schulte an operator's permit. The IDOT also considered the opinion of an independent medical review board in determining whether Schulte was competent to drive. In providing the IDOT with Schulte's visual acuity reports and their professional medical recommendations, the physicians could not have foreseen whether the IDOT would ultimately issue Schulte the permit. . . .

In finding a physician does not owe a duty to unknown third persons, we heavily relied upon these public policy reasons. It is of utmost importance that we do not compromise the physician's first loyalty and duty to his or her patient. See *Webb v. Jarvis*, 575 N.E.2d 992, 997 (Ind.1991); *Praesel v. Johnson,* 967 S.W.2d 391, 396 (Tex.Sup.Ct.1998) (. . . holding physicians do not have a common law duty to third parties to warn epileptic patients not to drive).

[I]t is highly likely ... physicians treating patients with seizure disorders will become reluctant to allow them to drive or engage in any other activity in which a seizure could possibly harm a third party. In order to curtail liability, physicians may become prone to make overly restrictive recommendations concerning the activities of their patients and will exercise their role as reporters to the department of transportation in an inflexible manner not in their patient's best interests.

2. What is required of the physician who concludes a patient is dangerous? The Medline abstract of M.G. Huber, et al, *A Survey of Police Officers' Experience With* Tarasoff *Warnings in Two States*, 51 Psychiatric Services 807 (2000), reports:

A desk sergeant at each of 48 Michigan police stations and 52 South Carolina police stations was surveyed about knowledge and experience of *Tarasoff* warnings. Respondents at 45 stations reported receiving warnings from mental health professionals, with a mean+/-SD of 3. 7+/-8.4 warnings a year. Only three respondents were familiar with the *Tarasoff* ruling. Twenty-four stations had a specific policy on such warnings. Twenty-seven stations would not warn a potential victim. . . . Because police apparently have limited experience with *Tarasoff* warnings, calling them may not be the best way to protect potential victims from patients making threats.

3. Plaintiffs' daughter was being treated by a psychiatrist who concluded she was disposed to suicide. The psychiatrist did not tell plaintiffs, who were temporarily living across the country and were unaware of the severity of their daughter's condition. Nor did the psychiatrist warn plaintiffs their daughter was inviting heroin addicts into plaintiffs' house. The daughter committed suicide. The California Court of Appeal said "*Tarasoff* requires only that a therapist disclose the contents of a confidential communication where the risk to be prevented thereby is the danger of violent assault, and not where the risk of harm is self-inflicted harm or mere property damage." *Bellah v. Greenson*, 141 CalRptr 92 (1977).

4. In *Peavy v. Texas Home Management*, 7 SW3d 795 (1999), "Anthony Tyrone Dixon shot and killed Elizabeth Ann Peavy in Houston, Texas while stealing her car. Dixon was on weekend leave to visit his mother from his court-mandated residence" at an institution owned by Texas Home Management (THM). Peavy's survivors brought a negligence action against THM. The court held

> that a special relationship existed between THM and Dixon sufficient to impose a duty on THM to control Dixon's behavior. Clearly, THM was responsible for controlling Dixon when he became a resident of its facility . . . ; thus, it was under a duty to use reasonable care in determining whether Dixon was allowed to continue unsupervised home visits. . . . THM had a choice other than allowing Dixon to go home. . . .
>
> [T]he risk, foreseeability, and likelihood of injury were within the knowledge of THM. . . . Dixon's behavior worsened during home visits. The record is replete with incidents of violence by Dixon of which THM was aware, including an incident in which Dixon possessed a gun. Further, THM had superior knowledge of Dixon's violent behavior. Therefore, the trier of fact in this case should be left free to decide whether THM acted reasonably . . . .

5. Please reread carefully *A Hidden Agenda* (the story in Chapter I.1.B about a patient's refusal to consent to an HIV test).

    a. The patient denies being in any of the risk groups and therefor refuses to be tested. You are convinced from the clinical evidence that he is infected. You know he is married. What do you do? You are practicing in New York City. N.Y. Pub. Health Law §§ 2130 & 2133 (McKinney Supp 1999) provide:

> § 2130. AIDS and HIV infection; duty to report
>
> 1. Every physician or other person authorized by law to order diagnostic tests or make a medical diagnosis, or any laboratory performing such tests shall immediately (a) upon initial determination that a person is infected with human immunodeficiency virus (HIV), or (b) upon initial diagnosis that a person is afflicted with the disease known as acquired immune deficiency syndrome (AIDS), or (c) upon initial diagnosis that a person is afflicted with HIV related illness, report such case to the commissioner.
>
> 2. The commissioner shall promptly forward such report to the health commissioner of the municipality where such disease, illness or infection occurred. . . .
>
> 3. Such report shall contain such information . . . as shall be required by the commissioner . . . [including] information identifying the protected individual as well as the names, if available, of any contacts of the protected individual . . . known to the physician or provided to the physician by the infected person.
>
> § 2133. Contact tracing of cases of AIDS, HIV related illness or HIV infection
>
> 1. Every municipal health commissioner or the department's district health officer, upon determination that such reported case or, any other known case of HIV infection merits contact tracing in order to protect the public health, shall personally or through their qualified representatives notify the known contacts of the protected individual. . . .
>
> 2. Such contact shall also be informed of (a) the nature of HIV, (b) the known routes of transmission of the virus, (c) as circumstances may require, the risks of prenatal and perinatal transmission, (d) actions he or she can take to limit further transmission of the virus, (e) other facilities . . . which are accessible to the person that provide counseling, medical

care and treatment, further information or other appropriate services for persons infected with HIV.

3. In notifying any contact . . . , the physician or public health officer shall not disclose the identity of the protected individual . . . .

4. A physician or public health officer making a notification to a contact pursuant to this section shall make such notification in person except where circumstances reasonably prevent doing so.

What are you obliged to do by your ethics, the statute, and *Tarasoff*?

b. Your patient now concedes he has known for eight years that he tests positive for HIV. He also acknowledges that on weekends he often has anal sexual relations with multiple partners, none of whom he can name. He tells you he does not tell his partners he has HIV. You have just read Donald C. Ainslie, *Questioning Bioethics: AIDS, Sexual Ethics, and the Duty to Warn*, 29 HCR 26 (Sept/Oct 1999): "[A]ccording to the *safer sex* ethic accepted by many in the gay community, those who are HIV positive are not required to disclose their status to their sexual partners so long as they practice safer sex." Many gay men have

> tried to adapt their pre-existing erotophilic values to the age of AIDS. . . . Importantly, this has meant that even people who know that they are HIV positive are not viewed as sexual outcasts . . . [E]ach sexual agent is to determine ahead of time a safer sex policy concerning the risks he is willing to take and then to apply it to *all of his sexual partners*. . . .
>
> The fact that asking a potential partner about his HIV status is discouraged reinforces the solidarity and shared responsibility between those who are and are not infected, for it allows those who know that they are HIV positive to reveal their status on their own terns. . . . And in most situations, while lying about one's HIV status would surely be wrong, the safer sex ethic helps those who are HIV positive to avoid succumbing to this wrong by reducing the likelihood that the question of HIV status will come up.

What are you obliged to do by your ethics, the statute quoted above, and *Tarasoff*? Is your analysis affected by N Y Pub Health Law §2307 (McKinney 1993): "Any person who, knowing himself or herself to be infected with an infectious venereal disease, has sexual intercourse with another shall be guilty of a misdemeanor." By *Doe v. Johnson*, 817 FSupp 1382 (WD Mich 1993):

> [A] defendant owes a plaintiff a legal duty to, at the very least, disclose the fact that s/he may have the HIV virus, if: (1) the defendant has actual knowledge that s/he has the HIV virus; (2) the defendant has experienced symptoms associated with the HIV virus; or (3) the defendant has actual knowledge that a prior sex partner has been diagnosed as having the HIV virus. When an individual has knowledge that rises to the level of one of these three fact scenarios, the burden on that individual in revealing his or her HIV virus information is minimal when compared to the high risks of the disease.

Would your ethical and legal duties change if your patient said he always uses a condom? The abstract of one study reports:

> HIV-positive persons face significant challenges to disclosing their HIV serostatus, and failure to disclose can place their sex partners at risk. The current study examined HIV serostatus disclosure in 266 sexually active HIV-positive persons recruited from the community. Results showed that 41% had not disclosed their HIV serostatus to sex partners. Men who had not disclosed to partners indicated lower rates of condom use during anal intercourse and scored significantly lower on a measure of self-efficacy for condom use compared to individuals who had disclosed.

S.C. Kalichman & D. Nachimson, *Self-Efficacy and Disclosure of HIV-Positive Serostatus to Sex Partners,* 18 Health Psychology 281 (1999). Is your analysis of these questions affected by Michael Warner, *Unsafe: Why Gay Men Are Having Risky Sex*, Village Voice, January 31, 1995, at 33? He estimates "that about 50 per cent of gay men my age in New York have HIV. These odds occurred to him during an unprotected sexual encounter in a kind of instant calculus that was not even recognizable as thinking, much less as making a decision. The quality of consciousness was more like impulse shoplifting. "When I talked to my best friends about the episode, I mentioned only how explosive the sex had been; not that it was unsafe. I recoiled so much from what I had done that it seemed to be not my choice at all. A mystery, I thought. A monster did it.

The next time I saw the same man, we went back to his apartment again. I thought to myself to take precautions, but I could tell by the heady thrill that my monster was in charge. Even scarier than the risk itself was the realization that shame and fear had not been enough to keep me safe. . . .

Usually, men who know they are positive will either tell you . . . or take on themselves the burden of keeping things safe. He hadn't. But he would have been quite reasonable to think, since I went along, either that I was making my own decisions or that I, too, was already positive and wasn't worried . . . .

There were other possibilities, consolation theories for me. Plenty of men, usually young, want unprotected sex because they trust the people they're with to be negative. But this was no ingenue . . . . Of course, it was also possible that, like me, he was negative or didn't know his status, and was simply willing to take a risk. These other possibilities, I now understand, preserved the level of uncertainty I wanted in order to take a risk; I dwelt on them just long enough to think that I didn't know what I thought I knew I was doing.

Gay men are so aware of the language of responsibility, guilt, and shame — remember homophobia? – that we go to great lengths to avoid it. . . . . "When people get high and have unprotected sex," he [Richard Elovich] asks, "which comes first? People assume that drugs lead to unsafe sex. But often the desire is there from the beginning. Men get high or drunk because they can't acknowledge that desire, or because they want someone else to be in control, or because they just don't want to make a choice."

c. Your patient has been in the hospital for prolonged testing. Do you have any obligation to inform any of the people treating him who may encounter his bodily fluids? Is your analysis affected by the fact that all those people are instructed to use "universal precautions"? (In other words, to take the precautions with everyone they would take with infected patients.)

6. In *Molloy v. Meier*, 679 NW3d 711 (2004), the Minnesota Supreme Court considered a malpractice suit parents brought against doctors "claiming they were negligent in failing to diagnose a genetic disorder (Fragile X syndrome, which causes retardation) in Molloy's daughter and their negligence caused Molloy to conceive another child with the same genetic disorder." The court observed that

> only a few other jurisdictions have addressed the question of whether a physician owes a legal duty to the family of a patient who received negligent care in the field of genetics. . . . The New Jersey Supreme Court held that a physician owes a duty to members of the patient's immediate family who might be injured by the physician's breach of duty to the patient. *Schroeder v. Perkel,* 432 A.2d 834 (1981). The court held that liability could extend to the patient's family where a doctor's failure to diagnose a first-born child with cystic fibrosis led to the birth of a second child with that disorder and it was foreseeable that the parents would rely on the diagnosis.
>
> The Supreme Court of Florida has also held that a duty exists where "the prevailing standard of care creates a duty that is obviously for the benefit of certain identified third parties and the physician knows of the existence of those third parties." *Pate v. Threlkel,* 661 So.2d 278 (Fla.1995). In *Pate,* the defendant physician diagnosed the plaintiff's mother with medullary thyroid carcinoma, a genetically inheritable disease. When the plaintiff learned that she also carried the disease, she sued, alleging that the defendant should have known of the inheritable nature of the disease and owed a duty to inform her mother that the plaintiff may have carried it as well. The plaintiff presented expert testimony that the prevailing standard of care required physicians to inform patients of the genetically transferable nature of their conditions. The Florida Supreme Court noted that the standard of care was developed for the benefit of third parties and therefore held that a physician owes a duty to those third parties of whom the physician has knowledge.
>
> Other courts have drawn upon the prevailing standard of care to define the duties physicians owe in the context of genetic counseling. For example, the California Court of Appeals found no duty to parents to disclose the possibility of having a child with

Tay-Sachs disease when the physicians did not have any reason to suspect that the parents were in a high-risk group for the disease. *Munro v. Regents of Univ. of Cal.*, 215 Cal.App.3d 977 (1989). That court recognized that it was impossible to test all patients and relied on expert testimony that the prevailing standard of care required testing only when parents had specific ethnic backgrounds. Similarly, the New Jersey Court of Appeals relied upon "the presumed medical knowledge at the time [of treatment]" to find a duty to warn the patient's immediate family of a patient's genetically transferable condition. *Safer v. Estate of Pack,* 677 A.2d 1188 (App.Div.1996). . . .

Our decision today is informed by the practical reality of the field of genetic testing and counseling; genetic testing and diagnosis does [sic] not affect only the patient. Both the patient and her family can benefit from accurate testing and diagnosis. And conversely, both the patient and her family can be harmed by negligent testing and diagnosis. Molloy's experts indicate that a physician would have a duty to inform the parents of a child diagnosed with Fragile X disorder. The appellants admit that their practice is to inform parents in such a case. The standard of care thus acknowledges that families rely on physicians to communicate a diagnosis of the genetic disorder to the patient's family. It is foreseeable that a negligent diagnosis of Fragile X will cause harm not only to the patient, but to the family of the patient as well. . . .

We therefore hold that a physician's duty regarding genetic testing and diagnosis extends beyond the patient to biological parents who foreseeably may be harmed by a breach of that duty. In this case, the patient suffered from a serious disorder that had a high probability of being genetically transmitted and for which a reliable and accepted test was widely available. The appellants should have foreseen that parents of childbearing years might conceive another child in the absence of knowledge of the genetic disorder. The appellants owed a duty of care regarding genetic testing and diagnosis, and the resulting medical advice, not only to S.F. but also to her parents. . . . [T]he duty arises where it is reasonably foreseeable that the parents would be injured if the advice is negligently given.

How ought an attorney advise the physician in the following case, which is taken from Kenneth Offit et al, *The "Duty to Warn" a Patient's Family Members About Hereditary Disease Risks*, 292 JAMA 1469 (2004)?

A 40-year-old woman presents for a follow-up consultation. She has a family history of breast cancer, heart disease, and Alzheimer disease. At her first visit, the physician had counseled her and provided genetic testing and now tells the patient that she was found to have an inherited *BRCA2* mutation. Although the physician had discussed the importance of familial risk notification before testing, the patient declines the strong recommendation that she share the results of her genetic tests with her sister and asks that this information be kept completely confidential.

Does this physician have an obligation to tell the patient's sister that she, too, may have inherited these genetic predispositions? If this sister later develops advanced breast cancer, or has a "preventive surgery" unnecessarily, can she take legal action, claiming that the physician had an obligation to contact her about her genetic risk?

7. Many jurisdictions have adopted statutes that speak to *Tarasoff* claims. According to Claudia Kachigian & Alan R. Felthous, *Court Responses to* Tarasoff *Statutes*, 32 Journal of the American Academy of Psychiatry 263 (2004), courts

> have taken diverse approaches in interpreting their state's . . . statutes. Only in a small number of cases did courts interpret the statutes to circumscribe the duties owed to third parties. Most, either by ignoring the statute in what seem to be applicable cases or by finding that a common law duty remains independent of it, left the duty to protect ill defined. . . . There are even cases that seemingly expand the protective duty to non-mental health professional physicians. Although these physicians traditionally have duties to warn others of potentially contagious diseases or disorders that may affect their ability to drive, they have not had a duty to protect others from the intentional violent acts of their patients or their patients, relatives. . . .

Notes and Questions on Confidentiality and Lawyers

Earlier, we compared the law's treatment of the doctor's and the lawyers's duty of informed consent, and we found that the law imposed more onerous burdens on doctors than lawyers. Can the same be said of the law's treatment of confidentiality in the two professions.

Lawyers and the Duty to Reveal Confidences. First, what kinds of duties of disclosure do lawyers impose on themselves? Does law impose on lawyers? Rule 1.6(b) of the ABA Model Rules of Professional Conduct states that a

> lawyer may reveal such information to the extent the lawyer reasonably believes necessary:
>
> > (1) to prevent the client from committing a criminal act that the lawyer believes is likely to result in imminent death or substantial bodily harm; or
> >
> > (2) to establish a claim or defense on behalf of the lawyer in a controversy between the lawyer and the client, to establish a defense to a criminal charge or civil claim against the lawyer based upon conduct in which the client was involved, or to respond to allegations in any proceeding concerning the lawyer's representation of the client.

This rule was exceptionally controversial, not least because it creates an exceptionally narrow duty to reveal information. "The ABA's Committee on Ethics and Professional Responsibility recommended that language . . . [permitting broader disclosure] be added to M.R. 1.6(b). . . . The House of Delegates rejected the committee's proposal, 251–158." Geoffrey C. Hazard, Jr., et al, *The Law and Ethics of Lawyering* 287 (Foundation, 1999) (3rd ed). Hazard et al report that the ALI "explicitly rejected a proposed subparagraph of Restatement § 73 which would have endorsed a *Tarasoff* duty when disclosure was necessary 'to prevent the client from committing a crime imminently threatening to cause death or serious bodily injury to an identifiable person who is unaware of the risk and the lawyer's act has facilitated the crime,' such as assisting the client in a release from custody." Furthermore, Hazard et al are "unaware of any decision holding a lawyer civilly liable for damages for failure to warn a victim of the client's intended dangerous conduct."

Fred C. Zacharias, *Rethinking Confidentiality*, 74 Iowa L Rev 351 (1989), comments mordantly:

> When the strict general prohibitions against disclosure affected the personal and economic convenience of lawyers most directly, code drafters were prompted to insert exceptions. These exceptions—now part and parcel of most strict state codes—do not take into account

clients' actual secrecy expectations. A lawyer may disclose when confidences threaten to embroil the lawyer in a future crime. The lawyer may use client communications when "necessary . . . to collect his fee." When the lawyer's conduct is itself called into question—even through no fault of the client—the lawyer also has recourse to the client's information. That is so even though the lawyer could not, under most codes, use the same information to save the life or reputation of an innocent third party.

What is more: "The same lawyer who is prohibited from disclosing information learned while representing a client to exonerate someone falsely accused of a capital crime . . . is perfectly free to disclose confidential information where he or she is the one accused, falsely or not. Nor is there any requirement that the lawyer's liberty be at stake, or even that the lawyer be accused of anything criminal." Daniel R. Fischel, *Lawyers and Confidentiality*, 65 U Chicago Law Review 1, 10 (1998). *Cui bono? Quis custodiet ipsos custodes?*

In light of this, how should you resolve this classic puzzle in lawyer's duties of confidentiality? You are the lawyer for a defendant in a tort case arising out of an automobile accident. You hire a doctor to examine the plaintiff. The doctor discovers the plaintiff has an aneurysm which was probably caused by the accident. The plaintiff does not know about this life-threatening injury. Because the plaintiff was a minor, a court had to approve a settlement in the case. Does the lawyer have any obligation to disclose the aneurysm to the plaintiffs? To the court? Did the doctor have such an obligation? What do your answers to these questions suggest about the differences between the lawyer's and the doctor's duties of confidentiality? Are those differences justifiable? (These facts are taken from *Spaulding v. Zimmerman*, 116 NW2d 704 (Minn 1962). For thoughtful commentary on that case and the confidentiality problems it raises, see Roger C. Cramton & Lori P. Knowles, *Professional Secrecy and Its Exceptions:* Spaulding v. Zimmerman *Revisited*, 83 Minn L Rev 63 (1998).)

Lawyers and Testimonial Privilege. What kinds of privileges do lawyers and law accord clients' disclosures to lawyers? Consider *Upjohn v. United States*, 449 US 383 (1980):

> The attorney-client privilege is the oldest of the privileges for confidential communications known to the common law. Its

purpose is to encourage full and frank communication between attorneys and their clients and thereby promote broader public interests in the observance of law and administration of justice. The privilege recognizes that sound legal advice or advocacy serves public ends and that such advice or advocacy depends upon the lawyer's being fully informed by the client. . . . " We [have] recognized the purpose of the privilege to be "to encourage clients to make full disclosure to their attorneys." This rationale for the privilege has long been recognized by the Court, see *Hunt v. Blackburn*, 128 U.S. 464, 470 (1888) (privilege "is founded upon the necessity, in the interest and administration of justice, of the aid of persons having knowledge of the law and skilled in its practice, which assistance can only be safely and readily availed of when free from the consequences or the apprehension of disclosure").

How does the attorney-client privilege differ from the doctor-patient privilege? How does the lawyers' duty of disclosure of threats clients pose differ from the doctors' duty? Are the differences justifiable? Why do they exist? Consider Fred C. Zacharias, *Harmonizing Privilege and Confidentiality*, 41 S Texas L Rev 69 (1999):

> The general notion that attorneys should keep client secrets started as matter of etiquette. As legal ethics became more legislative in nature, confidentiality became a principle promulgated by lawyer organizations. Confidentiality rules developed according to the unique vision of the bar about who lawyers are, their importance to the legal system, and how their relationships with clients should evolve to best serve that system.
>
> Accordingly, professional confidentiality rules developed extremely broadly, in all jurisdictions. The bar wants clients to come to lawyers and wants to enable lawyers to provide as many services for clients as possible. As a result, virtually everything having to do with a case is deemed a secret held by the lawyer for the client's behalf. Confidentiality applies in most contexts. Exceptions are narrow. When in doubt, the bar interprets the scope of confidentiality expansively.
>
> In contrast, attorney-client privilege rules are products of lawsuits. Courts and legislators make the rules. Whoever

adopts the rules initially, it is judges who interpret them and flesh them out. Because privilege applies only when one client attempts to prevent the other side's access to potentially probative evidence in litigation, courts implementing privilege are cognizant of secrecy's negative attributes.

Thus, judges tend to interpret attorney-client privilege narrowly. It covers only specified types of communications, not other information that might come to a lawyer's attention. Attorney-client privilege has numerous exceptions, which courts apply liberally. Much of what would be confidential ultimately proves to be subject to discovery or production in court.

Like the doctor-patient privilege and the doctor's duty of confidentiality, the attorney-client privilege and the lawyer's duty of confidentiality are justified in significant part on the theory that without them the client would not confide in the lawyer and hence would not receive adequate legal representation. We saw that this proposition is dubious applied to doctors and patients. Is it more persuasive applied to lawyers and clients? "To accept the modern systemic arguments in favor of confidentiality, one must reach one of two conclusions: first, that clients would use lawyers significantly less if more exceptions existed; second, that clients who employ lawyers would reveal substantially less information. Both conclusions are questionable." Fred C. Zacharias, *Rethinking Confidentiality*, 74 Iowa Law Review 351, 363–364 (1989). Professor Zacharias conducted empirical research which, while hardly national, produced some useful but not surprising results. "Of the lawyer pool, 22.6% confessed that they 'almost never' inform clients of attorney-client confidentiality; 59.7% stated that they inform their clients in less than 50% of their cases. . . . Clients responded that 72.9% of their first attorneys never told them anything about confidentiality." Clients widely misunderstood confidentiality rules (over 42% thought they were absolute). Most lawyers "believed that they would get the same information from clients even if they never informed the clients about confidentiality," and many clients thought so too. Presented with hypotheticals in which the local rules prohibited disclosure but in which disclosure served clear social goals, many lawyers said they would disclose and clients "overwhelmingly" thought they should. Professor Zacharias concludes: "That a significant and often large number of New York attorneys . . . would disclose in all but one of the cases suggests either that attorneys are using confidentiality to mislead clients and induce disclosures under false pretenses or that attorneys themselves do not understand the rules."

Furthermore, "[s]tated broadly, the claim that lawyers can be effective only when informed of all relevant facts is simply untrue. Attorneys do without information in a broad variety of contexts." (And sometimes they actively avoid receiving information.) In the Zacharias survey, 85.9% of lawyers thought

> "they would get enough information to represent clients competently" even were there no confidentiality rules. Nor are clients anywhere near fully protected by their privileges. [O]nce the client tells the lawyer a fact, the lawyer no longer is in a position to let the client hide the fact from discovery. Moreover, even if the communication involves an otherwise non-discoverable type of communication (e.g., about a non-fact), there are special privilege exceptions. Thus, for example, a client who learns that the Model Rule version of confidentiality governs his representation and tells a lawyer of his intent to commit a financial crime suddenly may find his lawyer called before the grand jury to testify to the communications."

Recall Shaw's unhappy dictum that all professions are conspiracies against the laity. Are lawyers using their authority as a profession and their special access to the law to write rules that serve their own interests? "Another way to ask why encouraging communications with the legal profession is so important is to inquire who benefits from these communications. . . . . Confidentiality benefits lawyers because it increases the demand for legal services [by allowing lawyers to offer a benefit – confidentiality – that cannot be offered by some other counsellors). The legal profession, not clients or society as a whole, is the primary beneficiary of confidentiality rules." Daniel R. Fischel, *Lawyers and Confidentiality*, 65 U Chicago Law Review 1, 3 (1998). Furthermore, a strong duty of confidentiality reduces the likelihood that lawyers will have to risk displeasing clients and saves them from some moral quandaries. ("Lawyers know that harming a client to protect the superior interest of a third party will lead to the ending of the lawyer-client relationship, probable non-payment of fees, client bitterness and recrimination, and possible loss of repute with other lawyers and clients. . . . Lawyers are extraordinarily reluctant to risk these consequences." Hazard et al.)

C. The National Administrative Regulation of Privacy: HIPAA

HHS REGULATIONS ISSUED ON THE AUTHORITY OF THE HEALTH INSURANCE PORTABILITY AND ACCOUNTABILITY ACT

45 CFR 160

§ 160.102 Applicability.

(a) Except as otherwise provided, the standards, requirements, and implementation specifications adopted under this subchapter apply to the following entities:

(1) A health plan.

(2) A health care clearinghouse.

(3) A health care provider who transmits any health information in electronic form in connection with a transaction covered by this subchapter. . . . .

§ 160.103 Definitions . . . .

Business associate:

(1) . . . [A] person who:

> (i) On behalf of such covered entity or of an organized health care arrangement . . . in which the covered entity participates, but other than in the capacity of a member of the workforce of such covered entity or arrangement, performs, or assists in the performance of:
>
> > (A) A function or activity involving the use or disclosure of individually identifiable health information . . . or

(B) Any other function or activity regulated by this subchapter; or

(ii) Provides . . . legal, actuarial, accounting, consulting, data aggregation . . . , management, administrative, accreditation, or financial services to or for such covered entity, or to or for an organized health care arrangement in which the covered entity participates, where the provision of the service involves the disclosure of individually identifiable health information from such covered entity or arrangement, or from another business associate of such covered entity or arrangement, to the person. . . . .

Covered entity means:

(1) A health plan.

(2) A health care clearinghouse.

(3) A health care provider who transmits any health information in electronic form in connection with a transaction covered by this subchapter.

Disclosure means the release, transfer, provision of, access to, or divulging in any other manner of information outside the entity holding the information. . . .

Group health plan (also see definition of health plan in this section) means an employee welfare benefit plan (as defined in section 3(1) of the Employee Retirement Income and Security Act of 1974 (ERISA), 29 U.S.C. 1002(1)), including insured and self-insured plans, to the extent that the plan provides medical care (as defined in section 2791(a)(2) of the Public Health Service Act (PHS Act), 42 U.S.C. 300gg-91(a)(2)), including items and services paid for as medical care, to employees or their dependents directly or through insurance, reimbursement, or otherwise, that:

(1) Has 50 or more participants (as defined in section 3(7) of ERISA; or

(2) Is administered by an entity other than the employer that established and maintains the plan. . . .

Health care means care, services, or supplies related to the health of an individual. Health care includes, but is not limited to, the following:

(1) Preventive, diagnostic, therapeutic, rehabilitative, maintenance, or palliative care, and counseling, service, assessment, or procedure with respect to the physical or mental condition, or functional status, of an individual or that affects the structure or function of the body; and

(2) Sale or dispensing of a drug, device, equipment, or other item in accordance with a prescription. . . .

Health care provider means . . . , a provider of medical or health services . . . , and any other person or organization who furnishes, bills, or is paid for health care in the normal course of business.

Health information means any information, whether oral or recorded in any form or medium, that:

(1) Is created or received by a health care provider, health plan, public health authority, employer, life insurer, school or university, or health care clearinghouse; and

(2) Relates to the past, present, or future physical or mental health or condition of an individual; the provision of health care to an individual; or the past, present, or future payment for the provision of health care to an individual. . . .

Health plan means an individual or group plan that provides, or pays the cost of, medical care . . . .

(1) Health plan includes the following, singly or in combination:

(i) A group health plan, as defined in this section.

(ii) A health insurance issuer . . . .

(iii) An HMO . . . .

(iv) Part A or Part B of the Medicare program under title XVIII of the Act.

(v) The Medicaid program under title XIX of the Act. . . .

(vii) An issuer of a long-term care policy, excluding a nursing home fixed-indemnity policy.

(viii) An employee welfare benefit plan or any other arrangement that is established or maintained for the purpose of offering or providing health benefits to the employees of two or more employers.

(ix) The health care program for active military personnel . . . .

(x) The veterans health care program . . . .

(xiii) The Federal Employees Health Benefits Program . . . .

(xvii) Any other individual or group plan, or combination of individual or group plans, that provides or pays for the cost of medical care . . . .

Individually identifiable health information is information that is a subset of health information, including demographic information collected from an individual, and:

(1) Is created or received by a health care provider, health plan, employer, or health care clearinghouse; and

(2) Relates to the past, present, or future physical or mental health or condition of an individual; the provision of health care to an individual; or the past, present, or future payment for the provision of health care to an individual; and

(i) That identifies the individual; or

(ii) With respect to which there is a reasonable basis to believe the information can be used to identify the individual. . . .

Protected health information means individually identifiable health information:

(1) . . . [T]hat is:

(i) Transmitted by electronic media;

(ii) Maintained in electronic media; or

(iii) Transmitted or maintained in any other form or medium. . . .

§ 160.203 General rule and exceptions.

A standard, requirement, or implementation specification adopted under this subchapter that is contrary to a provision of State law preempts the provision of State law. This general rule applies, except if one or more of the following conditions is met: . . .

(b) The provision of State law relates to the privacy of individually identifiable health information and is more stringent than a standard, requirement, or implementation specification adopted under subpart E of part 164 of this subchapter.

(c) The provision of State law, including State procedures established under such law, as applicable, provides for the reporting of disease or injury, child abuse, birth, or death, or for the conduct of public health surveillance, investigation, or intervention.

(d) The provision of State law requires a health plan to report, or to provide access to, information for the purpose of management audits, financial audits, program monitoring and evaluation, or the licensure or certification of facilities or individuals.

§ 164.502 Uses and disclosures of protected health information: general rules.

(a) Standard. A covered entity may not use or disclose protected health information, except as permitted or required by this subpart or by subpart C of part 160 of this subchapter.

(1) Permitted uses and disclosures. A covered entity is permitted to use or disclose protected health information as follows:

(i) To the individual;

(ii) For treatment, payment, or health care operations, as permitted by and in compliance with § 164.506 . . . .

(b) Standard: Minimum necessary.

(1) Minimum necessary applies. When using or disclosing protected health information or when requesting protected health information from another covered entity, a covered entity must make reasonable efforts to limit protected health information to the minimum necessary to accomplish the intended purpose of the use, disclosure, or request. . . . .

(e)(1) Standard: Disclosures to business associates.

(i) A covered entity may disclose protected health information to a business associate and may allow a business associate to create or receive protected health information on its behalf, if the covered entity obtains satisfactory assurance that the business associate will appropriately safeguard the information. . . .

(2) Implementation specification: documentation. A covered entity must document the satisfactory assurances required by paragraph (e)(1) of this section through a written contract or other written agreement or arrangement with the business associate that meets the applicable requirements of § 164.504(e). . . .

§ 164.506 Uses and disclosures to carry out treatment, payment, or health care operations.

(a) Standard: Permitted uses and disclosures. Except with respect to uses or disclosures that require an authorization under § 164.508(a)(2) and (3), a covered entity may use or disclose protected health information for treatment, payment, or health care operations as set forth in paragraph (c) of this section, provided that such use or disclosure is consistent with other applicable requirements of this subpart.

(b) Standard: Consent for uses and disclosures permitted.

(1) A covered entity may obtain consent of the individual to use or disclose protected health information to carry out treatment, payment, or health care operations.

(2) Consent, under paragraph (b) of this section, shall not be effective to permit a use or disclosure of protected health information when an authorization, under § 164.508, is required or when another condition must be met for such use or disclosure to be permissible under this subpart.

(c) Implementation specifications: Treatment, payment, or health care operations.

(1) A covered entity may use or disclose protected health information for its own treatment, payment, or health care operations.

(2) A covered entity may disclose protected health information for treatment activities of a health care provider.

(3) A covered entity may disclose protected health information to another covered entity or a health care provider for the payment activities of the entity that receives the information.

(4) A covered entity may disclose protected health information to another covered entity for health care operations activities of the entity that receives the information, if each entity either has or had a relationship with the individual who is the subject of the protected health information being requested, the protected health information pertains to such relationship, and the disclosure is:

> (i) For a purpose listed in paragraph (1) or (2) of the definition of health care operations; or

> (ii) For the purpose of health care fraud and abuse detection or compliance.

(5) A covered entity that participates in an organized health care arrangement may disclose protected health information about an individual to another covered entity that participates in the organized health care arrangement for any health care operations activities of the organized health care arrangement.

§ 164.508 Uses and disclosures for which an authorization is required.

(a) Standard: authorizations for uses and disclosures.--

(1) Authorization required: general rule. . . . [A] covered entity may not use or disclose protected health information without an authorization that is valid under this section. . . .

(3) Authorization required: Marketing.

> (i) . . . [A] covered entity must obtain an authorization for any use or disclosure of protected health information for marketing, except if the communication is in the form of:
>
>> (A) A face-to-face communication made by a covered entity to an individual; or
>>
>> (B) A promotional gift of nominal value provided by the covered entity.
>
> (ii) If the marketing involves direct or indirect remuneration to the covered entity from a third party, the authorization must state that such remuneration is involved.

(b) Implementation specifications: general requirements.– . . . .

(4) Prohibition on conditioning of authorizations. A covered entity may not condition the provision to an individual of treatment, payment, enrollment in the health plan, or eligibility for benefits on the provision of an authorization, except:

> (i) A covered health care provider may condition the provision of research-related treatment on provision of an authorization for the use or disclosure of protected health information for such research under this section;
>
> (ii) A health plan may condition enrollment in the health plan or eligibility for benefits on provision of an authorization requested by the health plan prior to an individual's enrollment in the health plan, if:

(A) The authorization sought is for the health plan's eligibility or enrollment determinations relating to the individual or for its underwriting or risk rating determinations; and

(B) The authorization is not for a use or disclosure of psychotherapy notes under paragraph (a)(2) of this section . . . .

(6) Documentation. A covered entity must document and retain any signed authorization under this section as required by § 164.530(j).

(c) Implementation specifications: Core elements and requirements.--

(1) Core elements. A valid authorization under this section must contain at least the following elements:

(i) A description of the information to be used or disclosed that identifies the information in a specific and meaningful fashion.

(ii) The name or other specific identification of the person(s), or class of persons, authorized to make the requested use or disclosure.

(iii) The name or other specific identification of the person(s), or class of persons, to whom the covered entity may make the requested use or disclosure.

(iv) A description of each purpose of the requested use or disclosure. The statement "at the request of the individual" is a sufficient description of the purpose when an individual initiates the authorization and does not, or elects not to, provide a statement of the purpose.

(v) An expiration date or an expiration event that relates to the individual or the purpose of the use or disclosure. The statement "end of the research study," "none," or similar language is sufficient if the authorization is for a use or disclosure of protected health information for research . . . .

(vi) Signature of the individual and date. If the authorization is signed by a personal representative of the individual, a description of such representative's authority to act for the individual must also be provided.

(2) Required statements. In addition to the core elements, the authorization must contain statements adequate to place the individual on notice of all of the following:

(i) The individual's right to revoke the authorization in writing, and either:

(A) The exceptions to the right to revoke and a description of how the individual may revoke the authorization; or

(B) To the extent that the information in paragraph (c)(2)(i)(A) of this section is included in the notice required by § 164.520, a reference to the covered entity's notice.

(ii) The ability or inability to condition treatment, payment, enrollment or eligibility for benefits on the authorization, by stating either:

(A) The covered entity may not condition treatment, payment, enrollment or eligibility for benefits on whether the individual signs the authorization when the prohibition on conditioning of authorizations in paragraph (b)(4) of this section applies; or

(B) The consequences to the individual of a refusal to sign the authorization when, in accordance with paragraph (b)(4) of this section, the covered entity can condition treatment, enrollment in the health plan, or eligibility for benefits on failure to obtain such authorization.

(iii) The potential for information disclosed pursuant to the authorization to be subject to redisclosure by the recipient and no longer be protected by this subpart.

(3) Plain language requirement. The authorization must be written in plain language. [This is Professor Schneider's favorite provision.]

(4) Copy to the individual. If a covered entity seeks an authorization from an individual for a use or disclosure of protected health information, the covered entity must provide the individual with a copy of the signed authorization.

§ 164.510 Uses and disclosures requiring an opportunity for the individual to agree or to object.

A covered entity may use or disclose protected health information, provided that the individual is informed in advance of the use or disclosure and has the opportunity to agree to or prohibit or restrict the use or disclosure, in accordance with the applicable requirements of this section. The covered entity may orally inform the individual of and obtain the individual's oral agreement or objection to a use or disclosure permitted by this section.

(a) Standard: use and disclosure for facility directories.

(1) Permitted uses and disclosure. Except when an objection is expressed in accordance with paragraphs (a)(2) or (3) of this section, a covered health care provider may:

>(i) Use the following protected health information to maintain a directory of individuals in its facility:

>>(A) The individual's name;

>>(B) The individual's location in the covered health care provider's facility;

>>(C) The individual's condition described in general terms that does not communicate specific medical information about the individual; and

>>(D) The individual's religious affiliation; and

>(ii) Disclose for directory purposes such information:

>>(A) To members of the clergy; or

(B) Except for religious affiliation, to other persons who ask for the individual by name.

(2) Opportunity to object. A covered health care provider must inform an individual of the protected health information that it may include in a directory and the persons to whom it may disclose such information (including disclosures to clergy of information regarding religious affiliation) and provide the individual with the opportunity to restrict or prohibit some or all of the uses or disclosures permitted by paragraph (a)(1) of this section.

(3) Emergency circumstances.

(i) If the opportunity to object to uses or disclosures required by paragraph (a)(2) of this section cannot practicably be provided because of the individual's incapacity or an emergency treatment circumstance, a covered health care provider may use or disclose some or all of the protected health information permitted by paragraph (a)(1) of this section for the facility's directory, if such disclosure is:

(A) Consistent with a prior expressed preference of the individual, if any, that is known to the covered health care provider; and

(B) In the individual's best interest as determined by the covered health care provider, in the exercise of professional judgment.

(ii) The covered health care provider must inform the individual and provide an opportunity to object to uses or disclosures for directory purposes as required by paragraph (a)(2) of this section when it becomes practicable to do so.

(b) Standard: uses and disclosures for involvement in the individual's care and notification purposes.

(1) Permitted uses and disclosures.

(i) A covered entity may, in accordance with paragraphs (b)(2) or (3) of this section, disclose to a family member, other relative, or a close personal friend of the individual, or any other person identified by the individual, the protected health information directly relevant to such person's involvement with the individual's care or payment related to the individual's health care.

(ii) A covered entity may use or disclose protected health information to notify, or assist in the notification of (including identifying or locating), a family member, a personal representative of the individual, or another person responsible for the care of the individual of the individual's location, general condition, or death. Any such use or disclosure of protected health information for such notification purposes must be in accordance with paragraphs (b)(2), (3), or (4) of this section, as applicable.

(2) Uses and disclosures with the individual present. If the individual is present for, or otherwise available prior to, a use or disclosure permitted by paragraph (b)(1) of this section and has the capacity to make health care decisions, the covered entity may use or disclose the protected health information if it:

(i) Obtains the individual's agreement;

(ii) Provides the individual with the opportunity to object to the disclosure, and the individual does not express an objection; or

(iii) Reasonably infers from the circumstances, based the exercise of professional judgment, that the individual does not object to the disclosure.

(3) Limited uses and disclosures when the individual is not present. If the individual is not present, or the opportunity to agree or object to the use or disclosure cannot practicably be provided because of the individual's incapacity or an emergency circumstance, the covered entity may, in the exercise of professional judgment, determine whether the disclosure is in the best interests of the individual and, if so, disclose only the protected health information that is directly relevant to the person's involvement with the individual's health care. A covered entity may use professional judgment and its experience with common practice to make reasonable inferences of the individual's best interest in allowing a person to act on behalf of the

individual to pick up filled prescriptions, medical supplies, X-rays, or other similar forms of protected health information.

(4) Use and disclosures for disaster relief purposes. A covered entity may use or disclose protected health information to a public or private entity authorized by law or by its charter to assist in disaster relief efforts, for the purpose of coordinating with such entities the uses or disclosures permitted by paragraph (b)(1)(ii) of this section. The requirements in paragraphs (b)(2) and (3) of this section apply to such uses and disclosure to the extent that the covered entity, in the exercise of professional judgment, determines that the requirements do not interfere with the ability to respond to the emergency circumstances.

§ 164.512 Uses and disclosures for which an authorization or opportunity to agree or object is not required. . . .

(j) Standard: Uses and disclosures to avert a serious threat to health or safety.

(1) Permitted disclosures. A covered entity may, consistent with applicable law and standards of ethical conduct, use or disclose protected health information, if the covered entity, in good faith, believes the use or disclosure:

>   (i)

>   >   (A) Is necessary to prevent or lessen a serious and imminent threat to the health or safety of a person or the public; and

>   >   (B) Is to a person or persons reasonably able to prevent or lessen the threat, including the target of the threat; or

>   (ii) Is necessary for law enforcement authorities to identify or apprehend an individual:

>   >   (A) Because of a statement by an individual admitting participation in a violent crime that the covered entity reasonably believes may have caused serious physical harm to the victim; or

(B) Where it appears from all the circumstances that the individual has escaped from a correctional institution or from lawful custody, as those terms are defined in § 164.501.

(2) Use or disclosure not permitted. A use or disclosure pursuant to paragraph (j)(1)(ii)(A) of this section may not be made if the information described in paragraph (j)(1)(ii)(A) of this section is learned by the covered entity:

(i) In the course of treatment to affect the propensity to commit the criminal conduct that is the basis for the disclosure under paragraph (j)(1)(ii)(A) of this section, or counseling or therapy; or

(ii) Through a request by the individual to initiate or to be referred for the treatment, counseling, or therapy described in paragraph (j)(2)(i) of this section.

(3) Limit on information that may be disclosed. A disclosure made pursuant to paragraph (j)(1)(ii)(A) of this section shall contain only the statement described in paragraph (j)(1)(ii)(A) of this section and the protected health information described in paragraph (f)(2)(i) of this section.

(4) Presumption of good faith belief. A covered entity that uses or discloses protected health information pursuant to paragraph (j)(1) of this section is presumed to have acted in good faith with regard to a belief described in paragraph (j)(1)(i) or (ii) of this section, if the belief is based upon the covered entity's actual knowledge or in reliance on a credible representation by a person with apparent knowledge or authority.

["The Privacy Regulations address a host of other situations in which a university may use or disclose PHI without an individual's authorization or the opportunity for the individual to agree or object to the disclosure. These include uses or disclosures of PHI as required by law, for public health activities, in connection with abuse, neglect, or domestic violence, for health oversight activities, for judicial and administrative proceedings, for law enforcement purposes, about decedents, for cadaveric organ, eye, or tissue donation purposes, for research purposes, to avert a serious threat to health or safety, for specialized government functions, and for workers' compensation. Each category of permitted use and disclosure of PHI carries with it its own special (and sometimes complicated) provisions and requirements for when such PHI may be released, under what circumstances, and to whom." Pietrina Scaraglino, *Complying With HIPAA: A Guide for the University and Its Counsel*, 29 J College & University Law 525 (2003).]

§ 164.520 Notice of privacy practices for protected health information.

(a) Standard: notice of privacy practices.

(1) Right to notice. . . . [A]n individual has a right to adequate notice of the uses and disclosures of protected health information that may be made by the covered entity, and of the individual's rights and the covered entity's legal duties with respect to protected health information. . . .

(b) Implementation specifications: content of notice.

(1) Required elements. The covered entity must provide a notice that is written in plain language and that contains the elements required by this paragraph.

> (i) Header. The notice must contain the following statement as a header or otherwise prominently displayed: "THIS NOTICE DESCRIBES HOW MEDICAL INFORMATION ABOUT YOU MAY BE USED AND DISCLOSED AND HOW YOU CAN GET ACCESS TO THIS INFORMATION. PLEASE REVIEW IT CAREFULLY."
>
> (ii) Uses and disclosures. The notice must contain:
>
>> (A) A description, including at least one example, of the types of uses and disclosures that the covered entity is permitted by this subpart to make for each of the following purposes: treatment, payment, and health care operations.

(B) A description of each of the other purposes for which the covered entity is permitted or required by this subpart to use or disclose protected health information without the individual's written authorization.

(C) If a use or disclosure for any purpose described in paragraphs (b)(1)(ii)(A) or (B) of this section is prohibited or materially limited by other applicable law, the description of such use or disclosure must reflect the more stringent law as defined in § 160.202 of this subchapter.

(D) For each purpose described in paragraph (b)(1)(ii)(A) or (B) of this section, the description must include sufficient detail to place the individual on notice of the uses and disclosures that are permitted or required by this subpart and other applicable law.

(E) A statement that other uses and disclosures will be made only with the individual's written authorization and that the individual may revoke such authorization as provided by § 164.508(b)(5).

(iii) Separate statements for certain uses or disclosures. If the covered entity intends to engage in any of the following activities, the description required by paragraph (b)(1)(ii)(A) of this section must include a separate statement, as applicable, that:

(A) The covered entity may contact the individual to provide appointment reminders or information about treatment alternatives or other health-related benefits and services that may be of interest to the individual;

(B) The covered entity may contact the individual to raise funds for the covered entity; or

(C) A group health plan, or a health insurance issuer or HMO with respect to a group health plan, may disclose protected health information to the sponsor of the plan.

(iv) Individual rights. The notice must contain a statement of the individual's rights with respect to protected health information and a brief description of how the individual may exercise these rights, as follows:

(A) The right to request restrictions on certain uses and disclosures of protected health information as provided by § 164.522(a), including a statement that the covered entity is not required to agree to a requested restriction;

(B) The right to receive confidential communications of protected health information as provided by § 164.522(b), as applicable;

(C) The right to inspect and copy protected health information as provided by § 164.524;

(D) The right to amend protected health information as provided by § 164.526;

(E) The right to receive an accounting of disclosures of protected health information as provided by § 164.528; and

(F) The right of an individual, including an individual who has agreed to receive the notice electronically in accordance with paragraph (c)(3) of this section, to obtain a paper copy of the notice from the covered entity upon request.

(v) Covered entity's duties. The notice must contain:

(A) A statement that the covered entity is required by law to maintain the privacy of protected health information and to provide individuals with notice of its legal duties and privacy practices with respect to protected health information;

(B) A statement that the covered entity is required to abide by the terms of the notice currently in effect; and

(C) For the covered entity to apply a change in a privacy practice that is described in the notice to protected health information that the covered entity created or received prior to issuing a revised notice, in accordance with § 164.530(i)(2)(ii), a statement that it reserves the right to change the terms of its notice and to make the new notice provisions effective for all protected health information that it maintains. The statement must also describe how it will provide individuals with a revised notice.

(vi) Complaints. The notice must contain a statement that individuals may complain to the covered entity and to the Secretary if they believe their privacy rights have been violated, a brief description of how the individual may file a complaint with the covered entity, and a statement that the individual will not be retaliated against for filing a complaint.

(vii) Contact. The notice must contain the name, or title, and telephone number of a person or office to contact for further information as required by § 164.530(a)(1)(ii). . . .

(2) Optional elements.

(i) In addition to the information required by paragraph (b)(1) of this section, if a covered entity elects to limit the uses or disclosures that it is permitted to make under this subpart, the covered entity may describe its more limited uses or disclosures in its notice, provided that the covered entity may not include in its notice a limitation affecting its right to make a use or disclosure that is required by law or permitted by § 164.512(j)(1)(i).

(ii) For the covered entity to apply a change in its more limited uses and disclosures to protected health information created or received prior to issuing a revised notice, in accordance with § 164.530(i)(2)(ii), the notice must include the statements required by paragraph (b)(1)(v)(C) of this section.

(3) Revisions to the notice. The covered entity must promptly revise and distribute its notice whenever there is a material change to the uses or disclosures, the individual's rights, the covered entity's legal

duties, or other privacy practices stated in the notice. Except when required by law, a material change to any term of the notice may not be implemented prior to the effective date of the notice in which such material change is reflected.

(c) Implementation specifications: Provision of notice. A covered entity must make the notice required by this section available on request to any person and to individuals as specified in paragraphs (c)(1) through (c)(3) of this section, as applicable.

(1) Specific requirements for health plans.

    (i) A health plan must provide notice:

        (A) No later than the compliance date for the health plan, to individuals then covered by the plan;

        (B) Thereafter, at the time of enrollment, to individuals who are new enrollees; and

        (C) Within 60 days of a material revision to the notice, to individuals then covered by the plan.

    (ii) No less frequently than once every three years, the health plan must notify individuals then covered by the plan of the availability of the notice and how to obtain the notice.

    (iii) The health plan satisfies the requirements of paragraph (c)(1) of this section if notice is provided to the named insured of a policy under which coverage is provided to the named insured and one or more dependents.

    (iv) If a health plan has more than one notice, it satisfies the requirements of paragraph (c)(1) of this section by providing the notice that is relevant to the individual or other person requesting the notice.

(2) Specific requirements for certain covered health care providers. A covered health care provider that has a direct treatment relationship with an individual must:

    (i) Provide the notice:

(A) No later than the date of the first service delivery, including service delivered electronically, to such individual after the compliance date for the covered health care provider; or

(B) In an emergency treatment situation, as soon as reasonably practicable after the emergency treatment situation.

(ii) Except in an emergency treatment situation, make a good faith effort to obtain a written acknowledgment of receipt of the notice provided in accordance with paragraph (c)(2)(i) of this section, and if not obtained, document its good faith efforts to obtain such acknowledgment and the reason why the acknowledgment was not obtained;

(iii) If the covered health care provider maintains a physical service delivery site:

(A) Have the notice available at the service delivery site for individuals to request to take with them; and

(B) Post the notice in a clear and prominent location where it is reasonable to expect individuals seeking service from the covered health care provider to be able to read the notice; and

(iv) Whenever the notice is revised, make the notice available upon request on or after the effective date of the revision and promptly comply with the requirements of paragraph (c)(2)(iii) of this section, if applicable.

(3) Specific requirements for electronic notice.

(i) A covered entity that maintains a web site that provides information about the covered entity's customer services or benefits must prominently post its notice on the web site and make the notice available electronically through the web site.

(ii) A covered entity may provide the notice required by this section to an individual by e-mail, if the individual agrees to electronic notice and such agreement has not been withdrawn.

If the covered entity knows that the e-mail transmission has failed, a paper copy of the notice must be provided to the individual. Provision of electronic notice by the covered entity will satisfy the provision requirements of paragraph (c) of this section when timely made in accordance with paragraph (c)(1) or (2) of this section.

(iii) For purposes of paragraph (c)(2)(i) of this section, if the first service delivery to an individual is delivered electronically, the covered health care provider must provide electronic notice automatically and contemporaneously in response to the individual's first request for service. The requirements in paragraph (c)(2)(ii) of this section apply to electronic notice.

(iv) The individual who is the recipient of electronic notice retains the right to obtain a paper copy of the notice from a covered entity upon request. . . .

(e) Implementation specifications: Documentation. A covered entity must document compliance with the notice requirements, as required by § 164.530(j), by retaining copies of the notices issued by the covered entity and, if applicable, any written acknowledgments of receipt of the notice or documentation of good faith efforts to obtain such written acknowledgment, in accordance with paragraph (c)(2)(ii) of this section. . . .

§ 164.524 Access of individuals to protected health information.

(a) Standard: Access to protected health information.

(1) Right of access. . . . [A]n individual has a right of access to inspect and obtain a copy of protected health information about the individual in a designated record set, for as long as the protected health information is maintained in the designated record set . . . . [There follows a list of exceptions and provision in some circumstances for review of a denial of access.]

§ 164.528 Accounting of disclosures of protected health information.

(a) Standard: Right to an accounting of disclosures of protected health information.

(1) An individual has a right to receive an accounting of disclosures of protected health information made by a covered entity in the six years prior to the date on which the accounting is requested, except for [numerous specified] disclosures . . . .

(b) Implementation specifications: Content of the accounting. The covered entity must provide the individual with a written accounting that meets the following requirements. . . .

(2) . . . [T]he accounting must include for each disclosure:

> (i) The date of the disclosure;
>
> (ii) The name of the entity or person who received the protected health information and, if known, the address of such entity or person;
>
> (iii) A brief description of the protected health information disclosed; and
>
> (iv) A brief statement of the purpose of the disclosure that reasonably informs the individual of the basis for the disclosure . . . .

42 U.S.C. § 1320(d)(5)

(a) General penalty

(1) In general

Except as provided in subsection (b) of this section, the Secretary shall impose on any person who violates a provision of this part a penalty of not more than $100 for each such violation, except that the total amount imposed on the person for all violations of an identical requirement or prohibition during a calendar year may not exceed $25,000.

42 U.S.C. § 1320(d)(6)

(a) Offense

A person who knowingly and in violation of this part--

(1) uses or causes to be used a unique health identifier;

(2) obtains individually identifiable health information relating to an individual; or

(3) discloses individually identifiable health information to another person,

shall be punished as provided in subsection (b) of this section.

(b) Penalties

A person described in subsection (a) of this section shall--

(1) be fined not more than $50,000, imprisoned not more than 1 year, or both;

(2) if the offense is committed under false pretenses, be fined not more than $100,000, imprisoned not more than 5 years, or both; and

(3) if the offense is committed with intent to sell, transfer, or use individually identifiable health information for commercial advantage, personal gain, or malicious harm, be fined not more than $250,000, imprisoned not more than 10 years, or both.

NORTHWESTERN MEMORIAL HOSPITAL v. ASHCROFT
362 F3d 923 (7th Cir 2004)

POSNER, J.

The government appeals from an order by the district court quashing a subpoena commanding Northwestern Memorial Hospital in Chicago to produce the medical records of certain patients on whom Dr. Cassing Hammond had performed late-term abortions at the hospital using the controversial method known variously as "D & X" (dilation and extraction) and "intact D & E" (dilation and evacuation). . . .

The subpoenaed records, apparently some 45 in number, are sought for use in the forthcoming trial . . . of a suit challenging the constitutionality of the Partial-Birth Abortion Ban Act of 2003. . . . Dr. Hammond is one of the plaintiffs in that suit and will also be testifying as an expert witness. The district court held that the production of the records is barred by [HIPAA]. . . .

The particular focus of the appeal is an HHS regulation entitled "Standard: Disclosures for Judicial and Administrative Proceedings," § 164.512(e), which authorizes a "covered entity" . . . to disclose private health information in judicial or administrative proceedings "in response to an order of a court." § 164.512(e)(1)(i). The regulation also allows the disclosure of such information in those proceedings "in response to a subpoena, discovery request, or other lawful process," § 164.512(e)(1)(ii), if the party seeking the information either notifies the patient (or at least makes a good faith effort to do so) or makes a "reasonable effort" to secure a qualified protective order, that is, an order that prohibits the use or disclosure of the information outside the litigation and requires the return or destruction of the information at the end of the litigation. 45 C.F.R. § 164.512(e)(1)(v).

The district judge presiding over the case in New York issued an order authorizing, although not directing, the hospital to provide the records to the government after redaction to remove information identifying the patients. The parties agree that his order is an "order" within the meaning of the "in response" provision. It hardly matters; the government didn't need such an order because it had obtained a protective order, thus qualifying under the alternative procedure for disclosure of medical records. But under Illinois law, even redacted medical records are not to be disclosed in judicial proceedings, with immaterial exceptions. The district court in our case ruled that the Illinois law, because it sets a "more stringent" standard for disclosure than the HIPAA regulation, trumps that regulation by virtue of HIPAA's supersession provision. So he quashed the subpoena, precipitating this appeal.

Although the issue is not free from doubt, we agree with the government that the HIPAA regulations do not impose state evidentiary privileges on suits to enforce federal law. Illinois is free to enforce its more stringent medical-records privilege (there is no comparable federal privilege) in suits in state court to enforce state law . . . . The enforcement of federal law might be hamstrung if state-law privileges more stringent than any federal privilege regarding medical records were applicable to all federal cases. . . . [W]e think it improbable that HHS intended to open such a can of worms when it set forth a procedure for disclosure of medical records in litigation--intended, that is, to be regulating, actually or potentially (depending on other statutory provisions regulating subpoenas), the litigation of federal employment discrimination cases, social security disability cases, ERISA cases, Medicare and Medicaid fraud cases, Food and Drug Administration cases, and the numerous other classes of federal case in which medical records whether of the parties or of nonparties would not be privileged under federal evidence law.

All that 45 C.F.R. § 164.512(e) should be understood to do, therefore, is to create a procedure for obtaining authority to use medical records in litigation. Whether the records are actually admissible in evidence will depend among other things on whether they are privileged. And the evidentiary privileges that are applicable to federal-question suits are given not by state law but by federal law, Fed.R.Evid. 501, which does not recognize a physician-patient (or hospital-patient) privilege. . . .

The purely procedural character of the HIPAA standard for disclosure of medical information in judicial or administrative proceedings is indicated by the procedure for disclosure in response to a subpoena or other process; the notice to the patient must contain "sufficient information about the litigation or proceeding in which the protected health information is requested to permit the individual to raise an objection to the court." § 164.512(e)(1)(iii)(B). The objection in court would often be based on a privilege--the source of which would be found elsewhere than in the regulations themselves.

As an alternative basis for quashing the subpoena, the district judge undertook to craft a new federal common law privilege for abortion records. He based this ruling on their sensitivity, which he compared to that of psychotherapists' treatment records, held privileged in *Jaffee v. Redmond*. . . . . [W]e are reluctant to embark on a case-by-case determination of the relative sensitivity of medical records of different ailments or procedures. Most medical records are sensitive, and many are as sensitive as late-term abortion records, such as the records of AIDS patients. Proceeding down the path taken by the district court would inevitably result in either arbitrary line drawing or the creation of an Illinois-type comprehensive privilege for medical records.

The district court did not reach a further ground urged by Northwestern Memorial Hospital for quashing the government's subpoena, which is simply that the burden of compliance with it would exceed the benefit of production of the material sought by it. However, in support of his ruling expanding the federal common law of privilege to embrace the medical records of abortion patients, the judge made findings that are highly germane to--indeed arguably dispositive of--the Rule 45(c) issue. He pointed out that the "government seeks these records on the *possibility* that it may find something therein which would affect the testimony of Dr. Hammond adversely, that is, for its potential value in impeaching his credibility as a witness. What the government ignores in its argument is how little, if any, probative value lies within these patient records." He contrasted the dearth of probative value "with the potential loss of privacy that would ensue were these medical records used in a case in which the patient was not a party" and concluded that "the balance of harms resulting from disclosure severely out-weighs the loss to the government through non-disclosure." . . .

Ordinarily when a district judge has not addressed an issue committed to his discretion, such as the balance of benefit and burden in complying with a subpoena . . . the appellate court must remand to give the judge a chance to exercise his discretion. We do not follow that course, here, however, for two reasons. The first is that the judge, in the passages we quoted from his opinion . . . "weigh[ed the] competing hardships." True, he did so in the course of addressing a different issue from whether Rule 45(c) required that the subpoena be quashed; but, realistically, the result of a remand is foreordained.

The second reason is that with the trial in New York scheduled to begin on March 29 and to last only four weeks, the practical effect of a remand would be to moot the issue of compliance with the subpoena. . . .

The government . . . argues that since it is seeking only a limited number of records and they would be produced to it minus the information that would enable the identity of the patient to be determined, there is no hardship to either the hospital or the patients of compliance. . . . The natural sensitivity that people feel about the disclosure of their medical records . . . is amplified when the records are of a procedure that Congress has now declared to be a crime. Even if all the women whose records the government seeks know what "redacted" means, they are bound to be skeptical that redaction will conceal their identity from the world. . . . [T]he Partial-Birth Abortion Ban Act and the litigation challenging its constitutionality . . . have generated enormous publicity. These women must know that, and doubtless they are also aware that hostility to abortion has at times erupted into violence, including criminal obstruction of entry into abortion clinics, the firebombing of clinics, and the assassination of physicians who perform abortions.

Some of these women will be afraid that when their redacted records are made a part of the trial record in New York, persons of their acquaintance, or skillful "Googlers," sifting the information contained in the medical records concerning each patient's medical and sex history, will put two and two together, "out" the 45 women, and thereby expose them to threats, humiliation, and obloquy. . . .

Even if there were no possibility that a patient's identity might be learned from a redacted medical record, there would be an invasion of privacy. Imagine if nude pictures of a woman, uploaded to the Internet without her consent though without identifying her by name, were downloaded in a foreign country by people who will never meet her. She would still feel that her privacy had been invaded. The revelation of the intimate details contained in the record of a late-term abortion may inflict a similar wound.

If Northwestern Memorial Hospital cannot shield the medical records of its abortion patients from disclosure in judicial proceedings, moreover, the hospital will lose the confidence of its patients, and persons with sensitive medical conditions may be inclined to turn elsewhere for medical treatment. . . .

The question whether the D & X procedure is ever medically indicated will be resolved as a matter of legislative fact not requiring the taking of trial-type testimony at all or will pivot on the clash of expert witnesses at the New York trial, or perhaps, as suggested in *Stenberg,* will be answered by some combination of these two approaches to ascertaining facts. The medical records of expert witnesses are irrelevant to the first inquiry; and, so far as we can determine after having listened to the government's arguments at length, those records will not figure significantly in the resolution of experts' disagreements either.

The fact that quashing the subpoena comports with Illinois' medical-records privilege is a final factor in favor of the district order's action. . . . [C]omity "impels federal courts to recognize state privileges where this can be accomplished at no substantial cost to federal substantive and procedural policy." Patients, physicians, and hospitals in Illinois rely on Illinois' strong policy of privacy of medical records. They cannot rely completely, for they are not entitled to count on the state privilege's being applied in federal court. But in a case such as this in which, so far as we can determine, applying the privilege would not interfere significantly with federal proceedings, comity has required us not to apply the Illinois privilege, but to consider with special care the arguments for quashing the subpoena on the basis of relative hardship under Fed.R.Civ.P. 45(c).

MANION, J., concurring in part, dissenting in part.

I agree with the court that HIPPA [*sic* throughout] does not adopt state privilege law in a federal question suit brought in federal court, but rather Rule 501 of the Federal Rules of Evidence governs the evidentiary privileges applicable in such suits. Opinion at 925. I also agree that it is not for us to create a federal common law physician-patient privilege where none exists, and that the redacted medical records are not privileged.. However, for several reasons, I disagree with the court's conclusion that enforcing the subpoena creates an undue burden under Fed.R.Civ.P. 45(c)(3)(A)(iv). . . .

Both Congress and HHS define "individually identifiable health information" as information that . . . *(i) identifies the individual; or (ii) with respect to which there is a reasonable basis to believe the information can be used to identify the individual."* 42 U.S.C. 1320d(6); 45 C.F.R. § 160.103 (emphasis added).

In this case, the government seeks only redacted medical records and agrees that all identifying information may be removed before Northwestern makes the records available for its review. Because the records will be redacted, they will not identify the individual. Nor is there a reasonable basis to believe that the information can be used to identify the individual. Section 164.514(b) confirms the latter conclusion. Section 164.514(b)(2)(i) sets forth specific identifiers which, if removed, "de-identify," the health records . . . .

[E]ven if the records were "individually identifiable," they would still be subject to the general privacy rules governing use and disclosure of protected health information set forth in § 164.502. . . . [T]he privacy protection afforded in that section provides several exceptions. . . . [T]he government obtained a court order authorizing the disclosure of the medical records. Under the regulations, such an order negates any need to redact identifying information.[2] 45 C.F.R. § 164.512(e)(1)(i). Yet, as the government stressed at oral argument, it has no need for, nor desire to know, the individual identities of the patients. Therefore, it is only seeking the relevant redacted medical records. Such redacted records are afforded no privacy protection under HIPPA, logically so because the redacted records have no identifiably private information to expose. . . .

That should end the inquiry. But instead the court resurrects the privacy question through the "undue burden" language of Fed.R.Civ.P. 45(c)(3)(A)(iv). Rule 45(c)(3)(A)(iv) provides that a court may quash or modify a subpoena if it "subjects a person to undue burden." In the court's view, compliance with the subpoena would impose an undue burden (i.e. "potential psychological cost") on the

---

[2] As the court also recognizes, the government did not need a court order in this case because it obtained a protective order securing the confidentiality of the redacted records. Thus, the government complied with the privacy protections established by HIPPA in three independent ways: by obtaining a court order; by obtaining a protective order; and by seeking only redacted records.

women whose redacted records were subpoenaed. . . . This conclusion is wrong on several levels. . . .

HIPPA and the implementing regulations recognize that there is no loss of privacy where the medical records are redacted . . . . Nor is it reasonable to believe that the unidentified 45 women have "acquaintances ... who will put two and two together, 'out' the 45 women, and thereby expose them to threats, humiliation, and obloquy." In fact, there is no reason to believe that the women themselves have any idea that their records are among the few sought by the government in this case. But even if they knew, no one else ever would, because all of the information that could reasonably be used to identify them will be redacted, and none of the information--not even the redacted non-identifying information--will ever be made public, much less paraded in court or placed on the Internet within the reach of "skillful Googlers." That is guaranteed by the additional security of the protective order entered in this case in the Southern District of New York. *See, e.g., Reproductive Serv., Inc. v. Walker,* 439 U.S. 1307, 1308 (Brennan, J., in chambers) (dissolving stay of subpoena seeking abortion records of non-party patients on condition that patient names were redacted and parties agreed to a protective order to ensure privacy of all patients).

The court's erroneous conclusion that a privacy interest exists in the redacted documents leads to the unnecessary attempt to assess the probative value of the evidence. Notably, the district court did not reach the undue burden of compliance issue of Fed.R.Civ.P. 45(c)(3)(A)(iv). . . . Based on the complaint, Dr. Hammond's declaration, the congressional findings when it passed the law, and the arguments made by the government and the hospital (both very limited since privilege, not probative value, was the issue argued below), there is significant probative value. But that is not for us to decide, as the probative value of the evidence has already been determined. . . . Judge Casey, who is presiding over the underlying case, believes the information is relevant, so much so, that he has indicated that if it is not produced, he would consider lifting the stay and dismissing the case (or at least dismissing Dr. Hammond from the case). . . . If any deference is owed, it is to the presiding judge--the judge who handled this case pre-trial and who knows the arguments presented by both sides, and the judge who will need all (non-privileged) relevant evidence available to allow him to make the necessary factual findings to determine this difficult and contentious constitutional case. . . .

[T]he court nonetheless interjects its own theory of the case and its own judgment of the probative value of the evidence. For instance, the court states: "What the government would like to show, in refutation of Dr. Hammond's impending testimony, is that D & E is always an adequate alternative, from the standpoint of a pregnant woman's health, to the D & X procedure. The government has failed to explain how the record of a D & X abortion would show this." But the government's document request was not so structured: The government did not ask for the records of the D & X abortions identified by Dr. Hammond, but rather requested the redacted medical records of patients who had abortions--both the D & E and D & X variety--for the reasons asserted by Dr. Hammond as justifying a partial-birth abortion. For instance, Dr. Hammond stated that he sometimes performed abortions for women to protect their health after they learned that "their fetuses have anomalies that are often quite severe." The government requested the patient records for 2003 of any women who had an abortion during their 19th or 20th week of pregnancy, (whether partial-birth or D & E) for that reason. As the government explained at oral argument, those records are highly relevant to the question of medical necessity because, if they show that Dr. Hammond did not regularly perform partial-birth abortions under those circumstances, that would demonstrate that Dr. Hammond does not believe a partial-birth abortion is necessary to protect the women's health. . . . [T]he only way the government (and the trial judge) can assess Dr. Hammond's contention that partial-birth abortions are medically necessary to protect the women's health is to review the medical records of the patients with the conditions that Dr. Hammond referenced. . . .

In fact, the relevance here cannot be overstated: Congress made explicit findings that a partial-birth abortion is never medically necessary to protect a women's health. Yet, Dr. Hammond claims Congress is wrong. The court concisely lays out Dr. Hammond's argument: In a D & X (partial-birth) abortion, "the fetus is destroyed after the lower extremities, and sometimes the torso, have emerged from the womb and only the head remains inside," and this, according to Dr. Hammond is safer then the D & E procedure, where "the fetus is destroyed while it is still entirely within the womb . . . ." . . . Dr. Hammond seeks to testify accordingly, and it is therefore imperative that the government be able to determine the veracity of his testimony. There is no better way than by determining if Dr. Hammond's actual practice supports his testimony. And this is not a question only of impeachment, but rather concerns the heart of this case.

Moreover, as the government explained during oral argument, the medical records are highly relevant to its case because its experts must be able to review Dr. Hammond's files to determine whether, in their expert opinion, a D & X procedure was the most appropriate procedure, as Dr. Hammond claims. . . .

The medical records are also highly relevant to a second congressional finding, namely, that a "partial-birth abortion poses serious risks to the health of a woman undergoing the procedure." Congress detailed numerous risks it found posed by partial-birth abortions. . . . Northwestern's attorney alerted the court to the fact that the medical records will show whether there were any complications from the abortion, and this evidence is highly probative to the underlying constitutional challenge.

The court also questions whether the government sincerely wants to determine "whether D & X abortions are ever medically indicated," because the government did not seek summary statistics of all circumstances in which such abortions are performed. But as the government pointed out at oral argument, it was trying to limit the burden on Northwestern by confining its document request to those specific situations where Dr. Hammond claimed a partial birth abortion was necessary to preserve the mother's health. And it succeeded, maybe even better than the government had hoped: During oral argument, the government learned for the first time that there are only 45 records that satisfy its document request. Given that Dr. Hammond stated in his declaration that he performs, teaches or supervises about 300 abortions a year, and that the government sought the records for a two- to three-year time frame, it probably surprised the government to learn that there were only 45 relevant records, with the rest apparently unrelated to the mother's or fetus's health. . . .

Under Rule 45, a court may quash a subpoena where it creates an undue burden. There is no such burden in this case because HIPPA establishes that there is no privacy interest in redacted records and those records are highly relevant to the constitutional challenge to the Partial Birth Abortion Ban Act. The only burden identified by the court seems to be a "potential psychological cost." Even assuming that is the kind of "burden" Rule 45 contemplates, reliance on that as a burden in effect creates a privilege where none exists.

Finally, contrary to the court's conclusion, quashing the subpoena in this case does come at a "substantial cost to federal substantive and procedural policy." The court's ruling may well be the death knell for Dr. Hammond's claim, as the district court made clear that it believed the records relevant and that it would consider dismissing the case if the records were not produced. Given that the government cannot adequately cross-examine Dr. Hammond, the district court would be well within its rights to bar Dr. Hammond's testimony, which will not only harm his case, but also the other plaintiffs'. The court's decision also comes at a substantial cost to the federal policy adopted by HIPPA. Lastly, and most significantly, it comes at a cost to the truth of Congress' findings that a partial-birth abortion is never necessary to protect a woman's health and poses significant health risks, and to the constitutionality of such a law. . . .

Notes and Questions on Life After HIPAA

1. What is the problem HIPAA solves? Richard A. Epstein, *HIPPA on Privacy: Its Unintended and Intended Consequences*, 22 Cato J 13 (2002), contends that the years before HIPAA saw no "explosion of improper disclosures of sensitive information, and no systematic unwillingness to deal with the problems that do arise by private organization or even by more limited and focused regulatory responses. It is hard to see a less fertile ground for comprehensive government regulation; yet that is exactly what has happened in the privacy regulations promulgated by HHS under HIPAA."

In justifying the HIPAA regulations, HHS centrally relied on nine anecdotes. For example: "A Michigan-based health system accidentally posted the medical records of thousands of patients on the Internet." "The health insurance claims forms of thousands of patients blew out of a truck on its way to a recycling center . . . ." "A patient in a Boston-area hospital discovered that her medical record had been read by more than 200 of the hospital's employees." "An employee of the Tampa, Florida health department took a computer disk containing the names of 4,000 people who had tested positive for HIV . . . ." 65 Fed Reg 82462 - 82829 (2000). Were remedies for any of these incidents available under state law? Which, if any, sections of HIPAA prevent such problems from arising?

2. When lawmakers encounter a problem, they may choose from a variety of kinds of responses. Here, the federal government chose to act through an elaborate system of administrative regulations. What other lawmakers might have acted and did act, and what other kinds of legal approaches were available? How do you evaluate Professor Epstein's criticism that HHS

> did not take an incremental view of the entire problem and decide to regulate where the dangers were greatest. Far from acting incrementally, it opted from the start for the most comprehensive system of regulation to solve a wide number of problems without any evidence of systematic and sustained abuse. It also acted before it understood the interactive effects between its regulations and thousands of other regulations that are elsewhere on the books, or which could be added in short order with the expansion of other programs.

3. The administrative regulations HHS promulgated extensively use a familiar technique – our old friend disclosure. Does it work here? Do the regulations call for dumping masses of information on patients exactly at the time when they are least able to use it?

4. It is conventionally said that courts regulate exercises of eminent domain lightly because the obligation to pay for any property that is taken disciplines government's zeal for exercising that power. In HIPAA, however, the costs are not paid out of government's coffers. Has this made HHS unduly willing to impose duties on private actors? What will HIPAA cost in direct financial terms and in terms of the efficiency of medical care and the productivity of medical research? Is HIPAA worth the cost? Might it have achieved its purposes more cheaply and effectively some other way?

5. Polls regularly report considerable public concern for privacy and a desire to have the government protect that privacy. But what do these polls mean? Is the word "privacy" so plain that everyone (anyone?) knows what it means? What price are people willing to pay to get some level of privacy? What should we make of the case Professor Scott describes:

In January 1999, the Maine legislature enacted a tough new law prohibiting the release of a patient's medical information without her written permission. This simple and direct prohibition was backed up with heavy fines for violation. The impact was swift and dramatic: hospitals refused to give any information over the telephone to family and friends inquiring about a patient's status; florists said they could not deliver flowers; priests said they could not see patients for last rites; newspapers said they would be hindered in reporting on accident victims. Even doctors could not compare notes on the same patient without getting written permission from the patient, and clinical labs refused to give patients their results over the telephone. The law was repealed within two weeks and replaced with a less restrictive version, and one of its original drafters commented, "What we really did . . . [was] protect patients more than they wanted to be protected." Maine citizens seem to have concluded that too much privacy could be bad for their health.

6. You are the general counsel of the American Hospital Association. The president of that organization wants you to prepare testimony to present to Congress on whether HIPAA should be revoked or amended. (If you Google "American Hospital Association," the first thing you get is the AHA's HIPAA page.) What will you advise the organization to say to Congress?

A Modest HIPAA Problem

You have just been appointed the general counsel of the Hutchins University Medical Center. The HIPAA regulations have been promulgated and are about to go into effect. You are shocked to discover that little preparation has been made by your office for this change in the law, since you know that one of the most basic lawyers' jobs is to stay abreast of changes in the law. (Your only consolation is that your institution is not alone in its failure.) So, what advice will you give your client about how it should respond to HIPAA? Observe how difficult this question is. First, you have to understand the current law so that you can identify the areas that have changed. Then you have master the new law. You need to describe the things the client must unequivocally do to comply with the law. You need to tell the client where the borderlands of the law are and prepare advice about behavior in it. You need to anticipate legal issues that are not present on the face of the regulations but that may arise as the regulations are applied and litigated. Furthermore, you need to know your client's business situation well enough to help it respond to the regulations not just as a matter of law but also as a matter of economics and good care for patients.

As you are pondering these worrying facts, you are called to meet with the President of Hutchins University (formerly the dean of the law school) and the Medical Center CEO. They ask you a series of questions:

1. Some universities have appointed quite senior people to oversee HIPAA compliance. Should Hutchins? What structure should be created to run and monitor compliance? Should you hire consultants? "There are many consultants, including law firms and others, that provide HIPAA-related services . . . rang[ing] from assistance in analyzing whether and to what extent an entity is covered by the Regulations to assistance in drafting policies and procedures and training employees." Pietrina Scaraglino, *Complying With HIPAA: A Guide for the University and Its Counsel*, 29 J College & University Law 525 (2003).

2. The President wants to know whether the university is a "covered entity." All of it or just parts? Does it matter? If the university is a "hybrid," which parts are covered? What, for example, about the university's general counsel and IT office?

3. What information falls within HIPAA's purview? The Medical Center runs a managed-care organization which is one of the principal options available to employees eligible for health insurance. Are records which show that an employee has elected that coverage PHI under HIPAA? Worker's compensation records? Americans With Disabilities Act records? The results of drug tests on the football team and the university's med-evac helicopter pilots? Does it matter whether the university administers those tests itself or the tests are performed elsewhere? What if the university holds health information which it acquired through both covered and non-covered channels? Are student medical records in the Student Health Service covered? What is the relationship between the Family Educational Rights and Privacy Act, 20 USC § 1232(g) (2000), and HIPAA? What other questions of this sort should you ask?

4. The university must hand out hundreds of thousands of privacy notices annually. The president reminds you of the evidence that people (1) do not read such handouts, (2) do not understand

them, and (3) do not heed them. A study of thirty-one HIPAA privacy notices found them written at the reading level of a second or third year college student. Only one "scored any better than 'difficult.'" Mark Hochhauser, *Readability of HIPAA Privacy Notices*, www.benefitslink.com/articles/hipaareadability.pdf (visited July 21, 2005). The analysis included sentences from the forms, the first of which reads:

> Examples of these activities include obtaining accreditation from independent organizations like the Joint Commission for the Accreditation of Healthcare Organizations, the National Committee for Quality Assurance and others, outcomes evaluation and development of clinical guidelines, operation of preventive health, early detection and disease management programs, case management and care coordination, contacting of health care providers and patients with information about treatment alternatives, and related functions; evaluations of health care providers (credentialing and peer review activities) and health plans; operation of educational programs; underwriting, premium rating and other activities relating to the creation, renewal or replacement of health benefits contracts; obtaining reinsurance, stop-loss and excess loss insurance; conducting or arranging for medical review, legal services, and auditing functions, including fraud and abuse detection and compliance programs; business planning and development; and business management and general administrative activities, including data and information systems management, customer service, resolution of internal grievances, and sales, mergers, transfers, or consolidations with other providers or health plans or prospective providers or health plans.

Developing disclosure statements that work is expensive, if it is possible at all. Should the university worry about comprehensibility and effectiveness?

5. How does HIPAA deal with the ways in which patients' personal privacy is most frequently and even painfully breached – in the hospital itself? In one fascinating study, the researchers rode for hours on hospital elevators. Peter A. Ubel et al, *Elevator Talk: Observational Study of Inappropriate Comments in a Public Space*, 99 Am J Med 190 (1995). Of 259 rides, "36 (13.9 percent) contained at least one inappropriate comment. On three rides, observers recorded two inappropriate comments, making a total of 39 inappropriate comments in 259 rides."

We observed 18 comments in which hospital employees discussed confidential patient information. Physicians were involved in 11 of these, nurses in 2 . . . . These comments usually took the form of statements such as, "Mr. X was readmitted last night for more chemo." Some comments did not refer to patients by name but provided other identifying information. For example, one passenger referred to a hospitalized patient as "the Admiral" and another was described as "the guy who runs company X," which was a well-known local establishment. . . . [On other] occasions, the . . . conversations, although not directly violating confidentiality, were so detailed that friends or family overhearing the comments may have been able to identify the patient . . . . For example, one team of physicians on rounds entered the elevator in the middle of a detailed discussion of a patient's presenting symptoms, complete with the results of a thallium stress test and the plan for how to proceed. The clinical discussions in these cases were so detailed, even graphic, that they could raise legitimate concerns among passengers regarding the value which health care professionals place on confidentiality. For instance, two physicians had a heated debate discussing the relative merits of removing parts of either one or two lungs from a patient. . . .

We observed 10 comments in which hospital employees talked about themselves in ways that could raise questions about their ability or desire to provide quality care. Nurses were involved in 6 . . . , physicians in 3 . . . . Several nurses and physicians complained that they were too tired to do their jobs well. One said: "I worked 16 hours yesterday, went home, had some beer, and before I knew it, I was back here. I don't think I can make it all night." . . . On two occasions, physicians riding elevators made it clear that they were biding their time until they could make large amounts of money, raising questions about whether their primary motivations were to provide quality medical care. As one physician said: "That's it, I'm getting out of here. I'm going where I can make big bucks. No more running after patients." Another physician responded by saying: "You need a magnifying glass to see your paycheck." . . .

We observed 5 derogatory comments about patients or their families. One physician snidely referred to 1 of his patients as "Mister Christian Dior," an allusion to the expensive clothes the patient wore . . . . On another ride, a nurse called a patient "a dump." . . . Physicians were involved in 2 of these comments, and nurses in 2; 1 commenter could not be identified.

In an ER study, the "patient's name was overheard [during check-in] for 81% (26/32). . . . The patient's name and diagnosis or presenting complaint were obtained for 53% (17/32). Insurance status was noted for 72% . . . . Occasionally, patients were associated with miscellaneous comments including their address, home telephone number and social security number." Privacy was often protected only by a curtain or glass through which everything could be heard and much seen: "Observations included a patient being sutured, with his face, legs, and buttocks readily in view; . . . a patient wheeled by with the announcement 'head CT to rule out tumor.'" What is more, "[a]ll members of the health care team, attending physicians, residents, medical students, nurses, paramedics, clerks, volunteers and other ancillary personnel, committed breaches . . . ." Edward J. Mlinek & Jessica Pierce, *Confidentiality and Privacy Breaches in a University Hospital Emergency Department*, 4 Academy of Emergency Medicine 1142 (1997). Finally: "Only small numbers of patients expected their cases to be shared with physicians' spouses (17%) or at parties (18%). House staff and medical students, however, indicated that such discussions occur commonly (57% and 70%, respectively)." Barry D. Weiss, *Confidentiality Expectations of Patients, Physicians, and Medical Students*, 247 JAMA 2695 (1982).

6. Lawrence Moore, the psychologist who treated Prosenjit Poddar, recently joined the Hutchins faculty. The president remembers *Tarasoff* from law school and asks how HIPAA might change the *Tarasoff* principle.

7. The president recently returned from a University Presidents' Conference which discussed *University of Colorado Hospital Authority v. Denver Publishing Company*, 340 FSupp2d 1142 (D Colo, 2004). The Rocky Mountain *News* had obtained "from an unknown source" a report produced in a University Hospital peer review. The *News* published articles using information from the report and posted a copy of it on its website. The hospital sought damages under HIPAA. The court said, "The statutory provision under which University Hospital seeks to hold DPC liable prohibits a person from knowingly obtaining or disclosing individually identifiable health information. 42 U.S.C. §§ 1320d-6(a)(2) & (3). The provision also establishes penalties for violations . . . ." However, neither "§ 1320d-6, nor any other section of HIPAA, contains any language conferring privacy rights upon, or identifying as the intended beneficiary of § 1320d-6, any specific class of persons (particularly

one which would include healthcare providers such as University Hospital)." Furthermore, the "statutory structure of HIPAA likewise precludes implication of a private right of action. § 1320d-6 expressly provides a method for enforcing its prohibition upon use or disclosure of individual's health information-the punitive imposition of fines and imprisonment for violations." Will other courts reach the same conclusion about private causes of action arising under HIPAA. Suppose that the plaintiff were a patient whose medical information had appeared in the *News*? Suppose the plaintiff is claiming breach of the duty of confidentiality under state law and wants to use HIPAA to establish the standard of care to which the defendant held?

8. The president's daughter is a Candystriper at the Hutchins Medical Center. She told her best friend that she had seen one of her high school teachers in the infectious diseases clinic in the hospital, seen the teacher receiving a prescription for AZT, seen the teacher filling that prescription at the hospital pharmacy, and seen a notation about the patient's HIV status on the patient's chart as a nurse was making entries. Are there any HIPAA issues here?

D. Confidentiality and the Innocent Bystander

In *Baptist Memorial Hospital v. Johnson*, 754 So2d 1165 (Miss 2000), the issue was whether a third party should be compelled to reveal her identity and medical information because of a problem to which she was a stranger. A child was born to plaintiffs. "Before she and her mother were released from the hospital a nurse employed by the hospital took Kayla to the wrong mother to be nursed (hereinafter "Mrs. X"). Before the staff recognized the error, Kayla was nursed by Mrs. X. Some hours later, the hospital disclosed the mix-up to the Johnsons but refused to reveal the identity of Mrs. X." The Johnsons' daughter "has experienced bad health since birth and they fear it has a connection with her breast feeding by Mrs. X." The Johnsons' brought a negligence action and asked the hospital to reveal Mrs. X's name. The hospital said that "Mrs. X chose to affirmatively assert her medical privilege of confidentiality. However, Mrs. X did waive her privilege to a limited degree, expressly stipulating which medical records she consented to disclose. . . .The documents included records of Mrs. X's pregnancy and delivery (discharge summary), past medical history, genetics screening, hematology and urinalysis profile, drug screen and HIV test."

The court held that Mrs. X's identity had to be revealed because she was "one of only a handful of potential witnesses to the hospital's actions. . . . To hold otherwise would allow hospitals to completely conceal the identity of any patient who was involved with or may have information regarding tortious conduct by a hospital." And the court ordered that Mrs. X's medical records should be "turned over to Judge Coleman for an in camera review to determine whether the health of Kayla Johnson may be at risk. If necessary, he may also choose to take advantage of protective orders . . . a familiar device used to preserve confidentiality in trade secret and other cases in which secrecy is of high importance or there is a need to protect a party from embarrassment."

Or consider the following situation, in which the issue is whether a hospital should must use confidential information to make it possible to induce a patient to do good:

> Plaintiff William Head is a leukemia victim who is currently undergoing chemotherapy in a Texas clinic. His illness is in relapse, and the prognosis is grim.
>
> The University of Iowa Hospitals and Clinics include a bone marrow transplant unit. That unit maintains a bone marrow transplant registry, listing persons whose blood has been tissue-typed by the hospital. The tissue typing reveals blood antigen characteristics which must be known for determining whether a donor's bone marrow will be a suitable match-up for the bone marrow of a donee. A bone marrow transplant consists of removing bone marrow from a healthy person and infusing it into the body of a patient in the hope it will generate healthy white blood cells. The procedure is experimental between unrelated persons.
>
> Late in 1982, plaintiff phoned the transplant unit and . . . learned that the hospital's registry included the name of a woman who might . . . prove to be a suitable donor to him. Only one in approximately 6,000 persons would have blood with the necessary antigen characteristics.
>
> The tissue typing of the woman, referred to in the record as "Mrs. X," had not been done for reasons of her own health but to determine her suitability as a blood platelet donor to a member of her family who was ill. The hospital subsequently placed her name in its platelet donor registry. Then, when it later established an experimental program involving bone marrow transplants between

unrelated persons, the hospital, without Mrs. X's knowledge or consent, placed her name in the bone marrow transplant registry. When the hospital established the new program, its institutional review board approved a procedure for contacting persons listed on the registry to determine whether they would act as donors. The procedure involved sending a letter informing the person of the program, its nature and goals, and inviting the person's participation in it. If the letter was not answered, a staff member was authorized to telephone the person and ask a series of general questions designed to determine whether the person would volunteer as a donor.

After plaintiff's contact with the bone marrow unit, the unit staff on December 31, 1982, sent Mrs. X the general letter informing her about the program and encouraging her to participate in it. When no response to the letter was received, a staff member telephoned Mrs. X on January 10, 1983, and asked her the series of questions. . . . Mrs. X said she was not interested in being a bone marrow donor. When asked if she might ever be interested in being a donor, she said, "Well, if it was for family, yes. Otherwise, no." Despite plaintiff's subsequent request that the hospital make a specific inquiry of Mrs. X in plaintiff's behalf or to disclose her identity to him so he could contact her, the hospital refused to contact her or to disclose her identity to plaintiff. . . .

Plaintiff asked for a mandatory injunction to require [the hospital] to disclose the name and identity of the potential donor either to the court or to his attorney. He proposed that the court or counsel then be permitted to write the woman to notify her of plaintiff's need and her possible suitability as a donor, asking her if she would consider being a donor to plaintiff.

What moral obligations, if any, does Mrs. X have to the plaintiff? Is Mrs. X a "patient" of the hospital who is entitled to the confidentiality protections accorded to patients? Should she have those protections even if she is not a "patient"? Would Mrs. X's confidentiality rights have been infringed had the plaintiff's request been granted? The plaintiff would presumably not learn her name unless she consented to be contacted. The hospital already knows who she is. Does "confidentiality" protect Mrs. X from being pressured to consider donating bone marrow? "Although the primary issue in this case may seem to be the question of invading the potential donor's privacy, we believe it is actually the protection of her initial decision from harassment and pressure." Charles W. Lidz, et al,

Commentary on *Mrs. X and the Bone Marrow Transplant*, 13 HCR 17 (June 1983). But how is this "pressure"? Lidz et al acknowledge that Mrs. X needs information in order to decide whether to donate marrow, but they argue that she already "presumably had enough general information to make a rational choice" and ask whether she also needed "the further information that there is a specific individual who needs her bone marrow." They continue:

> Whether such information is relevant to her decision and thus promotes rationality is debatable, but the pressure that such a letter would place on her certainly compromises her autonomy. . . . All the additional "information" would do is to engender guilty feelings about possibly being responsible for someone else's death. This type of information no longer promotes informed consent. Rather, it is a form of psychological coercion.

Lidz et al even suggest that contacting Mrs. X would violate "the spirit of federal regulations requiring efforts to 'minimize coercion and undue influence.'" Are these persuasive arguments? First, even Lidz et al decline to say the new information is irrelevant. Before being told of the plaintiff's need, Mrs. X might have thought a good match was improbable. Now she can know it is not. In addition, isn't it likely that Mrs. X didn't think very carefully about the hospital's request but that, told about a specific recipient, she might be inspired to do so? Second, wherein lies the "coercion"? The only pressure Mrs. X is likely to feel will come from her "guilty feelings about possibly being responsible for someone else's death." But no one would be telling Mrs. X anything that she had to feel that way or anything that was not true. Might she even be glad to learn of a chance to help someone so dramatically?

It was once normal for mothers giving children up for adoption to be promised their identity would be kept secret. Recently, however, provisions have been made for bringing those mothers and children together. Are there any significant differences between the mothers' confidentiality claims and Mrs. X's?

Finally, in *In re George*, 630 SW2d 614 (1982), Mr. George was dying of leukemia. His best remaining chance of a successful bone-marrow transplant seemed to lie in locating his father. However, Mr. George had been adopted. He asked to have his adoption records opened. Eventually, the trial judge and the judge's wife met for four to five hours with the person thought to be Mr. George's father and showed him letters from Mr. George and from Mr. George's wife. The trial judge described

> this man's reaction as one of disbelief, shock, and denial. As more information was given to him . . . , it was obvious to him who was the mother of the applicant.
>
> He stated to the Court that he was not the father of the applicant, that the circumstances were such that he could not be his father, and that under those circumstances, he could be of no help to him, and that he did not want to have anything more to do with the matter.
>
> We prevailed, however, that he should discuss this matter with his wife, that it was entirely appropriate for her to know what the situation was, and we asked him to inform her of this matter and to allow us to meet with he and she to discuss the problem further. He finally agreed to this . . . .
>
> We did hear from him indicating that we could come visit he and his wife, and we did. This meeting probably lasted another five to six hours . . . .
>
> We were hopeful that perhaps his wife would be supportive of us in our desire to get his blood tested, but she supported her husband, and accepted her husband – and accepted his statement that he was not the father of the applicant.

After the natural mother proved not to be a suitable donor, the judge again asked the alleged natural father to consent to blood test. Again the man refused.

> Persevering still in the effort to obtain the consent of the alleged natural father to such testing, the court wrote a letter to the alleged natural father. In that letter, the court again called attention to the plight of the applicant and his need for a donor. The court pointed out that regardless of paternity, the need justified help from anyone. . . . The court offered conditions of anonymity and guaranteed that the sex and identity of the persons tested would be unknown to anyone but the court and the alleged natural father. . . . The alleged natural father contacted the court and rejected the proposal and indicated he would put his statement in writing.

The supposed father wrote the judge

to say that I have every compassion for the person with the horrible disease, and I agree whole heartedly on our responsibility to serve and help others, but, in this case, I have been put in a special category. The only reason that I have been asked to do this is due to the thirty-five year old allegation which is mathematically impossible. I deny completely this allegation with a clear conscience. I am sure that I have been used to cover someone else's actions.

In December I will have been married (very happily) 35 years to the very same intelligent woman.

Judging from the newspaper clippings that you showed me, and from the TV coverage that you said occurred, one would conclude that this whole situation has become theater. This is a sad predicament and indicates that an unfortunate, seriously ill human being has become the pawn of a group dedicated to break Missouri's law of confidentiality. Shattering this law is more important than finding real and immediate help for this sick man.

Judge, I am aware of your position in this matter, and I have compassion for you. Surely you are aware of the position these allegations have put upon me and my family. I'll say again, as I did when I handed the letters and papers back to you, "You are talking to the wrong person; so look elsewhere, not here." Continuing this any further with me is useless. . . and could turn into a regular witch hunt. I can see now where the law is good in protecting the innocent.

I served my country about four years in World War II and came out with an honorable discharge as an enlisted man, also with a certificate of service as an officer and gentleman. So on my honor, I state the above is true to the best of my ability.

Eventually the trial court denied Mr. George's request to open the adoption records. The appellate court held that the trial court had not abused its discretion in doing so. Was this correct? Had the trial court already gone too far?

Chapter 2

THE PRINCIPLE OF AUTONOMY: LAW AT THE END OF LIFE

SECTION 2. STOPPING

233. Insert before Subpart 2.

The Case of Harold Shipman

The worst (by far) serial murderer in English history was Harold Shipman, a general practitioner much esteemed by his patients. He was convicted in January 2000 of killing 15 patients with heroin injections and sentenced to life imprisonment for each murder. "But an inquiry into the case, by High Court judge Dame Janet Smith, has found that a further 200 deaths were 'highly suspicious' while there was a 'real suspicion' he could have claimed a further 45 victims." His victims ranged in age from 93 to 41; 171 were women, 44 men. BBC News, July 19, 2002.

Shipman was born in 1946.[1] In 1970 he graduated from Leeds University and began practicing medicine. In 1974 he started working in Todmorden, Lancashire. In 1976 he pleaded guilty to obtaining pethidine by deception, to unlawful possession of pethidine, and to forging prescriptions. His convictions were reported to the General Medical Council, which took no disciplinary action. The Home Office did not inhibit him from dealing with controlled drugs. "He was, therefore, free to continue practising as a doctor without limitation or supervision."

In 1975, a bathroom fall left Shipman with a concussion. On other occasions he "suffered 'blackouts' or 'seizures,'" including blackouts in front of patients.

---

[1] In what follows, we draw on *Death Disguised*, which is the First Report of The Shipman Inquiry (www.the-shipman-inquiry.org.uk/fr_page.asp?p=1&id=1). Unless otherwise indicated, quotations are from that report.

In 1977, he joined a practice in Hyde, and in 1992 he set up a solo practice in that town. "Throughout his career as a general practitioner, Shipman enjoyed a high level of respect within the communities in which he worked." One reason for his popularity "was his willingness to visit his elderly patients at home." One of his partners, however, described "Shipman as tending to be 'individualistic' in his approach and [said] that he 'could become irritated' if confronted by any other of the doctors and other staff members."

By March 1988, "certain people in Hyde had begun to feel concern at the number of Shipman's elderly patients who were dying in curiously similar circumstances." A local doctor alerted the coroner, who "initiated a limited police investigation." That investigation (which was made in ignorance of Shipman's earlier convictions) found "no evidence to substantiate the concerns," and no further action was taken.

On June 24, 1988, Mrs. Kathleen Grundy died. Although she had, at age 81, been in good health, Shipman "certified the cause of her death as 'old age.'" Mrs. Grundy's daughter, Mrs. Angela Woodruff, was a solicitor who had done her mother's legal work and drafted her will. Mrs. Woodruff was the sole beneficiary. "Following Mrs Grundy's death, Mrs Woodruff became aware of the existence of what purported to be a new will." That will left everything to Shipman.

"Mrs. Woodruff was immediately suspicious about the new will and her suspicions deepened after she had visited and spoken to the two patients of Shipman whose signatures appeared on the will as witnesses." When Mrs. Woodruff reported her suspicions to the police, they recognized Shipman as the person they had investigated earlier. After an exhumation, a "post-mortem examination of Mrs. Grundy's body failed to establish the cause of her death and a decision was taken to carry out toxicological tests." These showed "the presence of an opiate." The police then began to expand their investigations to include other patients.

"After his arrest and questioning, Shipman refused to speak to anyone and continued to deny responsibility for the deaths." Aneez Esmail, *Physician as Serial Killer – The Shipman Case*, 352 NEJM 1843 (2005). Shipman was eventually tried for the murder of Mrs. Grundy and fourteen other patients (and for forging Mrs. Grundy's will).

He testified that one of his patients had died after he arrived at her house and found her collapsed. He decided not to resuscitate her "because she had a poor chance of making a full recovery." BBC News, November 29, 1999. The daughter of another victim testified that Shipman had made her "feel guilty for not knowing [her] mother was 'ill.'"

In her summation, Shipman's defense lawyer "said the forensic scientist working on the case had broken new ground. There was [sic] no comparable data available, and the samples were taken from the alleged victims' bodies after death, so they could have been subjected to changes." Guardian Unlimited, January 27, 2000. On January 31, 2000, Shipman was convicted of 15 counts of murder and one count of forging Mrs. Grundy's will. The judge recommended to the Home Secretary that Shipman spend the rest of his life in prison.

The subsequent inquiry concluded that "Shipman's usual method of killing was by the administration of a lethal dose of an opiate, most frequently diamorphine," and that he may have killed a few patients with large doses of a sedative. Shipman's detectable murders had started while he was working in the group practice, and "he was able to kill undetected over a period of many years." The victims "frequently died suddenly at home . . . . Such deaths should be reported to the coroner. Yet Shipman managed to avoid a referral to the coroner in all but a very few cases in which he had killed." The majority of Shipman's victims were cremated. "Before a cremation can be authorised, a second doctor must confirm the cause of death and the cremation documentation must be checked by a third doctor employed at the crematorium."

Meanwhile, the police

> had been attempting for some time to prevent Shipman from continuing to practise. They had informed the G[eneral] M[edical] C[ouncil] of the position in August 1998 but were told that the GMC could do nothing until Shipman had been convicted of an offence. On 18th August, the West Pennine Health Authority contacted the NHS Tribunal, which had the power to suspend him, but a hearing by the Tribunal could not be arranged before 29th September. After that hearing, the Tribunal's decision to suspend Shipman from practice was not communicated to the Health Authority until 15th October. The Health Authority was able to take control of the

practice only after the expiration of the period for an appeal against that decision, on 29th October 1998.

After Shipman's conviction in Mrs. Grundy's case, Shipman was suspended from practice and, later, deprived of his license. On January 13, 2004, Shipman committed suicide. Aneez Esmail, *Physician as Serial Killer – The Shipman Case*, 352 NEJM 1843 (2005).

239. Insert after the second block quotation.

A more anecdotal but painfully revealing datum comes from a sophisticated doctor's description of how he obtained a patient's consent to a DNR order. The physician had just begun to break to the patient the news that her chances of surviving her cancer were not good. He then told her:

> "Most people say that if they reach a point in the illness when their brain is impaired, and there is no likelihood of improving their quality of life, then nothing should be done to keep them artificially alive, through machines like respirators. It's essential, Maxine, that I know what you want done if we reach that point."
>
> "I—I don't think I would want that," she said haltingly."
>
> "You mean that you would want only comfort measures to alleviate pain, and nothing done to prolong your life, like a respirator or cardiac resuscitation?"
>
> "Yes, I think so," Maxine whispered.
>
> I nodded. This was her "end-of-life directive." I would put it in writing in her medical chart.

Jerome Groopman, *Dying Words*, New Yorker 64 (October 28, 2002). How do you analyze this exchange? Does the doctor try to influence the patient's choice? If so, is the patient likely to realize it? Does the patient understand what she is agreeing to? What is she agreeing to? Is she agreeing to anything?

256. Insert before "A Discourse on Depression."

3. When Ian Basnett was a junior doctor he encountered a quadriplegic. *Will to Live Wins Over the Right To Die*, The Observer (March 24, 2002). "My reaction was: 'How can anyone live like that?' I said to my then girlfriend: 'I'd rather be dead if I couldn't play sport.'" When he was about 26, a sports injury left him a quadriplegic. For a while he was kept alive on a ventilator "and at times said to people: 'I wish I was dead.'" Now, at age 43, he is "extraordinarily glad no one acted on that."

Why did he think he preferred death to disability? "I think the first difficulty I faced was the fact that, like many people, I had a terribly negative image of disability."
People tried to disabuse him of his misconceptions: "Hospital staff would tell me about how marvellous this or that individual was and how they organised a 'good life'. That rarely helped me. They were people I couldn't identify with. Furthermore, when someone wheeled his electric chair into me to say 'Hi, there are ways of doing this', I felt worse. I think I felt bad as these were mirrors for me and I so hated the thought of 'being like that.'" Today he says, "I've made friends I wouldn't otherwise have known, travelled in ways I wouldn't have thought about, written more than I'm sure I would have otherwise. Disability has strengthened me in my work as a public-health doctor." He needs personal assistants, but he is "dependent only if I don't have control over my personal assistants; in other words, able to choose who they are and what I can require them to do for me." And, "there are few people who wouldn't say there are things about their lives they'd like to change."

266. Insert at the bottom of the page.

(e) Analyzing Bouvia*: Coda*

As of February 13, 2005, Elizabeth Bouvia was apparently still alive. The latest news of her seems to be an interview published on September 30, 2002, on the Hemlock Society's website. www.hemlock.org/News/EditNews.asp:NewsID=57. The interview was conducted by Faye Girsh, a psychologist and ACLU board member who had assessed Ms. Bouvia's mental competence and who had eventually become president of the Hemlock Society.

In the interview, Ms. Girsh asked Ms. Bouvia whether she had been depressed in 1983. Ms. Bouvia said, "No. My decision to refuse food and hydration in 1983 was well thought out." She said she lived "a physically painful and arduous existence. My care costs the state and taxpayers thousands of dollars each. I – and, no doubt, many others – feel those funds could be put to more productive use." She thought nobody "in my physical situation (including myself) would be honest with him/herself if they said they enjoyed life. Over the last 18 years, I have had infections, spinal fractures, and a myriad of other complications. . . . I hope each day that before I have to endure continued excruciating pain and constant suffering, I will slip away as naturally and as peacefully as possible. . . . Unfortunately physician-assisted suicide is legal in only one state . . . ."

Asked what she thought about Not Dead Yet, Ms. Bouvia said that "if they're anything like most 'disability groups' – especially those which are run by actual disabled individuals – they tend to be whiny, fanatical freaks who are obsessed with whatever disability they may have. . . . Like many other 'socially militant' groups, they use precedent-setting legal cases, oftentimes twisting the facts to fit their own views."

323. Insert after Question 3.

4. Does your answer to these questions change if you consider the following information? People regularly fail to anticipate how illness and disability will affect their happiness. This is reasonable, because – in general – people seem to react to disease and disability less despairingly than our cultural understandings would lead us to expect. For example, Tsevat et al interviewed HIV-infected patients and found that 49% of them "said that their life was better currently than it was before they were aware that they had HIV," while only 29% said life was worse. Of course, if their lives were already wretched, these figures might not tell us much. But "[w]hen asked how they felt their life was going, 71% of patients were mostly satisfied, pleased, or delighted; only 6% were mostly dissatisfied or unhappy. No patient felt that life was terrible." Joel Tsevat et al, *The Will To Live Among HIV-Infected Patients*, 131 AIM 194 (1999).

Not only do patients' reactions to illness differ from those "common sense" would predict, but patients apparently evaluate their lives differently from other people. Discrepancies in these evaluations are not inevitable, but they are frequent. For example, "the general public estimates the health related quality of life (HRQoL) of dialysis at the value of 0.39 (on a scale where 0 represents death and 1 represents perfect health), whereas dialysis patients estimate their HRQoL at 0.56 . . . . Patients without colostomies estimate the HRQoL of living with a colostomy at 0.80, while patients with colostomies rate their own HRQoL at 0.92." Peter A. Ubel et al, *Whose Quality of Life? A Commentary Exploring Discrepancies Between Health State Evaluations of Patients and the General Public*, 12 Quality of Life Research 599 (Kluwer, 2003).

Well, perhaps these discrepancies arise because most people have little personal experience with the kinds of patients whose happiness is being assessed. No doubt, but apparently even people who work closely with the ill assess their happiness differently from the ill themselves. "In general, patients with experience with the health state assign the highest values, members of the general public or patients without experience the lowest values, and health care professionals values between the two." Anne M. Stiggelbout, *Assessing Patients' Preferences,* in Gretchen B. Chapman & Frank A. Sonnenberg, eds, *Decision Making in Health Care: Theory, Psychology, and Applications* 289 (Cambridge U P, 2000) More specifically, Pearlman and Uhlmann found that patients generally rated their quality of life to be slightly worse than 'good, no major complaints, but their physicians rated their quality of life as significantly worse . . . ." George Loewenstein & David Schkade, *Wouldn't It Be Nice? Predicting Future Feelings* in Daniel Kahneman et al, eds, *Well-Being: The Foundations of Hedonic Psychology* 92 (Russell Sage Foundation, 1999). In a large study of the seriously ill, "[p]atients gave higher ratings to their state of health than did their surrogates and physicians. Among the 959 patient-surrogate pairs that provided rating scores of the patient's health at day 3, the patients' mean rating score was 57.9 ± 23.9 (median, 60 [50, 75]), and the surrogates' mean rating score was 49.6 ± 22.2 (median, 50 [30, 65]; $P<0.0001$)." Joel Tsevat et al, *Health Values of the Seriously Ill*, 122 AIM 514 (1995).

In fact, despite the popularity of the slogan "quality is more important than quantity," many patients seem unwilling to trade much quantity even for real improvements in quality. Tsevat et al's HIV patients' "mean time-tradeoff score was 0.95 ± 0.1" over a five-year period, "indicating that, on average, patients did not have a clear preference between living 5 years in their current state of health and

4.75 years (0.95 x 5 years) in excellent health." In their study of seriously ill patients, Tsevat et al discovered that the "mean time-tradeoff score for the 1438 patients at day 3 was 0.73 ± 0.32 . . . , indicating that, on average, patients equated living 1 year in their current state of health with living 8.8 months . . . in excellent health." This sounds like an endorsement of the quality/quantity mantra. But a "total of 34.8% had utilities of 1.0, meaning that they were unwilling to give up any time in exchange for a shorter life in excellent health, and 9.0% had utilities of 0.04, indicating that they preferred living 2 weeks or less in excellent health to living 1 year in their current state of health."

Similarly, while "polls indicate that most Americans would prefer not to die attached to "life saving" machinery, "many ICU survivors state that they would be willing to return to an ICU if it would extend their life by even 1 week." Joan M. Teno et al, *Decision-Making and Outcomes of Prolonged ICU Stays in Seriously Ill Patients*, 48 J American Geriatrics Society S70 (2000). And in one study "16% of the patients would want resuscitation in the coma scenario even if the chance of awakening were less than 1%." Jeremiah Suhl et al, *Myth of Substituted Judgement*, 154 AIM 90 (1994). All this suggests that people contemplating a living will cannot count on being willing to sacrifice time for health.

Further evidence of the stubbornness with which human beings wish to live comes from a study in which

> different groups of respondents were asked whether they would accept a grueling course of chemotherapy if it would extend their lives by three months. No radiotherapists said that they would accept the chemotherapy, only 6 percent of oncologists, and 10 percent of healthy people; but 42 percent of current cancer patients say they would. Another study found that 58 percent of patients with serious illnesses said that when death was near they would want treatment, even if it prolonged life by just a week. Even after they had been subjected to the most advanced medical technology and seen little long-term benefit, a majority of families of patients who died were willing to undergo the intensive-care experience again.

George Loewenstein & David Schkade, *Wouldn't It Be Nice? Predicting Future Feelings*, supra.

What is sobering about these data is that life in the ICU and in a coma and on chemotherapy are exactly the kinds of situations living wills are classically intended to prevent. "As an insightful and articulate commentator said: 'in principle, people want a peaceful, dignified, comfortable death but . . . in reality, they do not want it quite yet. They prefer life prolonging care in the hope that their peaceful, dignified, comfortable death can occur later . . . .'" Judith E. Nelson & Marion Danis, *End-of-Life Care in the Intensive Care Unit: Where Are We Now?*, 29 Critical Care Medicine N2 (2001).

Chapter 3

KILLING

SECTION 1. AN INTRODUCTORY PROBLEM: THE CASE OF DIANE

332. *This is the last paragraph of Question 1.*

Stephen J. Ziegler, *At Risk?*, 33 J Law, Medicine & Ethics 349 (2005), reports a study which asked prosecutors in four states whether they would prosecute in the case of "a vignette where a dying patient was provided with a large prescription of sedatives by her physician along with instructions on how to consume them." In general,

> the likelihood of recommending a police investigation was small. Twenty-nine percent of prosecutors estimated the likelihood at 0 percent and 53.7 percent of the respondents set the likelihood of investigation between 0 and 20 percent. A small percentage of the respondents (22%), estimated the likelihood of recommending an investigation at 90-100 percent. The mean likelihood across all four states was 4.00 (40 percent chance of recommending a police investigation), and the median 2.00 (20 percent chance of recommending an investigation).

SECTION 3. ASSISTED SUICIDE AS A RIGHT

431. *Insert before Subsection D.*

3. The Pain of Death and the Death of Pain

> *So as I prepared for class by rereading the cases and statutes on law at the end of life and reading articles on planning for death, I could not repress the memory of one visit to the palliative-care unit of a hospital. The unit received a warning and shortly thereafter a patient from another hospital. He had only hours to live, and he was in apparently untreated pain. He had tried to tear out his IV, and blood smeared his sheets. He had writhed to find a painless position, and his gown hardly covered his nakedness. And as he lay dying he cried out, "Don't let*

your children die like this in pain. Don't let your children die like this in pain."

Carl E. Schneider
Benumbed

(a) Is Pain Undertreated?

As this Chapter suggests, vast efforts have been devoted in recent years to making it easy for patients – especially dying patients – to die, whether by refusing medical treatment or by committing suicide. Is this a good allocation of medical, legal, and reformist energies? Would those energies have been more productively spent elsewhere? This is our old friend the cost-benefit problem in fresh garb. Here, it particularly leads us to ask whether those energies might better have been devoted to addressing the medical and legal problem of pain.

Why is pain a medical and legal problem? In the scientific sense, pain is less problematic than one might think: Today, most pain is treatable. The medical problem is that it is often not treated. The legal problem is how to deal with that failure.

We begin with the recollection of a prominent palliative-care physician:

> At 9:00 pm on a bitter cold, wintry Chicago night I received a page from an ENT [ear, nose and throat] resident. He was admitting a young man with head and neck cancer to my service who was "endstage" and expected to die. He said there was "nothing to do." As I was overwhelmed by new admissions, a large clinical service, and had not yet learned to cope with the VA system where I was a new intern, I saw the patient last. When I arrived in his room at about 2:00 am, he was alone. His head was the size and shape of a pumpkin due to edema. He was restless and short of breath and he looked terrified. Because his tongue was swollen, he couldn't talk. I didn't know what to do for him, so I patted him on the shoulder, said something inane and left and at 7:00 am he died.
>
> The memory haunts me because now I know I could have helped him feel better in many ways. I failed to care for him properly because I was ignorant of palliative medicine. If I am known as a doctor who specializes in the care of the dying, then maybe a

frightened, overwhelmed intern will know to call me for help rather than walk away because he mistakenly thinks there is "nothing more that can be done ."

Charles F. Von Gunten, *Why I Do What I Do*, in American Board of Internal Medicine, *Caring for the Dying: Identification and Promotion of Physician Competency, Personal Narratives* 47- 48 (1996).

More systematically, Amy J. Dilcher, *Damned If They Do, Damned If They Don't: The Need for a Comprehensive Public Policy to Address the Inadequate Management of Pain*, 13 Annals of Health Law 81, (2004), reports: "The undertreatment of pain in the United States is well-documented in scientific literature." Studies "have demonstrated continued inadequacies in treatment (1) of those patient populations most likely to suffer from chronic and acute pain, including terminally ill patients, cancer patients, nursing home residents, elderly individuals, and chronic pain patients, and (2) in those medical environments where acute pain is routine, such as the emergency room, the post-operative unit, and the intensive care unit."

For example, the SUPPORT research, a large-scale "study of seriously ill hospitalized patients, demonstrated a high prevalence of pain. Half of the patients in this study complained of pain and one sixth reported extremely severe pain of any frequency or moderately severe pain occurring at least half of the time. Questioning suggested that pain was related to chronic conditions, as well as to the patients' acute illnesses and their treatment." Norman A. Desbiens et al, *Pain and Satisfaction With Pain Control in Seriously Ill Hospitalized Adults: Findings From the SUPPORT Research Investigations*, 24 Critical Care Medicine 1953 (1996). This study "found clinically important levels of pain and dissatisfaction with pain control in all disease categories, including chronic obstructive pulmonary disease and congestive heart failure, diseases that have not been traditionally associated with pain." While pain was virtually pervasive, some specialities failed more completely than others: "Surgeons' patients reported increased levels of pain compared with patients of other specialists. . . . Compared with oncologists' patients, patients of pulmonologists or intensivists were more dissatisfied with pain control."

And "[w]hat is the status of pain control in seriously ill patients five years after the completion of patient enrollment in SUPPORT? Unfortunately, our best estimate, based on the lack of temporal trend in the five years of the study, is that pain control persists as a major problem for hospitalized patients. These patients are still in pain many months after their hospitalization and experience pain and other symptoms even on their deathbeds." Norman A. Desbiens & Albert W. Wu, *Pain and Suffering in Seriously Ill Hospitalized Patients*, 48 JAGS S183 (2000).

Desbiens & Wu continue: "Generally, pain control is not a high priority for most hospitals or their physicians. Pain is not routinely monitored, and there are no protocols that are used routinely to treat pain. Regulatory agencies such as the Joint Commission on Accreditation of Health Care Organizations do not have process or outcome indicators for pain control. For patients, during short, diagnostically intense hospitalizations, pain is a concern whose treatment can complicate an otherwise busy physician's or nurse's life." However, there are differences among hospitals that suggest that significant improvements in the treatment of pain are quite possible: "Patients at the worst performing hospital reported about 75% higher levels of pain than those at the hospital with the best performance. Anecdotally, at the best performing hospital, pain control had been a major emphasis for several years before the onset of SUPPORT."

The undertreatment of pain has been documented for over a quarter of a century. Why does it persist?

- HCPs receive inadequate education on pain assessment, pain treatment and palliative care . . .

- HCPs face legal and regulatory pressures to restrict the use of narcotics . . .

- HCPs, patients, and families are concerned about the probable or possible side-effects of analgesics, such as sedation, dizziness, nausea, constipation, increased cardiac load, decreased renal function, tolerance, physical dependence, addiction . . .

- HCPs sometimes think that patients are overstating, imagining, or faking their pain . . .

- Patients are hesitant to talk to HCPs about pain because they do not want to distract HCPs from their "real" diseases or they think an increase in pain means that their disease is getting worse . . .

- Patients want to feel some pain because they view pain as an overall indicator of their health or they think it is virtuous to suffer . .

- Health care organizations, government agencies, and insurers do not provide adequate funding for pain control . . .

- The medical community has not conducted enough research on pain management and palliative care . . . .

David B. Resnik et al, *The Undertreatment of Pain: Scientific, Clinical, Cultural, and Philosophical Factors*, 4 Medicine, Health Care & Philosophy 277 (2001).

No small part of the problem is that too many physicians and nurses misunderstand the drugs used to treat pain. "[S]tudies of physicians, pharmacists, and medical regulators not only document serious gaps in knowledge, but provide evidence that many medical professionals are largely unaware of the positive role of opioids in the treatment of pain." Stephen J. Ziegler & Nicholas P. Lovrich, Jr., *Pain Relief, Prescription Drugs and Prosecution: A Four-State Survey of Chief Prosecutors*, 31 Journal of Law, Medicine & Ethics 75 (2003). For example, "several studies have indicated that physicians are often reluctant to prescribe opioids out of fear of iatrogenic addiction, despite the fact that the documented rate of addiction is extremely low."

(b) The Regulation of Medicine and the Undertreatment of Pain

We have been exploring some of the failures of understanding and organization that lead doctors and hospitals to undertreat pain. But when asked, doctors often say they are deterred from treating pain adequately by the fear that the medical boards that regulate physicians and the prosecutors who regulate us all will unfairly punish them. In this light, consider:

HOOVER v. AGENCY FOR HEALTH CARE ADMINISTRATION
676 So2d 1380 (Dist Ct App Fla 1996)

JORGENSON, Judge.

Dr. Katherine Anne Hoover, a board-certified physician in internal medicine, appeals a final order of the Board of Medicine penalizing her and restricting her license to practice medicine in the State of Florida. We reverse because the board has once again engaged in the uniformly rejected practice of overzealously supplanting a hearing officer's valid findings of fact regarding a doctor's prescription practices with its own opinion in a case founded on a woefully inadequate quantum of evidence.

FACTS

In March 1994, the ... Agency for Health Care Administration ... filed an administrative complaint alleging that Dr. Hoover (1) inappropriately and excessively prescribed various Schedule II controlled substances to seven of her patients. ... All seven of the patients had been treated by Dr. Hoover for intractable pain arising from various non-cancerous diseases or ailments. ...[4]

Dr. Hoover disputed the allegations of the administrative complaint and requested a formal hearing. At the hearing, the agency presented testimony of its investigator; several pharmacists from Key West, where the doctor was practicing at the time of the alleged infractions; and two agency expert physicians. The doctor testified

---

[4]. Persons suffering from chronic pain (as opposed to acute episodes of pain) for which there is no cure or treatment available that can alleviate the person's pain are said to suffer from "intractable pain." There are two types of intractable pain. The first group are patients with terminal, irreversible illnesses, such as cancer patients. Physicians generally give those patients whatever narcotics they need to alleviate the pain during the end stage of their lives. The second group is composed of patients who suffer from non-terminal disease processes who have tried different specialists and treatments available without achieving relief from their chronic pain. Those persons are generally not treated in family practice settings but rather are referred to pain management centers or pain clinics ... to have their pain alleviated by treatments such as receiving morphine implants or having doctors perform nerve blocks. Many physicians avoid caring for patients who require Schedule II substances to relieve their suffering.

and presented the testimony of two Key West pharmacists and her own expert physician.

The Agency's Case

The agency presented the testimony of two physicians as experts. Neither had examined any of the patients or their medical records. The sole basis for the opinions of the agency physicians was computer printouts from pharmacies in Key West where the doctor's patients had filled their prescriptions. . . . Both of these physicians practiced internal medicine and neither specialized in the care of chronic pain. In fact, both doctors testified that they did not treat but referred their chronic pain patients to pain management clinics. The hearing officer found that this was a common practice among physician — perhaps to avoid prosecutions like this case. Both doctors "candidly testified that without being provided with copies of the medical records for those patients they could not evaluate Respondent's diagnoses of what alternative modalities were attempted or what testing was done to support the use of the medication chosen by Respondent to treat those patients. "Despite this paucity of evidence, lack of familiarity, and seeming lack of expertise, the agency's physicians testified at the hearing that the doctor had prescribed excessive, perhaps lethal amounts of narcotics, and had practiced below the standard of care.

Dr. Hoover's Response

Dr. Hoover testified in great detail concerning the condition of each of the patients, her diagnoses and courses of treatment, alternatives attempted, the patients' need for medication, the uniformly improved function of the patients with the amount of medication prescribed, and her frequency of writing prescriptions to allow her close monitoring of the patients. She presented corroborating physician testimony regarding the appropriateness of the particular medications and the amounts prescribed and her office-setting response to the patients' requests for relief from intractable pain.

Disposition of the Administrative Complaint

Following post-hearing submissions, the hearing officer issued her recommended order finding that the agency had failed to meet its burden of proof on all charges. The hearing officer concluded, for instance, that "Petitioner failed to provide its experts with adequate information to show the necessary similar conditions and circumstances upon which they could render opinions that showed clearly and convincingly that Respondent failed to meet the standard of care required of her in her treatment of the patients in question."

The agency filed exceptions to the recommended findings of fact and conclusions of law as to five of the seven patients. The board of medicine accepted all the agency's exceptions, amended the findings of fact in accordance with the agency's suggestions, and found the doctor in violation . . . . The board imposed the penalty recommended by the agency: a reprimand, a $4,000 administrative fine, continuing medical education on prescribing abusable drugs, and two years probation. . . .

DISCUSSION

In a proceeding to suspend, revoke, or impose other discipline upon a professional license, the administrative agency must prove the charges by clear and convincing evidence. Section 120.57(1)(b)(10), Florida Statutes, sets forth the medical board's responsibility in reviewing and acting upon a recommended order submitted by a hearing officer: . . .

> The agency in its final order may reject or modify the conclusions of law and interpretation of administrative rules in the recommended order. *The agency may not reject or modify the findings of fact, including findings of fact that form the basis for an agency statement, unless the agency first determines from a review of the complete record, and states with particularity in the order, that the findings of fact were not based upon competent substantial evidence* or that the proceedings on which the findings were based did not comply with essential requirements of law. . . .

(Emphasis added.) In this case, the board "merely stated its conclusion that the [rejected] findings [of fact] were not supported by competent substantial evidence." This determination violated the requirement that the board must state valid reasons for rejecting findings with particularity.

Hearing Officer's Findings of Fact

For each of the five patients, the hearing officer found the prescribing practices of Doctor Hoover to be appropriate. This was based upon (1) the doctor's testimony regarding the specific care given, (2) the corroborating testimony of her physician witness, and (3) the fact that the doctor's prescriptions did not exceed the federal guidelines for treatment of intractable pain in cancer patients, though none of the five patients were [sic] diagnosed as suffering from cancer.

The board rejected these findings as not based on competent substantial evidence. As particular reasons, the board adopted the arguments of the agency's exceptions to the recommended order that (1) the hearing officer's findings were erroneously based on irrelevant federal guidelines, and (2) the agency's physicians had testified that the doctor's prescription pattern was below the standard of care and outside the practice of medicine. The board's purported reasons for the rejection of findings do not state in particular that the findings are not based on competent substantial evidence, but merely substitute the board's preference for the conclusions of its experts.

First, the board mischaracterizes the hearing officer's reference to the federal guidelines. The board reasoned in its final order that "[t]he record reflects that the federal guidelines relied upon by the Hearing Officer for this finding were designed for cancer patients and [the five patients at issue were] not being treated for cancer." It is true, as the hearing officer noted, that

> Respondent presented expert evidence that there is a set of guidelines which have been issued for the use of Schedule II controlled substances to treat intractable pain and that although those guidelines were established to guide physicians in treating cancer patients, those are the only guidelines available at this time. Utilizing those guidelines, because they exist, the amount of medication prescribed by Respondent to the patients in question was not excessive or inappropriate.

In so finding, however, the hearing officer did not, as the board suggests, rely solely upon the federal guidelines. . . . Rather, the federal guidelines merely buttressed fact findings that were independently supported by the hearing officer's determination of the persuasiveness and credibility of the physician witnesses on each side. For example, though he admitted he had not even reviewed the federal guidelines, one of the agency physicians asserted that the amounts prescribed constituted a "tremendous number of pills" and that the doses involved would be lethal. That Dr. Hoover's prescriptions fell within the guidelines for chronic-pained cancer patients may properly be considered to refute this assertion. . . .

Second, Dr. Hoover testified in great detail concerning her treatment of each patient, the patient's progress under the medication she prescribed, and that the treatment was within the standard of care and practice of medicine. The hearing officer, as arbiter of credibility, was entitled to believe what the doctor and her physician expert opined. The agency's witnesses' ultimate conclusions do not strip the hearing officer's reliance upon Dr. Hoover of its competence and substantiality. The hearing officer was entitled to give Dr. Hoover's testimony greater weight than that of the agency's witnesses, who did not examine these patients or regularly engage in the treatment of intractable pain.

This point was articulated by the First District Court of Appeal under similar facts in *Reese* [*v. Department of Prof Reg, Bd of Medical Examiners*, 471 So2d 601 (Fla 1st DCA 1985)]. In *Reese,* the agency charged the doctor with 83 counts of violating various provisions of Chapter 458. The allegations were based primarily on the agency's belief that the doctor was over-prescribing Schedule II drugs. Both sides presented the testimony of physician witnesses, which conflicted. . . . The hearing officer found the testimony of the doctor's witnesses more persuasive, found no deviation from the acceptable level of care, and further found that the "drugs were prescribed in appropriate quantities and duration, were for medically justifiable purposes, and were not prescribed outside the course of [the doctor's] medical practice." The board accepted most of the agency's exceptions to the hearing officer's recommended order, and rejected the hearing officer's findings of fact as not supported by competent substantial evidence. The *Reese* court held that the board's rejection of the findings was not valid because there was substantial competent evidence to support the findings, and the board did not state reasons for rejection with particularity, but "merely stated a conclusion substituting its opinion for that of the finder of fact."

It is surprising to see agency disciplinary action based upon such a paucity of evidence after our admonitions in *Sneij v. Department of Professional Regulation, Board of Medical Examiners,* 454 So.2d 795 (Fla. 3d DCA 1984). In *Sneij,* the board rejected the hearing officer's determination that the agency had failed to establish by clear and convincing evidence that the doctor had, among other things, inappropriately prescribed controlled substances or prescribed excessive amounts of controlled substances. This Court noted the sparse and inadequate medical records and investigative file upon which the agency's physician witness had based his opinion:

> The witness did not talk to any of the patients involved nor did these patients testify at the hearing. Dr. Sneij also testified at the hearing and admitted that his medical records were poorly kept. He denied any other wrongdoing, however, although his memory of the patients involved was somewhat shaky. No other witnesses testified at the hearing. Plainly, this evidence was woefully insufficient to establish any of the charges against Dr. Sneij, save for the record-keeping violations....

Beyond that, the law is clear that the Board was not free to reject the hearing examiner's findings when, as here, these findings were based on competent, substantial evidence. This being so, the Board had no authority, in any event, to reject summarily the hearing examiner's findings and to substitute its own findings therefor.
Similarly, in this case the board has again supplanted valid findings of fact regarding a doctor's prescription practices with its own opinion. . . .

* * * * * * * * * *

As *Hoover* suggests, "state medical boards lack sufficient knowledge about pain management." However, it is also true that, "health care professionals sometimes overestimate the level of regulatory scrutiny to which they are exposed." Stephen J. Ziegler & Nicholas P. Lovrich, Jr., *Pain Relief, Prescription Drugs and Prosecution: A Four-State Survey of Chief Prosecutors*, 31 Journal of Law, Medicine & Ethics 75 (2003). For example, doctors are "concerned that their prescribing practices will raise suspicions of pharmaceutical diversion. . . . [I]n a recent survey of Texas physicians,

26.4 percent of the respondents agreed with the following statement: 'Prescribing narcotics for patients with chronic pain is likely to trigger a drug enforcement agency investigation'; and 47.7 percent agreed with the statement: 'If I follow the same prescribing practices as other doctors in my field, I will not be investigated by a regulatory agency.'"

Ziegler and Lovrich conclude "that, while physicians' fear of prosecution or investigation is a barrier to pain relief in our society, as the social science literature and our results indicate, both the likelihood and frequency of either are extremely low. True, some doctors have abused their prescribing authority and have been prosecuted, but oftentimes the situations were patently illegal, such as the selling of prescriptions for cash or sex. Overall, prosecutions surrounding the prescription of opioids are rare."

The rarity with which physicians are prosecuted arises partly from the fact that "white-collar crimes are not given the same priority as street crimes despite the fact that white-collar crime/occupational crime is far more costly in human and financial terms. . . . First, unlike street crimes, white-collar crimes are usually not committed in public view and quite often go undetected by either the general public or the victim. Secondly, white-collar crimes are often complex and require specialized expertise in their detection, investigation, and successful prosecution." Even "in the context of Medicare fraud, where enforcement personnel are specially trained to investigate offenses, investigators believe that the number of physicians detected represents merely the 'tip of the iceberg' and those prosecuted tend to constitute only the most egregious cases." Furthermore, proving "intent also presents a special problem, particularly when the individual conduct stems from differences in 'professional opinion' (e.g., the method of treatment). Moreover, the existence of civil remedies as an alternative to criminal prosecution is often considered, particularly in light of the high standard of proof that is required in a criminal proceeding."

Ziegler and Lovrich warn that, "in some circumstances an investigation stemming from the aggressive treatment of pain is indeed likely. However, this conclusion must be understood within its proper context. For instance, although the likelihood of investigation in Scenario 1 [which involved the aggressive treatment of pain] is greater in Maryland than it is in Oregon, there was a great deal of variation among prosecutors within each state."

Crucially, "any increased likelihood of investigation is likely [sic] the result of insufficient knowledge regarding the legitimate use of opioids in the aggressive treatment of pain and the limited experience of prosecutors when dealing with such matters." In other words, prosecutors share doctors' and nurses' misconceptions about treating pain: "[M]any of our respondents held views similar to those held by pharmacists, drug regulators, and physicians concerning drug addiction and the diversion of pharmaceuticals. . . . . [P]rosecutors do not think about the dispensing of prescription drugs on a frequent basis. Consistent with the conclusions of Ann Alpers, we . . . found that a prosecutor's decision to investigate, refer, or prosecute is not motivated by overzealousness, but most likely stems from a lack of knowledge concerning appropriate prescribing practices and opioid use."

(c) Legal Responses to the Undertreatment of Pain

We have discussed regulatory impediments to the better treatment of pain. But merely changing the regulatory environment will not produce a world in which physicians treat pain adequately. Can the tort system to help solve this problem?

**AMY J. DILCHER
DAMNED IF THEY DO, DAMNED IF THEY DON'T
THE NEED FOR A COMPREHENSIVE PUBLIC POLICY TO
ADDRESS THE INADEQUATE MANAGEMENT OF PAIN**
13 Annals of Health Law 81 (2004)

E. Civil Liability for the Undertreatment of Pain

While there are a multitude of barriers that impede adequate pain management, until recently, there were no external incentives for providers to treat pain. Traditionally, state medical boards have declined to pursue disciplinary actions against health care providers for the undertreatment of pain. . . .

An Oregon case, the only instance to date in which a state medical board disciplined a health care provider for under-prescribing pain medication, may signal a shift in attitudes toward imposing liability for undertreating pain. In September 1999, the Oregon Board of Medical Examiners cited Dr. Paul Bilder, a fifty-four year old pulmonary specialist, for unprofessional or dishonorable conduct and gross or repeated acts of negligence for failing to adequately treat six seriously ill or dying patients with pain medication from 1993 to 1998. In at least three of the cases, Dr. Bilder purportedly failed to prescribe controlled substances for pain relief for fear that pain medication would suppress the respiratory drive of his patients despite medical research reflecting appropriate titration of controlled substances does not depress patient respirations. In one case, for example, Dr. Bilder refused to prescribe sedatives for a thirty-five year old woman with pulmonary disease and instead prescribed a paralytic agent, which relaxes the breathing muscles to accommodate the breathing tube. Dr. Bilder refused to prescribe pain medications or sedatives later that day when the patient became restless and fought the ventilator. When the woman subsequently pulled out her breathing tube, Dr. Bilder failed to respond to requests to re-intubate the patient. While the Board did not suspend or revoke Dr. Bilder's license to practice medicine, it required him to complete a one-year program in which another pulmonary specialist worked with him to assess his practice and make improvements; it also required him to attend a continuing medical education course on physician-patient communication and to meet with a psychiatrist who would give regular reports to the Board for at least one year.

Dr. Bilder's case demonstrates the extent to which providers' lack of knowledge about the appropriate use of narcotics to manage pain may negatively impact their use of narcotics to relieve pain or discomfort. Further, Dr. Bilder's story sends a message to providers that state medical boards may impose sanctions, pursuant to administrative actions, for undertreating pain. Accordingly, both the treatment and undertreatment of pain may prospectively result in penalties and the loss of external rewards (i.e., loss or suspension of license, fines, etc.). Nevertheless, health care providers may continue to perceive the potential penalties for undertreatment by medical boards less onerous than those penalties imposed when a provider overtreats, given that Oregon's medical board did not suspend or revoke Dr. Bilder's medical license . . . .

Aside from disciplinary actions, two other cases illustrate the potential civil penalties that providers may face for undertreating pain. In *Estate of Henry James v. Hillhaven*, a 1990 case, the court found a health care provider liable for failing to treat pain appropriately. Mr. James was admitted to Hillhaven nursing home with less than six months to live as a result of prostate cancer that had metastasized to his left femur and spine. Although a physician had ordered doses of oral morphine elixir every three hours as needed for pain, a Hillhaven nurse, based on her assessment that Mr. James was "addicted to morphine," substituted a mild tranquilizer and delayed or withheld altogether the administration of the oral morphine without the physician's authorization.

Mr. James' family filed a lawsuit alleging that the failure of the nurse and the nursing home to ensure the proper administration of pain medication in appropriate doses caused Mr. James to experience "inhuman treatment" inflicted "without regard to the consequences and without care as to whether or not the patient received analgesic relief and without care that the result and procedures were torture of the human flesh." During the trial, medical and nursing experts testified about the proper standard of care for the administration of opioid analgesics and specifically about the administration of morphine for the relief of intractable pain. In addition, a nurse specializing in quality assurance for nursing homes testified that health care institutions have an obligation to ensure that their health care providers properly manage pain. The jury awarded fifteen million dollars in damages to the family of Mr. James, which was subsequently resolved by settlement among the parties in an undisclosed amount. . . .

Bergman v. Eden Medical Center is the first case in which a physician was held liable for elder abuse under California's Bill of Patient's Rights for the undertreatment of pain based on the physician's failure to prescribe sufficient medication for a terminally ill patient. William Bergman, eighty-five years old, presented to Eden Medical Center in Northern California with complaints of severe back pain. Mr. Bergman had recently lost weight and had been suffering pain from a compression fracture of a spinal bone; a chest x-ray also revealed possible lung cancer. Dr. Wing Chin, an internal medicine specialist who had not previously treated Bergman, admitted him to the hospital for tests and prescribed intravenous Demerol, a narcotic for pain, to be given in twenty-five to fifty milligram doses as needed.

Nurses at the hospital periodically asked Mr. Bergman to rate his pain on a scale of one to ten and recorded his responses. All of the ratings in Mr. Bergman's medical chart ranged from seven to ten, corresponding with moderate to severe pain. However, progress notes recorded at other times by Dr. Chin and respiratory therapists indicated that Mr. Bergman said he "felt okay" or that his back pain was tolerable. Mr. Bergman underwent a procedure to obtain lung tissue--although not definitive, the results were suggestive of lung cancer. Subsequently, Mr. Bergman chose to forego treatment for lung cancer and returned home from the hospital for palliative care. Upon discharge, Mr. Bergman rated his pain a ten for which Dr. Chin prescribed Vicodin tablets, even though Mr. Bergman could not swallow pills and even though this medication had been ineffective for his back pain on previous occasions. Mr. Bergman's daughter complained that her father required stronger pain medication; accordingly, Dr. Chin ordered a single injection of Demerol and a slow-release patch containing fentanyl, a narcotic. After three days at home, a hospice nurse assessed Mr. Bergman's pain at level ten and called Dr. Chin to ask him to prescribe liquid morphine. According to court records, Dr. Chin did not prescribe the morphine. Later that afternoon, a doctor who had previously treated Mr. Bergman prescribed a single dose of morphine, which brought him immediate relief. Mr. Bergman died the next day.

Mr. Bergman's family sued both Eden Medical Center and Dr. Chin alleging violation of California's Elder Abuse and Dependent Adult Civil Protection Act Remedies, which allows patients to ask for painkillers of their choice. The act provides that "abuse" of an elder includes "neglect," which is defined to include the failure to provide medical care for physical and mental health needs. It allows for both criminal prosecutions and civil suits against those accused of elder abuse. It also allows a victim's family to bring a lawsuit, even after the victim's death. Because California's malpractice laws do not allow pain and suffering for the deceased, Mr. Bergman's family brought a lawsuit for elder abuse.

The jury found Dr. Chin liable for elder abuse and reckless negligence by not giving Mr. Bergman enough pain medication. Although the jury awarded Mr. Bergman's family $1.5 million in general damages, it did not find that Dr. Chin acted with malice or that he had intentionally caused emotional distress that would have supported an award of punitive damages. Subsequently, the trial judge reduced the $1.5 million damages to $250,000, applying California's medical malpractice cap, notwithstanding that the case had been characterized as one of abuse rather than malpractice. In April 2002, Judge Robert Hunter of the Superior Court of California for Alameda County denied defense motions to set aside the verdict and demand a new trial. The court also awarded attorney's fees to the plaintiff and applied a 1.5

multiplier to the fee award to emphasize the importance of the case to the public interest.

The *Bergman* decision has had a tremendous impact on the management of pain in California. Reacting to the case, California passed legislation requiring physicians to complete continuing medical education every four years. As stated by Dr. Russell Portenoy, former president of the American Pain Society and head of the pain management department of Beth Israel Medical Center in New York City, the *Bergman* case also sends a wake-up call to physicians that there are potential civil penalties for undertreating pain: "[i]t begins to create the reality of (punishment) . . . for physicians who don't respond to patients who have severe pain."

Professor Barry Furrow suggests that cases similar to Hillhaven and Bergman are likely to continue and even increase in the near future given the number of "politically savvy aging babyboomers with lower back pain," the sound scientific evidence for the proper assessment of pain, and the proliferation of practice management guidelines. Furrow and other scholars have proposed that pain management guidelines may be utilized as a tool by plaintiff's attorneys to establish the standard of care for pain management. Practice guidelines are standardized suggestions based on a consensus of current medical research about how to treat a particular medical condition. . . .

While cases premised on the undertreatment of pain are likely to continue, it is unlikely that these cases alone will be sufficient to diminish physician reluctance to manage pain with controlled substances given the factors that work in concert to impede pain management. Consequently, a comprehensive solution that addresses each of the barriers to pain management is needed to shift the environment to one that treats pain adequately.

Delete subsection 2 on pages 444 - 450 and substitute:

2. The Institutional Question Revisited: Drugs, Death, and Federalism

In this casebook and in this chapter, we have been centrally concerned with the institutional choices law must make when it encounters an issue. *Cruzan* and *Glucksberg* were, of course, crucially about an old and basic question in American law – the question of judicial review, of how the authority to regulate assisted suicide and other bioethical issues should be divided between courts and legislatures. But those cases were also about an even older and more basic question – the question of federalism. In recent years, the federalism question has leapt to the fore in the law of bioethics. Consider, for example, the following constitutional challenge to Oregon's assisted suicide regime:

At the heart of the disputes over federalism in bioethics has been (perhaps rather oddly) the Controlled Substances Act (CSA), 21 USC § 801 *et seq*, which states: "Except as authorized by this subchapter, it shall be unlawful for any person knowingly or intentionally . . . to manufacture, distribute, or dispense, or possess with intent to manufacture, distribute, or dispense, a controlled substance . . . ." And it is "unlawful for any person knowingly or intentionally to possess a controlled substance unless such substance was obtained directly, or pursuant to a valid prescription or order . . . ."

The CSA divides controlled substances into five schedules. Schedule 1 is the most restrictive. Drugs in it have "a high potential for abuse," "no currently accepted medical use in treatment," and no safe use. Schedule I drugs may be used only for federally approved research. By Congressional direction, marijuana is a Schedule I drug. Drugs on Schedules II – V, however, may be prescribed by doctors registered by the Drug Enforcement Agency. Registered physicians must use elaborate record-keeping and reporting procedures when handling and prescribing controlled substances.

The Act provides both civil and criminal penalties. A doctor who "dispenses" controlled substances in prohibited ways commits a crime. "Dispense" means "to deliver a controlled substance to an ultimate user . . . by, or pursuant to the lawful order of a practitioner, including the prescribing and administering of a controlled substance . . . ." A physician's registration may be revoked if "registration would be inconsistent with the public interest." More specifically, 21 USC §823(f) provides:

> The Attorney General shall register practitioners . . . to dispense, or conduct research with, controlled substances in schedule II, III, IV, or V, if the applicant is authorized to

dispense, or conduct research with respect to, controlled substances under the laws of the State in which he practices. The Attorney General may deny an application for such registration if he determines that the issuance of such registration would be inconsistent with the public interest. In determining the public interest, the following factors shall be considered:

> (1) The recommendation of the appropriate State licensing board or professional disciplinary authority
>
> (2) The applicant's experience in dispensing, or conducting research with respect to controlled substances.
>
> (3) The applicant's conviction record under Federal or State laws relating to the manufacture, distribution, or dispensing of controlled substances.
>
> (4) Compliance with applicable State, Federal, or local laws relating to controlled substances.
>
> (5) Such other conduct which may threaten the public health and safety.

(a) The Controlled Substances Act and the First Amendment

Much of the federalism dispute over the CSA has been provoked by California's Compassionate Use Act of 1996, which exempts from criminal liability "patients . . . who possess or cultivate marijuana for medicinal purposes with the recommendation or approval of a physician." Both the Clinton and Bush administrations have insisted that California's legalization of marijuana for medical uses does not affect federal drug laws. In 1998, for example, the United States sued to enjoin an organization that was distributing marijuana under the aegis of Proposition 215. The organization responded by arguing that distribution was medically necessary and that the CSA implicitly authorized such a defense. A Ninth Circuit panel thought this a "legally cognizable defense" the district (trial) court should consider. *US v. Oakland Cannabis Buyers' Cooperative*, 190 F3d 1109 (1999). (Judge Reinhardt, whose opinion in *Compassion in Dying* the Supreme Court unanimously rejected, was a panel member, as was Chief Judge Schroeder, the author of the opinion in *Conant*.) In *United States v. Oakland Cannabis Buyers' Cooperative*, 532 US 483

(2001), the Supreme Court unanimously disagreed. A necessity defense "traditionally covered the situation where physical forces beyond the actor's control rendered illegal conduct the lesser of two evils," but that was not the Cooperative's situation. And while the Cooperative alleged that marijuana was medically necessary, the CSA itself "reflects a determination that marijuana has no medical benefits worthy of an exception . . . ."

Another kind of challenge to the CSA was presented in

CONANT v. WALTERS
309 F3d 629 (2002)

Schroeder, C.J.

This is an appeal from a permanent injunction entered to protect First Amendment rights. . . .

I. The Federal Marijuana Policy

The federal government promulgated its policy in 1996 in response to initiatives passed in both Arizona and California decriminalizing the use of marijuana for limited medical purposes and immunizing physicians from prosecution under state law for the "recommendation or approval" of using marijuana for medical purposes. The federal policy declared that a doctor's "action of recommending or prescribing Schedule I controlled substances is not consistent with the 'public interest' (as that phrase is used in the federal Controlled Substances Act)" and that such action would lead to revocation of the physician's registration to prescribe controlled substances.

[The Departments of Justice and Health and Human Services] sent a letter . . . to national, state, and local practitioner associations . . . [that] cautioned that physicians who "intentionally provide their patients with oral or written statements in order to enable them to obtain controlled substances in violation of federal law ... risk revocation of their DEA prescription authority."

II. Litigation History . . .

[By 1999, the case had reached the trial court. Under its aegis, the plaintiff class] was modified to include only those patients suffering from specific symptoms related to certain illnesses and physicians who treat such patients. . . . [The court] issued an order permanently enjoining the government from:

> (i) revoking any physician class member's DEA registration merely because the doctor makes a recommendation for the use of medical marijuana based on a sincere medical judgment and (ii) from initiating any investigation solely on that ground. The injunction should apply whether or not the doctor anticipates that the patient will, in turn, use his or her recommendation to obtain marijuana in violation of federal law. . . .

III. Discussion . . . .

The dispute in the district court in this case focused on the government's policy of investigating doctors or initiating proceedings against doctors only because they "recommend" the use of marijuana. While the government urged that such recommendations lead to illegal use, the district court concluded that there are many legitimate responses to a recommendation of marijuana by a doctor to a patient. . . . For example, the doctor could seek to place the patient in a federally approved, experimental marijuana-therapy program. Alternatively, the patient upon receiving the recommendation could petition the government to change the law. By chilling doctors' ability to recommend marijuana to a patient, the district court held that the prohibition compromises a patient's meaningful participation in public discourse. . . .

On appeal, the government first argues that the "recommendation" that the injunction may protect is analogous to a "prescription" of a controlled substance, which federal law clearly bars. We believe this characterizes the injunction as sweeping more broadly than it was intended or than as properly interpreted. If, in making the recommendation, the physician intends for the patient to use it as the means for obtaining marijuana, as a prescription is used as a means for a patient to obtain a controlled substance, then a physician would be guilty of aiding and abetting the violation of federal law. That, the injunction is intended to avoid. . . .

The government on appeal stresses that the permanent injunction applies "whether or not the doctor anticipates that the patient will, in turn, use his or her recommendation to obtain marijuana in violation of federal law," and suggests that the injunction thus protects criminal conduct. A doctor's anticipation of patient conduct, however, does not translate into aiding and abetting, or conspiracy. A doctor would aid and abet by acting with the specific intent to provide a patient with the means to acquire marijuana. Similarly, a conspiracy would require that a doctor have knowledge that a patient intends to acquire marijuana, agree to help the patient acquire marijuana, and intend to help the patient acquire marijuana. Holding doctors responsible for whatever conduct the doctor could anticipate a patient *might* engage in after leaving the doctor's office is simply beyond the scope of either conspiracy or aiding and abetting.

The government also focuses on the injunction's bar against "investigating" on the basis of speech protected by the First Amendment and points to the broad discretion enjoyed by executive agencies in investigating suspected criminal misconduct. . . .

[W]e interpret this portion of the permanent injunction to mean only that the government may not initiate an investigation of a physician solely on the basis of a recommendation of marijuana within a bona fide doctor-patient relationship, unless the government in good faith believes that it has substantial evidence of criminal conduct. Because a doctor's recommendation does not itself constitute illegal conduct, the portion of the injunction barring investigations solely on that basis does not interfere with the federal government's ability to enforce its laws.

The government policy does, however, strike at core First Amendment interests of doctors and patients. An integral component of the practice of medicine is the communication between a doctor and a patient. Physicians must be able to speak frankly and openly to patients. That need has been recognized by the courts through the application of the common law doctor-patient privilege. . . .

Being a member of a regulated profession does not, as the government suggests, result in a surrender of First Amendment rights. . . .To the contrary, professional speech may be entitled to "the strongest protection our Constitution has to offer." *Florida Bar v. Went For It, Inc.,* 515 U.S. 618, 634 (1995). Even commercial speech by professionals is entitled to First Amendment protection. *See Bates v. Arizona,* 433 U.S. 350, 382-83 (1977). Attorneys have rights to speak freely subject only to the government regulating with "narrow specificity." *NAACP v. Button,* 371 U.S. 415, 433, 438-39 (1963).

In its most recent pronouncement on regulating speech about controlled substances, *Thompson v. Western States Medical Ctr.,* 122 S.Ct. 1497 (2002), the Supreme Court found that provisions in the Food and Drug Modernization Act of 1997 that restricted physicians and pharmacists from advertising compounding drugs violated the First Amendment. The Court refused to make the "questionable assumption that doctors would prescribe unnecessary medications" and rejected the government's argument that "people would make bad decisions if given truthful information about compounded drugs." The federal government argues in this case that a doctor-patient discussion about marijuana might lead the patient to make a bad decision, essentially asking us to accept the same assumption rejected by the Court in *Thompson.* . . .

The government's policy in this case seeks to punish physicians on the basis of the content of doctor-patient communications. Only doctor-patient conversations that include discussions of the medical use of marijuana trigger the policy. Moreover, the policy does not merely prohibit the discussion of marijuana; it condemns expression of a particular viewpoint, i.e., that medical marijuana would likely help a specific patient. Such condemnation of particular views is especially troubling in the First Amendment context. . . .

The government relies upon *Rust* [*v. Sullivan,* 500 U.S. 173 (1991)], and [*Planned Parenthood of Southeastern Pennsylvania v.*] *Casey,* [505 U.S. 833 (1992),] to support its position in this case. However, those cases did not uphold restrictions on speech itself. *Rust* upheld restrictions on federal funding for certain types of activity, including abortion counseling, referral, or advocacy. In *Casey,* a plurality of the Court upheld Pennsylvania's requirement that physicians' advice to patients include information about the health risks associated with an abortion and that physicians provide information about alternatives to abortion. The plurality noted that physicians did not have to comply if they had a reasonable belief that the information would have a "severely adverse effect on the physical or mental health of the patient," and thus the statute did not "prevent the physician from exercising his or her medical judgment." The government's policy in this case does precisely that. . . .

The government also relies on a case in which a district court refused to order an injunction against this federal drug policy. See *Pearson v. McCaffrey,* 139 F.Supp.2d 113, 125 (D.D.C.2001). The court did so, however, because the plaintiffs in that case did not factually support their claim that the policy chilled their speech. In this case, the record is replete with examples of doctors who claim a right to explain the medical benefits of marijuana to patients and whose exercise of that right has been chilled by the threat of federal investigation. The government even stipulated in the district court that a "reasonable physician would have a genuine fear of losing his or her DEA registration to dispense controlled substances if that physician were to recommend marijuana to his or her patients."

To survive First Amendment scrutiny, the government's policy must have the requisite "narrow specificity." Throughout this litigation, the government has been unable to articulate exactly what speech is proscribed, describing it only in terms of speech the patient believes to be a recommendation of marijuana. Thus, whether a doctor-patient discussion of medical marijuana constitutes a "recommendation" depends largely on the meaning the patient attributes to the doctor's words. This is not permissible under the First Amendment. . . .

Our decision is consistent with principles of federalism that have left states as the primary regulators of professional conduct. See *Whalen v. Roe,* 429 U.S. 589, 603 n. 30 (1977) (recognizing states' broad police powers to regulate the administration of drugs by health professionals); *Linder v. United States,* 268 U.S. 5, 18 (1925) ("direct control of medical practice in the states is beyond the power of the federal government"). We must "show [ ] respect for the sovereign States that comprise our Federal Union. That respect imposes a duty on federal courts, whenever possible, to avoid or minimize conflict between federal and state law, particularly in situations in which the citizens of a State have chosen to serve as a laboratory in the trial of novel social and economic experiments without risk to the rest of the country." *Oakland Cannabis,* 532 U.S. at 501 (Stevens, J., concurring). . . .

[The concurring opinion of Judge Kosinski is omitted.]

PEARSON v. McCAFFREY
139 FSupp2d 113 (DDC 2001)

BRYANT, Senior District Judge . . . .

[This was another suit by doctors and patients to enjoin the federal policy discussed in *Conant*.]

During the hearing, Defendants' counsel stated,

[t]he Federal Government has drawn a very clear line here that doctors are permitted--nothing in Federal law prevents doctors from discussing the possible risks and benefits of marijuana, but the line is that they cannot prescribe it, and they cannot recommend it to patients.

Thus, under current law, doctors, patients, and researchers may freely discuss the benefits and risks of the use of marijuana without fearing that the federal government will proceed against them with criminal, civil, or administrative penalties.

However, Plaintiffs also raised some question as to the meaning of the term "recommend" within the context of this discussion. Defendants note that in some states, such as California, the term "recommend" has a special significance under the law because patients are able to take a recommendation for medicinal marijuana to a buyers' club to receive the drug. In these situations, a recommendation is analogous to a prescription, therefore, the federal government will treat it as such. Since passage of its law, the State of California has issued guidelines to provide doctors with examples of physician-patient conversations about marijuana that are permitted under federal law. Defendants also referenced a letter from the American Medical Association stating that the medical establishment in this country understands the distinction between a "recommendation" for medicinal marijuana and mere discussion of its risks and benefits. The Court finds that the position taken by the Defendants alleviates the First Amendment concerns raised by Plaintiffs about the ability of doctors, patients, and researchers to be able to freely discuss the risks and benefits of medicinal marijuana. It is clear that, short of a prescription or recommendation for marijuana, the federal government will not get involved in communication between doctors, patients, and researchers regarding the potential medical benefits of marijuana use.

However, while the Plaintiffs are free to discuss the use of medicinal marijuana, the recommendation and prescription of the drug is a different issue. During a doctor-patient conversation, physicians are engaging in the practice of medicine, which has a long history of being regulated to protect the public safety. *See, e.g., Whalen v. Roe,* 429 U.S. 589, 603 n. 30 (1977) (stating, "[i]t is, of course, well-settled that the State has broad police powers in regulating the administration of drugs by health professionals.") As Defendants note, when a doctor's speech is part of his practice of medicine, it may be subject to "reasonable licensing and regulation." *Planned Parenthood of Southeastern Pennsylvania v. Casey,* 505 U.S. 833, 884 (1992).

In addition, there are no First Amendment protections for speech that is used "as an integral part of conduct in violation of a valid criminal statute." *Giboney v. Empire Storage & Ice Co.,* 336 U.S. 490, 498 (1949). This Court has recognized that:

> [m]any a crime is committed purely by word of mouth, such as obtaining money by false pretenses, extortion, broadcasting treasonable utterances, and many others.... The right of freedom of speech is not defense to a prosecution for any of these offenses.

United States v. Peace Information Ctr., 97 F.Supp. 255, 262 (D.D.C.1951). And, as this Circuit found in *National Org. of Women v. Operation Rescue,* 37 F.3d 646, 656 (D.C.Cir.1994), "[t]he First Amendment does not provide a defense to a criminal charge simply because the actor uses words to carry out his illegal purpose ..."

Even though state law may allow for the prescription or recommendation of medicinal marijuana within its borders, to do so is still a violation of federal law under the CSA. The fact that speech or writing is the mechanism used by physicians to carry out such a task does not make the conduct less violative of federal law. The First Amendment does not prohibit the federal government from taking action against physicians whose prescription or recommendation of medicinal marijuana violates the CSA.

Moreover, . . . Plaintiffs appear to overstate the position of the federal government. It appears to the Court that, above all else, the federal policy (and the media events related to it) are little more than a very public assertion of the government's intent to continue to enforce already existing federal laws. Therefore, it is not an unconstitutional prior restraint, it is a statement regarding the applicability of federal law to certain practices.

Finally, as Defendants note, the overbreadth doctrine has been used by the courts "sparingly and only as a last resort." *Broadrick v. Oklahoma,* 413 U.S. 601, 613 (1973). The federal policy only limits certain speech by physicians that violates federal law. The doctrine is only applicable in cases where the overbreadth is not only "real, but substantial as well, judged in relation to the statute's plainly legitimate sweep." *New York v. Ferber,* 458 U.S. 747, 770 (1982). . . .

Notes and Questions on Conant *and* Pearson

1. Is there really a first-amendment problem here? The federal government has now said in a variety of places and ways that it does not intend to deter doctors from discussing the merits of drugs with patients but only to prevent doctors from "prescribing" or "recommending" drugs to patients. Doesn't this leave doctors free to tell patients anything patients would need to know to make decisions about their own health or to participate in public discussions? Does a contrary result effectively prevent the federal government from enforcing the Controlled Substances Act, at least as to marijuana in states with statutes like California's?

2. In *U.S. v. Moore,* 423 US 122 (1975), a physician had in less than six months written 11,169 prescriptions for a total of some 800,000 tablets of methadone. The Court affirmed the doctor's conviction of violating § 841 even though he was registered, since his activities were plainly outside the ordinary scope of medical practice. The doctor was sentenced to one set of concurrent jail terms of 5 to 15 years and, consecutively, to another set of concurrent terms of 10 to 30 years, and he was fined $150,000. Similarly, *US v. Davis*, 564 F2d 840 (9th Cir 1977), held that "by creating the means by which controlled substances can be transferred, a doctor 'distributes' within the meaning of 21U.S.C. § 841(a) by the act of writing a prescription outside the usual course of professional practice and not for a legitimate medical purpose." If writing a prescription is so clearly a crime, "recommending" a Schedule 1 drug also criminal, at least under

the California scheme that gives a "recommendation" the effect of a prescription?

Is it impermissible for a statute to criminalize speech? Consider the passage on this subject in *Pearson*. Similarly, in *NOW v. Operation Rescue*, 37 F3d 646 (DC Cir 1994), the trial court enjoined Operation Rescue from obstructing access to abortion clinics and from "inducing, encouraging, directing, aiding, or abetting others" to do so. In affirming the injunction, the Court of Appeals acknowledged that the injunction "reaches appellants' speech and consequently raises . . . First Amendment concerns." It nevertheless found the injunction "unproblematic," since "[m]any criminal statutes prohibit directing, aiding, or abetting illegal acts, even though the directing, aiding, or abetting may be carried out through speech."

Is *Conant*'s argument that the injunction does not interfere with government's ability to enforce the criminal provisions of the CSA and that therefore the injunction does not trench on the government's legitimate activities? Is the assumption true? Does the conclusion follow? The CSA does more than prohibit some kinds of distribution of some substances. It gives doctors control of controlled drugs but imposes affirmative obligations on them to exercise their authority scrupulously. "Congress was particularly concerned with the diversion of drugs from legitimate channels to illegitimate channels. It was aware that registrants, who have the greatest access to controlled substances and therefore the greatest opportunity for diversion, were responsible for a large part of the illegal drug traffic." *U.S. v. Moore*, 423 US 122, 135 (1975). The CSA therefore establishes an elaborate regime of record-keeping and reporting procedures doctors must follow. Thus one court found that the DEA acted legitimately in revoking a doctor's registration for, *inter alia*, failing to maintain proper records. *Matter of Burka*, 684 FSupp 1300 (ED Pa 1988). Is the DEA thus entitled and even obliged to consider a physician's advice and acts concerning a drug Congress declared has no legitimate medical purpose, a declaration the Supreme Court left unmolested in *Oakland Cannabis Buyers' Cooperative*?

3. *Conant* is not an easy opinion to parse. (If you are having trouble with it, we think it is not because our editing has obscured the court's reasoning unduly.) But *Conant*'s response to the analysis suggested in Note 3 would apparently be that even though the government's criminal and civil enforcement of the CSA might not itself

affront the first amendment, that enforcement created a "chilling" effect which justified the injunction. *Conant* says the "record is replete with examples of doctors who claim a right to explain the medical benefits of marijuana to patients and whose exercise of that right has been chilled by the threat of federal investigation." This may well be. Doctors know little about the law, frequently misunderstand it, and regularly exaggerate its scope and ferocity. But are such misunderstandings a sufficient basis for declaring a statute unconstitutional?

Consider *Laird v. Tatum*, 408 US 1 (1972), which found that plaintiffs' allegation of a chilling effect did not present a justiciable controversy, since "[a]llegations of a subjective 'chill' are not an adequate substitute for a claim of specific present objective harm or a threat of specific future harm . . . ." And in *Polykoff v. Collins*, 816 F2d 1326 (9th Cir 1987), the plaintiffs argued that "the felony fine provisions [for selling obscene material] impermissibly chill[ed] protected speech because of the threat of large fines, " and they presented evidence that stores had taken presumably non-obscene materials off their shelves for fear of the fines. The Ninth Circuit retorted that that "argument is considerably weakened by the correct understanding of the felony fine provisions" and that "any chilling effect that may have been based on an incorrect understanding of the law is not constitutionally cognizable."

4. *Conant* suggests that doctors and patients have a first-amendment interest in unfettered speech for therapeutic reasons and because patients might use information from doctors to participate in public debates. How strong are those first-amendment interests? Are the doctors' and patients' interests congruent? Is the patient's interest primarily in receiving useful and reliable information, not whatever information a physician may proffer? Is this why Judge Reinhardt could write in *Compassion in Dying* that, "since doctors are highly-regulated professionals, it should not be difficult for the state or the profession itself to establish rules and procedures that will ensure that the occasional negligent or careless recommendation by a licensed physician will not result in an uninformed or erroneous decision by the patient or his family"? And why the Supreme Court could say in *Casey:* "To be sure, the physician's First Amendment rights not to speak are implicated, but only as part of the practice of medicine, subject to reasonable licensing and regulation by the State. We see no constitutional infirmity in the requirement that the physician

provide the information mandated by the State here." 505 US 833, 884 (1992).

Consider *Rust v. Sullivan*, 500 US 173 (1991). Title X of the Public Health Service Act provided that funds should not be used in programs where abortion was a method of family planning, and the Secretary of HHS prohibited Title X projects from encouraging, promoting, or advocating abortion for family planning. The Court rejected a first-amendment challenge. Under *Maher v. Roe*, 432 US 464 (1977), Congress could subsidize Medicaid services relating to childbirth without subsidizing abortion services, since government could "make a value judgment favoring childbirth over abortion, and . . . implement that judgment by the allocation of public funds." In Title X, the "Government has not discriminated on the basis of viewpoint; it has merely chosen to fund one activity to the exclusion of the other." Nor was the government impermissibly putting conditions on receipt of a benefit; it was "simply insisting that public funds be spent for the purposes for which they are authorized." Finally:

> It could be argued by analogy that traditional relationships such as that between doctor and patient should enjoy protection under the First Amendment from Government regulation, even when subsidized by the Government. We need not resolve that question here, however, because the Title X program regulations do not significantly impinge upon the doctor-patient relationship. Nothing in them requires a doctor to represent as his own any opinion that he does not in fact hold. Nor is the doctor-patient relationship established by the Title X program sufficiently all encompassing so as to justify an expectation on the part of the patient of comprehensive medical advice.

(b) The Controlled Substances Act and the Commerce Clause

GONZALES v. RAICH
545 US ___ (2005)

Justice STEVENS delivered the opinion of the Court.

California is one of at least nine States that authorize the use of marijuana for medicinal purposes. The question presented in this case is whether the power vested in Congress by Article I, § 8, of the Constitution "[t]o make all Laws which shall be necessary and proper for carrying into Execution" its authority to "regulate Commerce with foreign Nations, and among the several States" includes the power to prohibit the local cultivation and use of marijuana in compliance with California law.

I. . . .

In 1996, California voters passed Proposition 215, now codified as the Compassionate Use Act of 1996. . . . The Act creates an exemption from criminal prosecution for physicians, as well as for patients and primary caregivers who possess or cultivate marijuana for medicinal purposes with the recommendation or approval of a physician. [Raich and Monson used marijuana under the Act. After federal agents seized and destroyed six of Monson's cannabis plants, she, Raich, and two John Does sued for injunctive and declaratory relief prohibiting the enforcement of the federal Controlled Substances Act (CSA) against them. The district court denied the motion for a preliminary injunction because "respondents could not demonstrate a likelihood of success on the merits of their legal claims." A divided Ninth Circuit panel reversed because respondents had demonstrated a strong likelihood of success.]

III. . . .

[R]espondents' challenge is actually quite limited; they argue that the CSA's categorical prohibition of the manufacture and possession of marijuana as applied to the intrastate manufacture and possession of marijuana for medical purposes pursuant to California law exceeds Congress' authority under the Commerce Clause. . . .

Our case law firmly establishes Congress' power to regulate purely local activities that are part of an economic "class of activities" that have a substantial effect on interstate commerce. See, *e.g. Wickard v. Filburn,* 317 U.S. 111, 128-129 (1942). As we stated in *Wickard,* "even if appellee's activity be local and though it may not be regarded as commerce, it may still, whatever its nature, be reached by Congress if it exerts a substantial economic effect on interstate commerce." We have never required Congress to legislate with scientific exactitude. When Congress decides that the "total incidence" of a practice poses a threat to a national market, it may regulate the entire class. ("[W]hen it is necessary in order to prevent an evil to make the law embrace more than the precise thing to be prevented it may do so"). In this vein, we have reiterated that when "'a general regulatory statute bears a substantial relation to commerce, the *de minimis* character of individual instances arising under that statute is of no consequence.'"

Our decision in *Wickard* is of particular relevance. In *Wickard*, we upheld the application of regulations promulgated under the Agricultural Adjustment Act of 1938 which were designed to control the volume of wheat moving in interstate and foreign commerce in order to avoid surpluses and consequent abnormally low prices. The regulations established an allotment of 11.1 acres for Filburn's 1941 wheat crop, but he sowed 23 acres, intending to use the excess by consuming it on his own farm. Filburn argued that even though we had sustained Congress' power to regulate the production of goods for commerce, that power did not authorize "federal regulation [of] production not intended in any part for commerce but wholly for consumption on the farm." Justice Jackson's opinion for a unanimous Court rejected this submission. He wrote:

> "The effect of the statute before us is to restrict the amount which may be produced for market and the extent as well to which one may forestall resort to the market by producing to meet his own needs. That appellee's own contribution to the demand for wheat may be trivial by itself is not enough to remove him from the scope of federal regulation where, as here, his contribution, taken together with that of many others similarly situated, is far from trivial."

Wickard thus establishes that Congress can regulate purely intrastate activity that is not itself "commercial," in that it is not produced for sale, if it concludes that failure to regulate that class of activity would undercut the regulation of the interstate market in that commodity.

The similarities between this case and *Wickard* are striking. Like the farmer in *Wickard,* respondents are cultivating, for home consumption, a fungible commodity for which there is an established, albeit illegal, interstate market.[28] Just as the Agricultural Adjustment

---

[28] Even respondents acknowledge the existence of an illicit market in marijuana; indeed, Raich has personally participated in that market, and Monson expresses a willingness to do so in the future.

Act was designed "to control the volume [of wheat] moving in interstate and foreign commerce in order to avoid surpluses ..." and consequently control the market price, a primary purpose of the CSA is to control the supply and demand of controlled substances in both lawful and unlawful drug markets. In *Wickard,* we had no difficulty concluding that Congress had a rational basis for believing that, when viewed in the aggregate, leaving home-consumed wheat outside the regulatory scheme would have a substantial influence on price and market conditions. Here too, Congress had a rational basis for concluding that leaving home-consumed marijuana outside federal control would similarly affect price and market conditions.

More concretely, one concern prompting inclusion of wheat grown for home consumption in the 1938 Act was that rising market prices could draw such wheat into the interstate market, resulting in lower market prices. The parallel concern making it appropriate to include marijuana grown for home consumption in the CSA is the likelihood that the high demand in the interstate market will draw such marijuana into that market. While the diversion of homegrown wheat tended to frustrate the federal interest in stabilizing prices by regulating the volume of commercial transactions in the interstate market, the diversion of homegrown marijuana tends to frustrate the federal interest in eliminating commercial transactions in the interstate market in their entirety. In both cases, the regulation is squarely within Congress' commerce power because production of the commodity meant for home consumption, be it wheat or marijuana, has a substantial effect on supply and demand in the national market for that commodity.[29]

Nonetheless, respondents suggest that *Wickard* differs from this case in three respects: (1) the Agricultural Adjustment Act, unlike the CSA, exempted small farming operations; (2) *Wickard* involved a "quintessential economic activity"--a commercial farm--whereas respondents do not sell marijuana; and (3) the *Wickard* record made it clear that the aggregate production of wheat for use on farms had a significant impact on market prices. Those differences, though

---

[29] To be sure, the wheat market is a lawful market that Congress sought to protect and stabilize, whereas the marijuana market is an unlawful market that Congress sought to eradicate. This difference, however, is of no constitutional import. It has long been settled that Congress' power to regulate commerce includes the power to prohibit commerce in a particular commodity.

factually accurate, do not diminish the precedential force of this Court's reasoning.

The fact that Wickard's own impact on the market was "trivial by itself" was not a sufficient reason for removing him from the scope of federal regulation. That the Secretary of Agriculture elected to exempt even smaller farms from regulation does not speak to his power to regulate all those whose aggregated production was significant, nor did that fact play any role in the Court's analysis. Moreover, even though Wickard was indeed a commercial farmer, the activity he was engaged in--the cultivation of wheat for home consumption--was not treated by the Court as part of his commercial farming operation. And while it is true that the record in the *Wickard* case itself established the causal connection between the production for local use and the national market, we have before us findings by Congress to the same effect.

Findings in the introductory sections of the CSA explain why Congress deemed it appropriate to encompass local activities within the scope of the CSA. . . . [T]he national, and international, market for marijuana has dimensions that are fully comparable to those defining the class of activities regulated by the Secretary pursuant to the 1938 statute. Respondents nonetheless insist that the CSA cannot be constitutionally applied to their activities because Congress did not make a specific finding that . . . [this use of marijuana] would substantially affect the larger interstate marijuana market. Be that as it may, we have never required Congress to make particularized findings in order to legislate absent a special concern such as the protection of free speech. . . .

In assessing the scope of Congress' authority under the Commerce Clause, we stress that the task before us is a modest one. We need not determine whether respondents' activities, taken in the aggregate, substantially affect interstate commerce in fact, but only whether a "rational basis" exists for so concluding. Given the enforcement difficulties that attend distinguishing between marijuana cultivated locally and marijuana grown elsewhere and concerns about diversion into illicit channels, we have no difficulty concluding that Congress had a rational basis for believing that failure to regulate the intrastate manufacture and possession of marijuana would leave a gaping hole in the CSA. Thus, as in *Wickard,* when it enacted comprehensive legislation to regulate the interstate market in a fungible commodity, Congress was acting well within its authority to "make all Laws which shall be necessary and proper" to "regulate Commerce ... among the several States." U.S. Const., Art. I, § 8. That the regulation ensnares some purely intrastate activity is of no moment. . . .

IV

To support their contrary submission, respondents rely heavily on two of our more recent Commerce Clause cases[:] . . . . *United States v. Lopez,* 514 U.S. 549 (1995), and *United States v. Morrison,* 529 U.S. 598 (2000). As an initial matter, the statutory challenges at issue in those cases were markedly different from the challenge respondents pursue in the case at hand. Here, respondents ask us to excise individual applications of a concededly valid statutory scheme. In contrast, in both *Lopez* and *Morrison,* the parties asserted that a particular statute or provision fell outside Congress' commerce power in its entirety. This distinction is pivotal for we have often reiterated that "[w]here the class of activities is regulated and that class is within the reach of federal power, the courts have no power 'to excise, as trivial, individual instances' of the class."

At issue in *Lopez,* was the validity of the Gun-Free School Zones Act of 1990, which was a brief, single-subject statute making it a crime for an individual to possess a gun in a school zone. The Act did not regulate any economic activity and did not contain any requirement that the possession of a gun have any connection to past interstate activity or a predictable impact on future commercial activity. . . . We explained:

> "Section 922(q) is a criminal statute that by its terms has nothing to do with 'commerce' or any sort of economic enterprise, however broadly one might define those terms. Section 922(q) is not an essential part of a larger regulation of economic activity, in which the regulatory scheme could be undercut unless the intrastate activity were regulated. It cannot, therefore, be sustained under our cases upholding regulations of activities that arise out of or are connected with a commercial transaction, which viewed in the aggregate, substantially affects interstate commerce."

The statutory scheme that the Government is defending in this litigation is at the opposite end of the regulatory spectrum. . . . [T]he CSA, enacted in 1970 as part of the Comprehensive Drug Abuse Prevention and Control Act, was a lengthy and detailed statute creating a comprehensive framework for regulating the production, distribution, and possession of five classes of "controlled substances." . . . Our opinion in *Lopez* casts no doubt on the validity of such a program.

Nor does this Court's holding in *Morrison*. The Violence Against Women Act of 1994 created a federal civil remedy for the victims of gender-motivated crimes of violence. The remedy was enforceable in both state and federal courts, and generally depended on proof of the violation of a state law. Despite congressional findings that such crimes had an adverse impact on interstate commerce, we held the statute unconstitutional because, like the statute in *Lopez*, it did not regulate economic activity. We concluded that "the noneconomic, criminal nature of the conduct at issue was central to our decision" in *Lopez*, and that our prior cases had identified a clear pattern of analysis: " 'Where economic activity substantially affects interstate commerce, legislation regulating that activity will be sustained.' "

Unlike those at issue in *Lopez* and *Morrison,* the activities regulated by the CSA are quintessentially economic. . . . The CSA is a statute that regulates the production, distribution, and consumption of commodities for which there is an established, and lucrative, interstate market. Prohibiting the intrastate possession or manufacture of an article of commerce is a rational (and commonly utilized) means of regulating commerce in that product. . . . Because the CSA is a statute that directly regulates economic, commercial activity, our opinion in *Morrison* casts no doubt on its constitutionality.

The Court of Appeals was able to conclude otherwise only by isolating a "separate and distinct" class of activities that it held to be beyond the reach of federal power, defined as "the intrastate, noncommercial cultivation, possession and use of marijuana for personal medical purposes on the advice of a physician and in accordance with state law." The court characterized this class as "different in kind from drug trafficking." The differences between the members of a class so defined and the principal traffickers in Schedule I substances might be sufficient to justify a policy decision exempting the narrower class from the coverage of the CSA. The question, however, is whether Congress' contrary policy judgment, *i.e.,* its decision to include this narrower "class of activities" within the larger regulatory scheme, was constitutionally deficient. We have no difficulty concluding that Congress acted rationally in determining that none of the characteristics making up the purported class, whether viewed individually or in the aggregate, compelled an exemption from the CSA; rather, the subdivided class of activities defined by the Court of Appeals was an essential part of the larger regulatory scheme.

First, the fact that marijuana is used "for personal medical purposes on the advice of a physician" cannot itself serve as a distinguishing factor. The CSA designates marijuana as contraband for *any* purpose; in fact, by characterizing marijuana as a Schedule I drug, Congress expressly found that the drug has no acceptable medical uses. Moreover, the CSA is a comprehensive regulatory regime specifically designed to regulate which controlled substances can be utilized for medicinal purposes, and in what manner. Indeed, most of the substances classified in the CSA "have a useful and legitimate medical purpose." 21 U.S.C. § 801(1). . . .

More fundamentally, if, as the principal dissent contends, the personal cultivation, possession, and use of marijuana for medicinal purposes is beyond the "'outer limits' of Congress' Commerce Clause authority," it must also be true that such personal use of marijuana (or any other homegrown drug) for recreational purposes is also beyond those 'outer limits,' whether or not a State elects to authorize or even regulate such use. . . . The congressional judgment that an exemption for such a significant segment of the total market would undermine the orderly enforcement of the entire regulatory scheme is entitled to a strong presumption of validity. Indeed, that judgment is not only rational, but "visible to the naked eye," under any commonsense appraisal of the probable consequences of such an open-ended exemption. . . .

[T]hat the California exemptions will have a significant impact on both the supply and demand sides of the market for marijuana is not just "plausible" as the principal dissent concedes, it is readily apparent. The exemption for physicians provides them with an economic incentive to grant their patients permission to use the drug. In contrast to most prescriptions for legal drugs, which limit the dosage and duration of the usage, under California law the doctor's permission to recommend marijuana use is open-ended. The authority to grant permission whenever the doctor determines that a patient is afflicted with "any other illness for which marijuana provides relief" is broad enough to allow even the most scrupulous doctor to conclude that some recreational uses would be therapeutic. And . . . there are some unscrupulous physicians who overprescribe when it is sufficiently profitable to do so. . . .

So, from the "separate and distinct" class of activities identified by the Court of Appeals (and adopted by the dissenters), we are left with "the intrastate, noncommercial cultivation, possession and use of marijuana." Thus the case for the exemption comes down to the claim that a locally cultivated product that is used domestically rather than sold on the open market is not subject to federal regulation. Given the findings in the CSA and the undisputed magnitude of the commercial market for marijuana, our decisions in *Wickard v. Filburn* and the later cases endorsing its reasoning foreclose that claim.

V

Respondents also raise a substantive due process claim and seek to avail themselves of the medical necessity defense. These theories of relief were . . . not reached by the Court of Appeals. We therefore do not address . . . these alternative bases. We do note, however, the presence of another avenue of relief. . . . [T]he statute authorizes procedures for the reclassification of Schedule I drugs. But perhaps even more important than these legal avenues is the democratic process, in which the voices of voters allied with these respondents may one day be heard in the halls of Congress. . . .

[Justice Scalia's concurring opinion is omitted, as is Justice Thomas' dissent.]

Justice O'CONNOR, with whom THE CHIEF JUSTICE and Justice THOMAS join as to all but Part III, dissenting.

We enforce the "outer limits" of Congress' Commerce Clause authority not for their own sake, but to protect historic spheres of state sovereignty from excessive federal encroachment and thereby to maintain the distribution of power fundamental to our federalist system of government. *United States v. Lopez; NLRB v. Jones & Laughlin Steel Corp.*, 301 U.S. 1 (1937). One of federalism's chief virtues, of course, is that it promotes innovation by allowing for the possibility that "a single courageous State may, if its citizens choose, serve as a laboratory; and try novel social and economic experiments without risk to the rest of the country." *New State Ice Co. v. Liebmann,* 285 U.S. 262, 311 (1932) (Brandeis, J., dissenting).

This case exemplifies the role of States as laboratories. The States' core police powers have always included authority to define criminal law and to protect the health, safety, and welfare of their citizens. Exercising those powers, California (by ballot initiative and then by legislative codification) has come to its own conclusion about the difficult and sensitive question of whether marijuana should be available to relieve severe pain and suffering. Today the Court . . . extinguishes that experiment, without any proof that the personal cultivation, possession, and use of marijuana for medicinal purposes, if economic activity in the first place, has a substantial effect on interstate commerce . . . . [T]he Court announces a rule that gives Congress a perverse incentive to legislate broadly pursuant to the Commerce Clause--nestling questionable assertions of its authority into comprehensive regulatory schemes--rather than with precision. That rule and the result it produces in this case are irreconcilable with our decisions in *Lopez* and *Morrison*. . . .

II

A . . . .

Today's decision allows Congress to regulate intrastate activity without check, so long as there is some implication by legislative design that regulating intrastate activity is essential (and the Court appears to equate "essential" with "necessary") to the interstate regulatory scheme. Seizing upon our language in *Lopez* that the statute prohibiting gun possession in school zones was "not an essential part of a larger regulation of economic activity, in which the regulatory scheme could be undercut unless the intrastate activity were regulated," the Court appears to reason that the placement of local activity in a comprehensive scheme confirms that it is essential to that scheme. If the Court is right, then *Lopez* stands for nothing more than a drafting guide: Congress should have described the relevant crime as "transfer or possession of a firearm anywhere in the nation"--thus including commercial and noncommercial activity, and clearly encompassing some activity with assuredly substantial effect on interstate commerce. . . .

I did not understand our discussion of the role of courts in enforcing outer limits of the Commerce Clause for the sake of maintaining the federalist balance our Constitution requires as a signal to Congress to enact legislation that is more extensive and more intrusive into the domain of state power. If the Court always defers to Congress as it does today, little may be left to the notion of enumerated powers. . . .

A number of objective markers are available to confine the scope of constitutional review here. Both federal and state legislation--including the CSA itself, the California Compassionate Use Act, and other state medical marijuana legislation--recognize that medical and nonmedical (*i.e.,* recreational) uses of drugs are realistically distinct . . . . Moreover, because fundamental structural concerns about dual sovereignty animate our Commerce Clause cases, it is relevant that this case involves the interplay of federal and state regulation in areas of criminal law and social policy, where "States lay claim by right of history and expertise." California, like other States, has drawn on its reserved powers to distinguish the regulation of medicinal marijuana. To ascertain whether Congress' encroachment is constitutionally justified in this case, then, I would focus here on the personal cultivation, possession, and use of marijuana for medicinal purposes.

B . . . .

The Court's definition of economic activity is breathtaking. It defines as economic any activity involving the production, distribution, and consumption of commodities. And it appears to reason that when an interstate market for a commodity exists, regulating the intrastate manufacture or possession of that commodity is constitutional either because that intrastate activity is itself economic, or because regulating it is a rational part of regulating its market. Putting to one side the problem endemic to the Court's opinion--the shift in focus from the activity at issue in this case to the entirety of what the CSA regulates--the Court's definition of economic activity for purposes of Commerce Clause jurisprudence threatens to sweep all of productive human activity into federal regulatory reach. . . .

It will not do to say that Congress may regulate noncommercial activity simply because it may have an effect on the demand for commercial goods, or because the noncommercial endeavor can, in some sense, substitute for commercial activity. Most commercial goods or services have some sort of privately producible analogue. Home care substitutes for daycare. . . . Backyard or windowsill gardening substitutes for going to the supermarket. To draw the line wherever private activity affects the demand for market goods is to draw no line at all, and to declare everything economic. We have already rejected the result that would follow--a federal police power. *Lopez.*

In *Lopez* and *Morrison,* we suggested that economic activity usually relates directly to commercial activity. The homegrown cultivation and personal possession and use of marijuana for medicinal purposes has no apparent commercial character. . . . *Lopez* makes clear that possession is not itself commercial activity. And respondents have not come into possession by means of any commercial transaction; they have simply grown, in their own homes, marijuana for their own use, without acquiring, buying, selling, or bartering a thing of value.

The Court suggests that *Wickard,* which we have identified as "perhaps the most far reaching example of Commerce Clause authority over intrastate activity, established federal regulatory power over any home consumption of a commodity for which a national market exists. I disagree. *Wickard* involved a challenge to the Agricultural Adjustment Act of 1938 (AAA), which directed the Secretary of Agriculture to set national quotas on wheat production, and penalties for excess production. The AAA itself confirmed that Congress made an explicit choice not to reach--and thus the Court could not possibly have approved of federal control over--small-scale, noncommercial wheat farming. In contrast to the CSA's limitless assertion of power, Congress provided an exemption within the AAA for small producers. When Filburn planted the wheat at issue in *Wickard,* the statute exempted plantings less than 200 bushels (about six tons), and when he harvested his wheat it exempted plantings less than six acres. *Wickard*, then, did not extend Commerce Clause authority to something as modest as the home cook's herb garden. This is not to say that Congress may never regulate small quantities of commodities possessed or produced for personal use, or to deny that it sometimes needs to enact a zero tolerance regime for such commodities. It is merely to say that *Wickard* did not hold or imply that small-scale production of commodities is always economic, and automatically within Congress' reach.

Even assuming that economic activity is at issue in this case, the Government has made no showing in fact that the possession and use of homegrown marijuana for medical purposes, in California or elsewhere, has a substantial effect on interstate commerce. Similarly, the Government has not shown that regulating such activity is necessary to an interstate regulatory scheme. Whatever the specific theory of "substantial effects" at issue (*i.e.,* whether the activity substantially affects interstate commerce, whether its regulation is necessary to an interstate regulatory scheme, or both), a concern for dual sovereignty requires that Congress' excursion into the traditional domain of States be justified. . . .

There is simply no evidence that homegrown medicinal marijuana users constitute, in the aggregate, a sizable enough class to have a discernable, let alone substantial, impact on the national illicit drug market--or otherwise to threaten the CSA regime. . . . And here, in part because common sense suggests that medical marijuana users may be limited in number and that California's Compassionate Use Act and similar state legislation may well isolate activities relating to medicinal marijuana from the illicit market, the effect of those activities on interstate drug traffic is not self-evidently substantial.

In this regard, again, this case is readily distinguishable from *Wickard.* To decide whether the Secretary could regulate local wheat farming, the Court looked to "the actual effects of the activity in question upon interstate commerce." Critically, the Court was able to consider "actual effects" because the parties had "stipulated a summary of the economics of the wheat industry." After reviewing in detail the picture of the industry provided in that summary, the Court explained that consumption of homegrown wheat was the most variable factor in the size of the national wheat crop, and that on-site consumption could have the effect of varying the amount of wheat sent to market by as much as 20 percent. . . .

The Court refers to a series of declarations in the introduction to the CSA saying that (1) local distribution and possession of controlled substances causes "swelling" in interstate traffic; (2) local production and distribution cannot be distinguished from interstate production and distribution; (3) federal control over intrastate incidents "is essential to effective control" over interstate drug trafficking. These bare declarations cannot be compared to the record before the Court in *Wickard.*

They amount to nothing more than a legislative insistence that the regulation of controlled substances must be absolute. They are asserted without any supporting evidence--descriptive, statistical, or otherwise. "[S]imply because Congress may conclude a particular activity substantially affects interstate commerce does not necessarily make it so." If, as the Court claims, today's decision does not break with precedent, how can it be that voluminous findings, documenting extensive hearings about the specific topic of violence against women, did not pass constitutional muster in *Morrison,* while the CSA's abstract, unsubstantiated, generalized findings about controlled substances do? . . .

Because here California, like other States, has carved out a limited class of activity for distinct regulation, the inadequacy of the CSA's findings is especially glaring. The California Compassionate Use Act exempts from other state drug laws patients and their caregivers "who posses[s] or cultivat[e] marijuana for the *personal* medical purposes of the patient upon the written or oral recommendation of a physician" to treat a list of serious medical conditions. . . . We generally assume States enforce their laws, and have no reason to think otherwise here. . . .

III

We would do well to recall how James Madison, the father of the Constitution, described our system of joint sovereignty. . . : "The powers delegated by the proposed constitution to the federal government are few and defined. Those which are to remain in the State governments are numerous and indefinite .... The powers reserved to the several States will extend to all the objects which, in the ordinary course of affairs, concern the lives, liberties, and properties of the people, and the internal order, improvement, and prosperity of the State." The Federalist No. 45. . . .

If I were a California citizen, I would not have voted for the medical marijuana ballot initiative; if I were a California legislator I would not have supported the Compassionate Use Act. But whatever the wisdom of California's experiment with medical marijuana, the federalism principles that have driven our Commerce Clause cases require that room for experiment be protected in this case. . . .

Notes and Questions on Gonzales v. Raich

1. "Nationally, most marijuana arrests are made by state and local law-enforcement agencies, with federal arrests accounting for only about 1 percent of cases. However, soon after the decision was announced, federal agents raided 3 of San Francisco's more than 40 medical marijuana dispensaries. Nineteen people were charged with running an international drug ring; they allegedly were using the dispensaries as a front for trafficking in marijuana and in the illegal amphetamine 'ecstasy.'" California gives doctors greater latitude in prescribing marijuana than the other nine states that permit such prescriptions. "In San Francisco, some journalists or investigators who posed as patients have reported that they had little difficulty obtaining a recommendation for medical marijuana, which allows the holder to purchase the drug from a dispensary." Even before *Raich*, "many Californians had been calling for stricter state regulation of medical marijuana. Some cities have banned marijuana dispensaries, and many counties and cities — including San Francisco — have imposed moratoriums on the opening of new ones."

"Clinical research on marijuana has been hampered by the fact that the plant, which contains dozens of active substances, is an illegal drug classified as having no legitimate medical use." Researchers must get permission and the drug from the National Institute on Drug Abuse. In 1999, "an expert committee of the Institute of Medicine expressed concern about the adverse health effects of smoking marijuana, particularly on the respiratory tract," and "called for expanded research." Susan Okie, *Medical Marijuana and the Supreme Court*, 353 NEJM 648 (2005).

2. How far apart are the majority and the dissent in *Raich*?

(c) *The Controlled Substances Act and Assisted Suicide*

OREGON v. ASHCROFT
368 F3d 1118 (Ninth Circuit 2004)

Tallman, Circuit Judge . . . .

II

The CSA [the Controlled Substances Act] originally provided automatic federal registration for state-licensed health-care practitioners. The Attorney General could revoke a practitioner's federal registration only if the practitioner falsified his or her registration application, was convicted of a felony related to a controlled substance, or had his or her state license suspended or revoked.

In 1971, pursuant to his authority to issue rules regulating controlled substances under the CSA, then Attorney General John Mitchell promulgated the following regulation:

> A prescription for a controlled substance to be effective must be issued for a legitimate medical purpose by an individual practitioner acting in the usual course of his professional practice.... An order purporting to be a prescription issued not in the usual course of professional treatment ... is not a prescription within the meaning and intent of ... the Act . . . .

In 1984, Congress amended the CSA to give broader authority to the Attorney General. [The court here describes 21 USC §823(f), which we reprinted at the beginning of subsection 2.] . . . Although this provision gives the Attorney General new discretion over the registration of health care practitioners, Congress explained that "the amendment would continue to give deference to the opinions of State licencing authorities, since their recommendations are the first of the factors to be considered[.]" S.Rep. No. 98-225, at 267 (1984) . . . .

Oregon's Death With Dignity Act authorizes physicians to prescribe lethal doses of controlled substances to terminally ill Oregon residents according to procedures designed to protect vulnerable patients and ensure that their decisions are reasoned and voluntary. Oregon voters reaffirmed their support for the Death With Dignity Act on November 4, 1997, by defeating a ballot measure that sought to repeal the law. . . . .

On November 9, 2001, newly appointed Attorney General John Ashcroft reversed the position of his predecessor and issued the Directive at issue here. [66 Fed.Reg. 56,607.] The Ashcroft Directive proclaims that physician assisted suicide serves no "legitimate medical purpose" under 21 C.F.R. § 1306.04 and that specific conduct authorized by Oregon's Death With Dignity Act "may 'render [a practitioner's] registration ... inconsistent with the public interest' and therefore subject to possible suspension or revocation. The Directive specifically targets health care practitioners in Oregon and instructs the DEA to enforce this determination "regardless of whether state law authorizes or permits such conduct by practitioners." . . .

III . . . .

A

We begin with instructions from the Supreme Court that the "earnest and profound debate about the morality, legality, and practicality of physician-assisted suicide" belongs among state lawmakers. *Washington v. Glucksberg.* In *Glucksberg*, Justice O'Connor emphasized that "[s]tates are presently undertaking extensive and serious evaluation of physician-assisted suicide.... In such circumstances, the ... challenging task of crafting appropriate procedures for safeguarding ... liberty interests is entrusted to the 'laboratory' of the States ... in the first instance." (O'Connor, J., concurring); *cf. Cruzan v. Director* (Scalia, J., concurring) ("[W]hen it *is* demonstrated ... that a patient no longer wishes certain measures to be taken to preserve his or her life, it is up to the citizens[of the States] to decide, through their elected representatives, whether that wish will be honored."). Here, Oregon voters have twice declared their support for the legalization of physician assisted suicide in their state. We disagree with the dissent's suggestion that this court, rather than the Attorney General, is interfering with the democratic process. *See Glucksberg* ("Our holding permits this debate[about physician assisted suicide] to continue, as it should in a democratic society."). . . .

The principle that state governments bear the primary responsibility for evaluating physician assisted suicide follows from our concept of federalism, which requires that state lawmakers, not the federal government, are "the primary regulators of professional [medical] conduct." *Conant v. Walters*, 309 F.3d 629, 639 (9th Cir.2002) . . . . The Supreme Court has made the constitutional principle clear: "Obviously, direct control of medical practice in the states is beyond the power of the federal government." *Linder v. United States,* 268 U.S. 5, 18 (1925); *see also Barsky v. Bd. of*

Regents, 347 U.S. 442 (1954) ("It is elemental that a state has broad power to establish and enforce standards of conduct within its borders relative to the health of everyone there. It is a vital part of a state's police power."). The Attorney General "may not ... regulate [the doctor-patient] relationship to advance federal policy." *Conant,* 309 F.3d at 647 (Kozinski, J., concurring). . . .

Unless Congress' authorization is "unmistakably clear," the Attorney General may not exercise control over an area of law traditionally reserved for state authority, such as regulation of medical care. *Gregory v. Ashcroft, 501 U.S. 452, 460-61.* In divining congressional intent, it is a "cardinal principle" of statutory interpretation that "where an otherwise acceptable construction of a statute would raise serious constitutional problems, [federal courts shall] construe the statute to avoid such problems unless such construction is plainly contrary to the intent of Congress."

The Ashcroft Directive is invalid because Congress has provided no indication--much less an "unmistakably clear" indication--that it intended to authorize the Attorney General to regulate the practice of physician assisted suicide. By attempting to regulate physician assisted suicide, the Ashcroft Directive invokes the outer limits of Congress' power by encroaching on state authority to regulate medical practice. *See Conant,* 309 F.3d at 639. Because Congress has not clearly authorized such an intrusion, the Ashcroft Directive violates the clear statement rule. *See Solid Waste Agency,* 531 U.S. at 172-73. We need not, and therefore do not, decide whether the Ashcroft Directive actually exceeds Commerce Clause boundaries, but only that it "invokes the outer limits of Congress' power" without explicit authority from Congress.

B

The Ashcroft Directive not only lacks clear congressional authority, it also violates the plain language of the CSA. . . .

The CSA expressly limits federal authority under the Act to the "field of drug abuse." 21 U.S.C. § 801(2)-(6). Contrary to the Attorney General's characterization, physician assisted suicide is not a form of drug "abuse" that Congress intended the CSA to cover. . . .

We know that Congress intended to limit federal authority under the CSA to the field of drug abuse because the statute's non-preemption clause provides that the CSA shall be not be construed to preempt state law unless there is a "positive conflict" between the text of the statute and state law. 21 U.S.C. § 903. No provision of the CSA directly conflicts with Oregon's Death with Dignity Act. . . .

To the limited extent that the CSA does authorize federal regulation of medical practice, Congress carefully circumscribed the Attorney General's role. The Attorney General may not define the scope of legitimate medical practice. In [*U.S.*] *v. Moore,* the Supreme Court held that the CSA "requires" the Secretary of Health and Human Services "to determine the appropriate methods of professional practice" under the statute. 423 U.S. 122, 144 (1975). . . .

The Attorney General reasons that physician assisted suicide is inconsistent with the public interest because the practice threatens public health. Although threat to public health is one factor the Attorney General is to consider when determining the public interest, in this case he does not consider the other factors required by the statute.

The Attorney General misreads the CSA when he concludes that he may evaluate the public interest "based on *any* of the five factors identified in the statute." The CSA clearly provides that all five public interest factors "*shall* be considered." 21 U.S.C. § 823(f) (emphasis added). When the Attorney General declares that his Directive shall apply "regardless of whether state law authorizes or permits such conduct," he ignores the very first factor he is required to consider under the Act--*i.e.* "[t]he recommendation of the appropriate State licensing board or professional disciplinary authority." The Attorney General's categorical prohibition of physician assisted suicide also fails to consider the second and third public interest factors required under the CSA. . . .

C

The CSA's legislative record confirms that the Attorney General has exceeded the scope of his authority. . . .

Congress clearly intended to limit the CSA to problems associated with drug abuse and addiction. *See, e.g.,* H.R.Rep. No. 91-1444, 1970 U.S.C.C.A.N. at 4566; 116 Cong. Rec. 977-78 (Comments of Sen. Dodd, Jan. 23, 1970) ("[I]t cannot be overemphasized that the ... [CSA] is designed to crackdown hard on the narcotics pusher and the illegal diverters of pep pills and goof balls."). As we held in *Rosenberg,* "Congress was concerned with the diversion of drugs out of legitimate channels of distribution" when it enacted the CSA. 515 F.2d at 193. . . .

Furthermore, recognizing that this mandate may at times encroach on a state's traditional authority to regulate medical practices, Congress empowered "the principal health agency of the federal government," not the Attorney General, to make medical decisions under the Act. *See* H.R.Rep. No. 91-1444, 1970 U.S.C.C.A.N. at 4581 ("[T]he committee is concerned about the appropriateness of having federal officials determine the appropriate method of the practice of medicine. ... In view of this situation, this section will provide guidelines, determined by the principal health agency of the federal government[.]"). In *Moore,* the Court observed that "Congress pointed out that criminal prosecutions *in the past* had turned on the opinions of federal prosecutors. Under the [CSA], those physicians who comply with the recommendations *made by the Secretary* [of Health and Human Services] will no longer jeopardize their professional careers[.]"

In 1974, Congress amended the CSA to "cure the present difficulty in [resolving] ... the intricate and nearly impossible burden of establishing what is beyond the 'course of professional practice' for criminal law purposes." *Moore,* 423 U.S. at 140, n. 16. Although only tangentially related to this case, the 1974 amendment is noteworthy because it evinces Congress's intent to "preserve[ ] the distinctions found in the Controlled Substances Act between the functions of the Attorney General and the Secretary[of Health and Human Services].... *All decisions of a medical nature are to be made by the Secretary [of Health and Human Services].* Law enforcement decisions respecting the security of stocks of narcotic drugs and the maintenance of records on such drugs are to be made by the Attorney General." H.R.Rep. No. 93-884 (1974) (emphasis added).

Congress did not intend to expand the scope or general purpose of the CSA when it amended the statute in 1984 to give the Attorney General authority to revoke the federal registrations of physicians and pharmacists. *See* S.Rep. No. 98- 225 at 260, 261-62 ("In particular, the amendments ... are intended to address the severe problem of diversion of drugs of legitimate origin into the illicit market."). . . . By enacting the 1984 amendments, Congress merely intended to close "loop-holes" in the original legislation by authorizing the Attorney General to revoke physician registrations without depending on state licencing boards, which had proven ineffective regulators of physicians who were diverting drugs into the illicit market. . . .

The petitions for review are GRANTED. The injunction previously entered by the district court is ORDERED continued in full force and effect as the injunction of this court.

WALLACE, Senior Circuit Judge, dissenting:

As my colleagues in the majority suggest, this case is not about the ethics or public policy implications of physician-assisted suicide. We need not decide whether the federal government or the states is better equipped to regulate physician-assisted suicide. . . . [T]his case involves a single legal question: is the Attorney General's interpretation of 21 C.F.R. § 1306.04(a) entitled to deference? . . .

II. . . .

B.

The Petitioners . . . contend that the Ashcroft Directive violates 21 U.S.C. § 903, the Controlled Substances Act's non-preemption clause. Section 903 reads:

> No provision of this subchapter shall be construed as indicating an intent on the part of the Congress to occupy the field in which that provision operates ... to the exclusion of any State law on the same subject matter which would otherwise be within the authority of

the State, unless there is a positive conflict between that provision of this subchapter and that State law so that the two cannot consistently stand together.

21 U.S.C. § 903. The Petitioners argue that the Ashcroft Directive construes the Controlled Substances Act to preempt the Oregon Act and that this result violates 21 U.S.C. § 903 because there is no "positive conflict" between the Controlled Substances Act's text and the Oregon Act.

Petitioners are wrong; the Ashcroft Directive is consistent with section 903 because it does not utterly exclude state regulation of medical practice or even state regulation of physician-assisted suicide. The Ashcroft Directive does not effect a "positive conflict" with state law because it does not make "the federal role ... so pervasive that no room is left for the states to supplement it." *Sayles Hydro Assocs. v. Maughan,* 985 F.2d 451, 455 (9th Cir.1993). States may supplement the Ashcroft Directive by expanding the Controlled Substances Act's prohibitions, providing additional civil or criminal sanctions against physicians who assist suicide, or permitting conduct that the Ashcroft Directive does not prohibit.

More relevant for present purposes, the Ashcroft Directive proscribes only one method of assisting suicide: prescription, dispensation, and administration of controlled substances. The majority vastly exaggerates the Ashcroft Directive's scope by intimating that it "ban[s] physician-assisted suicide outright." A closer examination of the Ashcroft Directive's text reveals that "[assisting] suicide is not a 'legitimate medical purpose' " only "*within the meaning of 21 C.F.R. § 1306.04* " (prescription of controlled substances). Ashcroft Directive, 66 Fed.Reg. at 56,608 (emphasis added). The Ashcroft Directive avoids the sweeping prohibition claimed by the majority by assiduously limiting its reach to controlled substances; under its plain terms, only applications involving *controlled substances* may "render [a physician's] registration ... inconsistent with the public interest" and therefore subject to revocation. *Id., quoting* 21 U.S.C. § 824(a)(4). Oregon physicians may continue to assist suicide by other means without risking suspension or revocation of their registration to prescribe controlled substances. The Ashcroft Directive does not, therefore, "occupy the field" of physician-assisted suicide in violation of section 903

C.

Petitioners maintain--and the majority agrees--that the Ashcroft Directive is not entitled to deference because the Attorney General promulgated it "in excess of statutory jurisdiction, authority, or limitations, or short of statutory right."

1.

The Ashcroft Directive is not entitled to deference, the majority contends, because "Congress intended to limit federal authority under the [Controlled Substances Act] to the field of drug abuse" while preserving states' discretion to authorize other life-threatening applications of controlled substances. By what authority? True, the Controlled Substances Act's preamble arguably manifests Congress's intent "to strengthen existing law enforcement authority in the field of drug abuse," Comprehensive Drug Abuse Prevention and Control Act of 1970, Pub.L. No. 91-513, pmbl., 84 Stat. 1236, 1236, but it does not "expressly limit[ ] federal authority under the Act" to mainstream drug abuse, as the majority argues. Moreover, there is simply no textual support for the majority's conclusory assertion that "the field of drug abuse," as discussed in the Controlled Substances Act, does not encompass drug-induced, physician-assisted suicide.

The Controlled Substances Act's text furnishes ample evidence that Congress was concerned not only with street-variety drug trafficking and abuse but also with any other improper drug use that might have a "detrimental effect on the health and general welfare of the American people." 21 U.S.C. § 801(2). The Act targets all "improper use of controlled substances," *id.,* and gives the Attorney General discretion to decide whether registering a physician to dispense drugs is "consistent with the public health and safety," *id.* § 823(b)(5). Reasonable minds might disagree as to whether physician-assisted suicide constitutes an "improper use" of a controlled substance, but nothing in the Controlled Substances Act's text precludes its application to physician-assisted suicide.

Lacking a textual hook for its position, the majority attempts to patch the holes in its argument with inconclusive fragments of legislative history. Discerning congressional intent from legislative history is a speculative enterprise under the best of circumstances, and the risk of error is compounded in a case such as this when legislators' published statements do not squarely address the question presented-i.e., whether Congress intended to exclude drug-induced, physician-assisted suicide from regulation under the Controlled Substances Act. *See Chisom v. Roemer,* 501 U.S. 380, 406 (1991) (Scalia, J., dissenting) ("We are here to apply the statute, not legislative history, and certainly not the absence of legislative history.").

The Controlled Substances Act's legislative history suggests that some members of Congress envisioned the physician-registration provisions primarily as a mechanism to stem the flow of controlled substances into illicit channels, *Moore,* 423 U.S. at 135, but the record also specifically identifies "suicides and attempted suicides" as a "[m]isuse of a drug." H.R. REP. NO. 91-1444 (1970). Viewed holistically, the record "does not demonstrate a clear and certain congressional intent" to preclude physician-assisted suicide from regulation under sections 823 and 824. . . .

2.

The majority asserts that the Attorney General lacks authority to decide whether physician-assisted suicide is consistent with "the public interest" and a "legitimate medical practice" under the Controlled Substances Act and its implementing regulations because Congress intended to preserve the states' traditional authority to make these determinations. This argument ignores the Controlled Substances Act's text and controlling Supreme Court decisions. . . .

State law may be *relevant* to certain provisions of the Controlled Substances Act, *see, e.g.,* 21 U.S.C. § 823(f) (instructing the Attorney General to consider state-law violations when deciding whether a physician's registration would be contrary to the public interest), but nothing in the Controlled Substances Act plainly evinces a congressional intent to define "the public interest" solely according to state law. On the contrary, section 823 instructs the Attorney General to identify acts "inconsistent with the public interest" by reference to a variety of sources, including a physician's federal conviction record, compliance with "Federal ... laws relating to controlled substances," and "other conduct which may threaten public health and safety." . . .

The majority also cites *Washington v. Glucksberg* (O'Connor, J., concurring), for the position that the Attorney General must defer to the Oregon Act because "[p]hysician-assisted suicide is an unrelated, general medical practice to be regulated by the States in the first instance." *Glucksberg,* however, addressed states' authority to *prohibit* physician-assisted suicide *in the absence of federal regulation;* the case did not answer the question whether Congress may exercise its Commerce Clause power to deny physicians access to controlled substances for physician-assisted suicide. Rather than place federalism limitations on the federal government's authority to restrict physician-assisted suicide, Justice O'Connor's concurring opinion stressed that "[t]here is no reason to think the democratic process will not strike the proper balance between the interests of terminally ill ... individuals ... and the State's interests in protecting those who might seek to end life mistakenly or under pressure." Simply put, courts should defer to the political process instead of interposing hasty constitutional constraints.

Glucksberg does not require the Attorney General to interpret the Controlled Substances Act and its implementing regulations according to state standards of professional conduct. Rather, the Supreme Court's decision stands for the broader proposition that federal courts generally should keep their distance, allowing the political process to decide whether and how to regulate physician-assisted suicide. The majority's shortsighted decision to declare the Ashcroft Directive invalid has precisely the opposite effect.

3.

As an alternative, the majority contends that the Secretary of Health and Human Services (Secretary)--not the Attorney General--should decide whether medical practices are "legitimate" and consistent with the "public interest" under the Controlled Substances Act and its implementing regulations. The Controlled Substances Act's text directly contradicts this argument: "*The Attorney General* may deny an application for ... registration [of a practitioner to dispense drugs] if *he determines* that the issuance of such registration would be inconsistent with the public interest." 21 U.S.C. § 823(f) (emphasis added). Congress could not have stated more plainly that the Attorney General, not the Secretary, has authority to determine whether a physician's registration is consistent with the public interest.

The majority's reading of section 823 is a particularly astonishing exercise in statutory construction because the Controlled Substances Act specifically provides for the Secretary's participation in other discretionary judgments. *See, e.g.,* 21 U.S.C. § 811(b) (providing that the Secretary's determination with respect to the classification of controlled substances "shall be binding on the Attorney General"); *id.* § 823(f) (authorizing the Secretary to evaluate a practitioner's "qualifications and competency" to perform "research with controlled substances"); *id.* (stating that the Secretary "shall consult with the Attorney General as to effective procedures to adequately safeguard against diversion of ... controlled substances from legitimate medical or scientific use"); *id.* § 823(g)(2)(H)(i) (empowering the Secretary to "issue regulations ... or issue practice guidelines" for the approval of "additional credentialing bodies"). When Congress wished to entrust a discretionary judgment to the Secretary it said so explicitly. The Controlled Substances Act conspicuously omits any reference to the Secretary, however, when discussing the Attorney General's authority to assess "the public interest" for purposes of ordinary physician registrations. *Id.* § 823(f). The explanation for this omission is perfectly clear: section 823 authorizes the Attorney General--not the Secretary--to decide whether a physician's registration is consistent with the public interest.

The majority asserts that under the Controlled Substance Act all standards of legitimate professional conduct are set by the Secretary, not by the Attorney General. The majority's argument relies on a section of the Act entitled "Medical Treatment of Narcotic Addiction," which is located in a different title of the legislation. This section provides that the Secretary, "after consultation with the Attorney General ..., shall determine the appropriate methods of professional practice in the medical treatment of ... *narcotic addiction.*" 42 U.S.C. § 290bb 2a (emphasis added). Obviously, this is irrelevant to the issue before us. Yet from this narrow provision, the majority draws the sweeping, untenable conclusion that the Attorney General cannot enforce the Controlled Substances Act against a physician unless the Secretary first concludes that the prescription did not issue for a "legitimate medical purpose."

The Supreme Court rejected a similar challenge to the Attorney General's interpretive authority in *Moore.* The Court explained that Congress designed subsection 290bb 2a to function only as a limited safe-harbor for physicians who prescribe controlled substances to drug addicts; as long as physicians employ the treatment methods outlined in the Secretary's published standards of professional practice, the Attorney General may not prosecute them under the Controlled Substances Act. The Court recognized, however, that "[t]he negative implication [of this provision] is that physicians who go beyond approved practice remain subject to serious criminal penalties." In other words, section 290bb-2a prevents the Attorney General from enforcing the Controlled Substances Act and its implementing regulations only when the Secretary declares that a specific *narcotic addiction treatment* serves a "legitimate medical purpose." . . .

4. . . .

Contrary to the majority's assertion, the Ashcroft Directive does not sidestep subsection 823(f)'s five-factor inquiry. The Justice Department has yet to initiate an enforcement action against any individual physician pursuant to section 824, so the hour has not arrived for the Attorney General to consider subsections 823(f)(1)-(4) (i.e., the state licensing board's recommendation and physicians' relevant experience and criminal record). The Ashcroft Directive merely cautions that a physician who prescribes controlled substances to assist suicide "*may* 'render his registration ... inconsistent with the public interest'"; it does not declare that assisting suicide *shall* render a physician's registration inconsistent with the public interest. This word choice is significant, because it conclusively refutes the majority's contention that assisting suicide *automatically* renders a physician's registration "inconsistent with the public interest" under the Ashcroft Directive. Even if "assisting suicide is not a 'legitimate medical purpose' within the meaning of 21 C.F.R. § 1306.04 (2001)," the Attorney General remains free to consult all of section 823's five factors--including the recommendation of Oregon's licensing board or disciplinary authority--before making a final decision whether to suspend or revoke a particular physician's registration.

Significantly, the Ashcroft Directive's warning that assisting suicide could prompt Controlled Substances Act enforcement actions comports with fundamental administrative law principles:

> When a governmental official is given the power to make discretionary decisions under a broad statutory standard [e.g., "the public interest"], case-by-case

> decisionmaking may not be the best way to assure fairness. Here the [Attorney General] ... sought to define the statutory standard ... by the use of his rulemaking authority. The decision to use objective rules in this case provides [physicians] with more precise notice of what conduct will be sanctioned and promotes equality of treatment among similarly situated [individuals].

Dixon v. Love, 431 U.S. 105, 115 (1977). The Controlled Substances Act facilitates adherence to these principles by expressly authorizing the Attorney General to "promulgate and enforce any rules, regulations, and procedures which he may deem necessary and appropriate for the efficient execution of his functions under this subchapter." Thus, General Ashcroft acted well within the scope of his statutory authority in declaring that assisting suicide does not serve a "legitimate medical purpose" under 21 C.F.R. § 1306.04(a) and that this practice "may 'render [a physician's] registration ... inconsistent with the public interest' and therefore subject to possible suspension or revocation under [section] 824."

5.

Finally, the majority argues that the Ashcroft Directive exceeds the Attorney General's statutory authority because Congress has not clearly authorized the Attorney General to upset the delicate balance between federal regulation of controlled substances and state control of medical practices. As support for this conclusion, the majority invokes the Supreme Court's recent analysis in *Solid Waste Agency of Northern Cook County v. U.S. Army Corps of Engineers,* 531 U.S. 159 (2001):

> Where an administrative interpretation of a statute invokes the outer limits of Congress' power, we expect a clear indication that Congress intended that result. This requirement stems from our prudential desire not to needlessly reach constitutional issues and our assumption that Congress does not casually authorize administrative agencies to interpret a statute to push the limit of congressional authority. This concern is heightened where the administrative interpretation alters the federal-state framework by permitting federal encroachment upon a traditional state power.

Although the Court addressed the validity of "an administrative interpretation of a *statute*," its reasoning should apply equally to an administrative interpretation of an agency regulation. . . .

Not every colorable constitutional question triggers *Solid Waste's* clear statement rule. Our past decisions dictate that we must "scrutinize constitutional objections to [the] agency interpretation skeptically. Only if the agency's proffered interpretation raises *serious* constitutional concerns may [we] refuse to defer...." *Williams v. Babbitt,* 115 F.3d 657, 662 (9th Cir.1997). . . . Only if the Attorney General's proposed interpretation would likely render the statute unconstitutional do we apply *Solid Waste's* clear statement canon. Applying these principles, we should not require a clear statement in this case because controlling precedent compels the conclusion that the Attorney General's interpretation did not invoke "the outer limits" of Congress's Commerce Clause power. . . .

Turning to the specific issue raised here--whether the prescription or dispensation of controlled substances to assist suicide substantially affects interstate commerce--we base our assessment on four factors:

> 1) whether the statute in question regulates commerce or any sort of economic enterprise; 2) whether the statute contains any express jurisdictional element which might limit its reach to a discrete set of cases; 3) whether the statute or its legislative history contains express congressional findings that the regulated activity affects interstate commerce; and 4) whether the link between the regulated activity and a substantial effect on interstate commerce is attenuated.

United States v. McCoy, 323 F3d. 1114, 1119 (9th Cir. 2003). Of these four factors, the first and last are most important.

The Ashcroft Directive clearly satisfies *McCoy's* first and the last criteria. The Ashcroft Directive regulates economic transactions: physicians generally prescribe and dispense controlled substances for a fee. . . . Here Congress naturally and directly reduces the amount of a controlled substance that flows through the interstate channels when it prohibits the substance's distribution for a particular use. Thus, the link between drug prescriptions and interstate commerce is sufficiently direct and substantial even if the drugs ultimately are used in intrastate activities such as physician-assisted suicide and the activities' disaggregated effect on interstate commerce is small.

Because the Ashcroft Directive satisfies *McCoy's* first and last factors, we need not consider whether it meets the other, less important ones. . . .

The majority cannot have it otherwise. Their argument that "*direct* control of medical practice in the states is beyond the power of the federal government" misses the point. Unless and until the Supreme Court directs us differently, our opinions and other binding precedent compel the conclusion that Congress acts comfortably within its Commerce Clause power when it regulates the prescription and dispensation of controlled substances. General Ashcroft's interpretation of 21 C.F.R. § 1306.04(a) does not, therefore, "invoke [ ] the outer limits of Congress' power," the clear statement rule does not apply, and we must evaluate the Ashcroft Directive according to ordinary standards of deference.

D.

The Petitioners contend that the Ashcroft Directive constitutes an arbitrary and capricious interpretation of section 1306.04(a)'s "legitimate medical practice" requirement. General Ashcroft's determination is arbitrary and capricious, they argue, because he failed to examine the "wealth" of substantive data documenting the Oregon Act's effect on public health and safety. They point to a collection of studies which indicate that the Oregon Act's procedures have not been used disproportionately by the poor, uneducated, or uninsured. . . .

General Ashcroft had before him a single question: whether physician-assisted suicide is a "legitimate medical purpose" as defined in existing case law, federal policy, general state law, and medical opinion. Evidence that Oregon physicians used the Oregon Act's procedures disproportionally against the poor, uneducated, or uninsured could have strengthened his conclusion that physician-assisted suicide is not a "legitimate medical purpose," but it does not follow that the absence of such evidence means physician-assisted suicide is a "legitimate medical practice." . . .

Furthermore, Petitioners' assertion that General Ashcroft "entirely failed to consider" Oregon's position on the social benefits of physician-assisted suicide is plainly false. The Attorney General based his decision on a memorandum from the Office of Legal Counsel, which considered, but rejected, Oregon's position in favor of existing case law, federal policies and practices, the majority state position, and the dominant views of the American medical and nursing professions. Thus, Petitioners have not shown that General Ashcroft's decision to reject the Oregon Act's permissive approach to physician-assisted suicide was "arbitrary, capricious, an abuse of discretion, or otherwise not in accordance with law."

III.

If the Ashcroft Directive interprets an agency regulation, rather than the Controlled Substances Act itself, we must accord it "substantial deference." . . .

In my view, the Ashcroft Directive constitutes an interpretation of a regulation rather than a statutory interpretation. The Ashcroft Directive's single interpretive act is to "determine that assisting suicide is not a 'legitimate medical purpose' within the meaning of 21 C.F.R. § 1306.04 (2001)." . . .

Applying the *Thomas Jefferson* standard, I have no trouble upholding the Ashcroft Directive from Petitioners' attack. As the Office of Legal Counsel concluded:

> [T]he overwhelming weight of authority in judicial decisions, the past and present policies of nearly all of the States and of the Federal Government, and the clear, firm and unequivocal views of the leading associations within the American medical and nursing professions, establish that assisting in suicide is not an activity undertaken in the course of professional medical practice and is not a legitimate medical purpose. Indeed, we think it fair to say that physician-assisted suicide should not be considered a *medical* procedure at all.... It is plainly a fallacy to assume that a procedure must be "medical" because it is performed by a physician rather than, say, by a family member, or

because it involves the use of a drug that a physician has prescribed.

In *Glucksberg,* the Supreme Court offered a similar assessment . . . . Therefore, I would defer to the Ashcroft Directive's conclusion that physician-assisted suicide is not a "legitimate medical practice" under 21 C.F.R. § 1306.04(a) . . . .

Notes and Questions on Gonzales v. Oregon

1. At the time this supplement was written, the Supreme Court had agreed to hear what became (with the appointment of a new Attorney General) *Gonzales v. Oregon.* It had also handed down its opinion in *Gonzales v. Raich.* How does the latter case affect the arguments the Ninth Circuit made in *Oregon v. Ashcroft?*

Chapter 4

DECIDING FOR OTHERS: AUTONOMY OR BENEFICENCE?

SECTION 2. FORMERLY COMPETENT PATIENTS: WHO SHOULD DECIDE? WHAT STANDARDS SHOULD GOVERN?

Add at p. 525, following *Conservatorship of Wendland:*

In re GUARDIANSHIP OF Theresa Marie SCHIAVO, Incapacitated.
851 So.2d 182 (Fla. Dist. Ct. App., 2003)

ALTENBERND, CHIEF JUDGE.

Robert and Mary Schindler appeal the guardianship court's order denying their motion for relief from a judgment that ordered their daughter's guardian to withdraw life-prolonging procedures. We have carefully reviewed all aspects of the record on appeal. We conclude that the guardianship court complied with the instructions provided by this court in its last opinion. The guardianship court did not abuse its discretion in denying the motion for relief from judgment. Its ruling is supported by competent, substantial evidence and accords with the law of this state. Accordingly, we affirm the order on appeal.

I.

This is the fourth time that this court has reviewed an order from the guardianship court in this controversy. This case has a long and difficult history, which we will not detail in this opinion. As we explained in our last opinion, *Schiavo III*:

> In Schiavo I, we affirmed the trial court's decision ordering Mrs. Schiavo's guardian to withdraw life-prolonging procedures. In so doing, we affirmed the trial court's rulings that (1) Mrs. Schiavo's medical condition was the type of end-stage condition that permits the withdrawal of life-prolonging procedures, (2) she did not have a reasonable medical probability of recovering capacity so that she could make her own decision to maintain or withdraw life-prolonging procedures, (3) the trial court had the authority to make such a

decision when a conflict within the family prevented a qualified person from effectively exercising the responsibilities of a proxy, and (4) clear and convincing evidence at the time of trial supported a determination that Mrs. Schiavo would have chosen in February 2000 to withdraw the life-prolonging procedures.

. . . In *Schiavo III*, we held that the guardianship court must conduct an evidentiary hearing on the motion, limited to the fourth issue. . . . [Our opinion reflected the fact that the Schindlers had presented an medical affidavit alleging that there a potential new treatment for Schiavo's condition].

On remand, we permitted the parents to present evidence to establish by a preponderance of the evidence that the judgment was no longer equitable [because a] "new treatment offers sufficient promise of increased cognitive function in Mrs. Schiavo's cerebral cortex-- significantly improving the quality of Mrs. Schiavo's life--so that she herself would elect to undergo this treatment and would reverse the prior decision to withdraw life-prolonging procedures."

In order to minimize disputes between the parties, [w]e required an additional set of medical examinations of Theresa Schiavo and the selection of no more than five physicians to provide expert testimony on the issue presented. We instructed that one of the five physicians must be a new, independent physician selected either by the agreement of the parties or, if they could not agree, by the appointment of the guardianship court. We indicated that this physician should be board certified in neurology or neurosurgery, with expertise if possible "in the treatment of brain damage and in the diagnosis and treatment of persistent vegetative state."

On remand, the parents provided testimony from Dr. William Maxfield, a board-certified physician in radiology and nuclear medicine, and Dr. William Hammesfahr, a board-certified neurologist. Michael Schiavo, Mrs. Schiavo's husband and guardian, selected Dr. Ronald Cranford and Dr. Melvin Greer, both board-certified neurologists, to testify. The fifth physician, selected by the guardianship court when the parties could not agree, was Dr. Peter Bambakidis, a board-certified neurologist practicing in the Department of Neurology at the Cleveland Clinic Foundation in Cleveland, Ohio. He is a clinical professor of neurology at Case Western Reserve University. His credentials fulfilled the requirements of our prior opinion.

Through the assistance of Mrs. Schiavo's treating physician, Dr. Victor Gambone, the physicians obtained current medical information about Theresa Schiavo including high-quality brain scans. Each physician reviewed her medical records and personally conducted a neurological examination of Mrs. Schiavo. Lengthy videotapes of some of the medical examinations were created and introduced into evidence. Thus, the quality of the evidence presented to the guardianship court was very high, and each side had ample opportunity to present detailed medical evidence, all of which was subjected to thorough cross-examination. It is likely that no guardianship court has ever received as much high-quality medical evidence in such a proceeding.

On the issue that caused this court to reverse in our last decision, whether new treatment exists which offers such promise of increased cognitive function in Mrs. Schiavo's cerebral cortex that she herself would elect to undergo this treatment and would reverse the prior decision to withdraw life-prolonging procedures, the parents presented little testimony. Dr. William Hammesfahr claimed that vasodilation therapy and hyberbaric therapy "could help her improve." He could not testify that any "specific function" would improve. He did not claim that he could restore her cognitive functions. He admitted that vasodilation therapy and hyberbaric therapy were intended to increase blood and oxygen supply to damaged brain tissue to facilitate repair of such tissue. These therapies cannot replace dead tissue. Although the physicians are not in complete agreement concerning the extent of Mrs. Schiavo's brain damage, they all agree that the brain scans show extensive permanent damage to her brain. The only debate between the doctors is whether she has a small amount of isolated living tissue in her cerebral cortex or whether she has no living tissue in her cerebral cortex.

The evidentiary hearing held on remand actually focused on an issue that was not the issue we anticipated would be the primary issue on remand. The parents contended that Mrs. Schiavo was not in a persistent or permanent vegetative state. Both Dr. Maxfield and Dr. Hammesfahr opined that she was not in such a state. They based their opinions primarily upon their assessment of Mrs. Schiavo's actions or responses to a few brief stimuli, primarily involving physical and verbal contact with her mother. The three other physicians all testified that Mrs. Schiavo was in a permanent or persistent vegetative state. The guardianship court was most impressed with the testimony of Dr. Bambakidis, who concluded that Mrs. Schiavo remained in a permanent vegetative state. The guardianship court determined that Mrs. Schiavo remained in a permanent vegetative state. The guardianship court concluded that there was no evidence of a treatment in existence that offered such promise of increased cognitive function in Mrs. Schiavo's cerebral cortex that she herself would elect to undergo it at this time. Having concluded that the parents had failed to meet their burden to establish, by a preponderance of evidence, that the judgment was no longer equitable, the guardianship court denied the motion for relief from judgment and rescheduled the removal of the hydration and nutrition tube. When the parents appealed that order, the guardianship court stayed the removal of the nutrition and hydration tube pending review by this court.

II.

. . . A trial court has broad discretion in determining whether to grant relief from a judgment. An appellate court reviews that decision to determine whether the trial court abused its discretion. In this case, the guardianship court followed the instructions in our last decision. It conducted a thorough hearing and prepared an extensive order. We cannot conclude that the guardianship court abused its discretion when it denied the motion.

The Schindlers have urged this court to conduct a de novo review of the evidence in this case, primarily because of the finality of this decision for their daughter. . . . Despite our decision that the appropriate standard of review is abuse of discretion, this court has closely examined all of the evidence in this record. We have repeatedly examined the videotapes, not merely watching short segments but carefully observing the tapes in their entirety. We have examined the brain scans with the eyes of educated laypersons and considered the explanations provided by the doctors in the transcripts. We have concluded that, if we were called upon to review the guardianship court's decision de novo, we would still affirm it. . . . From our review of the videotapes of Mrs. Schiavo, despite the irrefutable evidence that her cerebral cortex has sustained the most severe of irreparable injuries, we understand why a parent who had raised and nurtured a child from conception would hold out hope that some level of cognitive function remained. If Mrs. Schiavo were our own daughter, we could not but hold to such a faith. But in the end, this case is not about the aspirations that loving parents have for their children. It is about Theresa Schiavo's right to make her own decision, independent of her parents and independent of her husband. In circumstances such as these, when families cannot agree, the law has opened the doors of the circuit courts to permit trial judges to serve as surrogates or proxies to make decisions about life-prolonging procedures. It is the trial judge's duty not to make the decision that the judge would make for himself or herself or for a loved one. Instead, the trial judge must make a decision that the clear and convincing evidence shows the ward would have made for herself. It is a thankless task, and one to be undertaken with care, objectivity, and a cautious legal standard designed to promote the value of life. But it is also a necessary function if all people are to be entitled to a personalized decision about life-prolonging procedures independent of the subjective and conflicting assessments of their friends and relatives. It may be unfortunate that when families cannot agree, the best forum we can offer for this private, personal decision is a public courtroom and the best decision-maker we can provide is a judge with no prior knowledge of the ward, but the law currently provides no better solution that adequately protects the interests of promoting the value of life. We have previously affirmed the guardianship court's decision in this regard, and we now affirm the denial of a motion for relief from that judgment.

At the conclusion of our first opinion, we stated:

> In the final analysis, the difficult question that faced the trial court was whether Theresa Marie Schindler Schiavo, not after a ew weeks in a coma, but after ten years in a persistent vegetative state that has robbed her of most of her cerebrum and all but the most instinctive of neurological functions, with no hope of a medical cure but with sufficient money and strength of body to live indefinitely, would choose to continue the constant nursing care and the supporting tubes in hopes that a miracle would somehow recreate her missing brain tissue, or whether she would wish to permit a natural death process to take its course and for her family members and loved ones to be free to continue their lives. After due consideration, we conclude that the trial judge had clear and convincing evidence to answer this question as he did.

Nothing in these proceedings has changed this conclusion. The extensive additional medical testimony in this record only confirms once again the guardianship court's initial decision. On remand, following the issuance of our mandate, the guardianship court should schedule another hearing solely for the purpose of entering a new order scheduling the removal of the nutrition and hydration tube.

Affirmed.

Notes and Questions

1. The trial court made these findings about the various treatments described by the Schindlers' experts:

> Dr. Hammesfahr feels his vasodilatation therapy will have a positive affect on Terry Schiavo. Drs. Greer, Bambakidis and Cranford do not feel it will have such an affect. It is clear that this therapy is not recognized in the medical community. Dr. Hammesfahr operates his clinic on a cash basis in advance which made the discussion regarding Medicare eligibility quite irrelevant. A lot of the time also was spent regarding his nominations for a Nobel Prize. While he certainly is a self-promoter and should have had for the court's review a copy of the letter from the Nobel committee in Stockholm, Sweden, the truth of the matter is that he is probably the only person involved in these proceedings who had a United States Congressman recommend him for such an award. Whether the committee "accepted" the nomination, "received" the nomination or whatever, it is not that significant. What is significant, however, and what undemises his creditability is that he did not present to this court any evidence other than his generalized statements as to the efficacy of his therapy on brain damaged individuals like Terry Schiavo. He testified that he has treated about 50 patients in the same or worse condition than Terry Schiavo since 1994 but he offered no names, no case studies, no videos and no tests results to support his claim that he had success in all but one of them. If his therapy is as effective as he would lead this court to believe, it is inconceivable that he would not produce clinical results of these patients he has treated. And surely the medical literature would be replete with this new, now patented, procedure. Yet, he has only published one article and that was in 1995 involving some 63 patients, 60% of whom were suffering from whiplash. None of these patients were in a persistent vegetative state and all were conversant. . . .

In re Guardianship of Schiavo, 2002 WL 31817960 (Fla. Cir. Ct., 2002). Dr. Maxwell also urged hyperbaric therapy, but "Drs. Greer, Bambakidis and Cranford. . . all . . .felt that such therapy would have no affect on Terry Schiavo. It is interesting to note the absence of any case studies since this therapy is not new and this condition has long been in the medical arena." *Id.*

2. *Substituted Judgment and Best Interests:* Some commentators have seen *Schiavo* as a "challenge[to] the view that incapacitated

patients' earlier general preferences are sufficient to guide contemporary treatment decisions." Rebecca Dresser, *Schiavo's Legacy: The Need for an Objective Standard,* 35 HCR 20, 21 (May-June, 2005). The evidence of Schiavo's preferences was undeniably thin. As commentator Joan Didion put it,

> . . .[A]ny notion about what Theresa Schiavo wanted or did not want remained essentially unconfirmable, notwithstanding the fact that a Florida court had in effect accepted the hearsay assertions that she had said, at one point, in reference to her husband's dying grandmother and at another while watching a television movie about someone with a feeding tube, "no tubes for me." (Imagine it. You are in your early twenties. You are watching a movie, say on Lifetime, in which someone has a feeding tube. You pick up the empty chip bowl. "No tubes for me," you say as you get up to fill it. What are the chances you have given this even a passing thought?)

Joan Didion, *The Case of Theresa Schiavo,* 52 NY Rev Books, June 9, 2005. Less pungently, one of the appellate judges who reviewed the evidence, commented that Theresa "had been raised in the Catholic faith, but did not regularly attend mass or have a religious advisor who could assist the court in weighing her religious attitudes about life-support methods. Her statements to her friends and family about the dying process were few and they were oral." Dresser, *supra,* at 20.

Professor Dressor concludes that "the best response to the conflict of Terri Schiavo would be intensified scholarly and public deliberation about the objective standard and its underlying moral judgments." Dresser, *supra*, at 21. Would such deliberation have aided Schiavo's parents and husband in reaching agreement on her best interests? If not, why not? On balance, is Dresser's suggested response to *Schiavo* likely to significantly reduce conflicts like that between Mr. Schiavo and the Schindlers?

3. *ADR as a solution for Schiavo-type controversies*: Other commentators have seen *Schiavo* as evidence pointing to the need for new conflict-resolution procedures:

> Terry Schiavo's case. . . shows that in quelling our fears, the adjudicatory model offers scant succor. . . . The ideas and techniques ADR has cultivated over the last thirty years offer us, and our families, a chance to do better. ADR can:
> - Help to resolve "misunderstandings" that the adjudicatory model tends to treat as full-blown "disputes";

- Identify intermediate options that satisfy both parties and remove the need for rights-oriented dispute resolution;
- Offer a lower-cost form of rights-oriented adjudication when a dispute must be "decided;"
- Enable the patient and free him from the debilitating "object" status accorded to him by adjudication; and
- Offer emotional settlement lacking in the typical litigation process.

I. Glenn Cohen, *Negotiating Death: ADR and End of Life Decision-making*, 9 Harv. Negotiation Rev. 253, 329-30 (2004). See also M. Gregg Bloche, *Managing Conflict at the End of Life*, 352 NEJM 2371 (2005). Would mediation and/or arbitration have been helpful in resolving the dispute between Mr. Schiavo and the Schindlers? What advantages and disadvantages do each of the dispute-resolution methods hold over traditional adjudication?

4. *PVS v. MCS*: Despite the thorough neurological review of Schiavo's condition reported by the appellate court, continuing controversy about her diagnosis continued right up to her death. In March, 2005, at the request of the Florida Department of Children and Families (which was seeking custody of Schiavo), she was seen by Dr. William P. Cheshire, a neurologist and director of the Florida Mayo Clinic's Autonomic Reflex Laboratory. Dr. Cheshire, who was apparently a conservative Christian, noted in his affidavit that Schiavo had not had a complete neurological examination in nearly three years, had never had such advanced testing as positron emission tomography (PET) or functional magnetic resonance imaging (fMRI), and that in the absence of such examination and imaging there remained "huge uncertainties" about her neurological status. *See* Didion, *supra*.

After Cheshire's evaluation, the Schindlers petitioned the court for fMRI evaluation of Schiavo, but the request was denied based on the court's finding that they had not established, as required in 2002, that new diagnostic techniques or treatment "would significantly improve the quality of her life." *See Schiavo, supra*.

Functional magnetic resonance imaging and PET scans do appear to offer greater diagnostic certainty than did older techniques of distinguishing MCS from PVS. *See* T. Bekinschtein et al, *Emotional Processing in the Minimally Conscious State*, 75 J Neurology

Neurosurgery & Psychiatry 788 (2004); Melanie Boly et al., *Auditory Processing in Severely Brain-Injured Patients,* 61 Arch Neurol 233 (2004).

Would consensus on diagnosis likely have resolved the dispute between Mr. Schiavo and the Schindlers? Certainly, medical experts do not universally agree that PVS is sufficiently distinctive to warrant sharply different treatment by the law. For example, Dr. Ronald Cranford, a neurological expert who testified in *Martin* and evaluated *Schiavo,* has written that

> . . . [T]he vegetative and minimally conscious states are actually quite similar in many respects. First, most persons in these conditions are unable to perform any of the typical activities of daily living such as walking or meaningfully communicating with others. Second, they are totally dependent upon others for care such as toileting, dressing, or feeding themselves. Third, as both groups of persons are profoundly physically and mentally limited and rendered largely inactive by their condition, both are subject to the medical complications of their inactivity, such as bedsores, infections, and contractures. Furthermore, the life expectancy of both groups is greatly shortened as a direct consequence of their medical conditions. The data supporting this claim, however, is much more extensive for vegetative patients than for the minimally conscious. In sum, persons in the vegetative and minimally conscious states are profoundly dysfunctional.
>
> . . . Although persons in both states are alive biologically, in neither state are they more than minimally alive personally or biographically. For all intents and purposes, both states equally obliterate an individual's personal and sapient existence, leaving him profoundly neurologically impaired. . . . The factual differences between the two states has generated an assumption on the part of the courts that persons in these two supposedly distinct states ought to be treated radically different in terms of the ethical and legal obligations of others to continue to maintain their lives with medical treatment. Adopting this position is a serious mistake. The assumption that any degree of consciousness in a person--no matter how minimal--makes a decision to forego life-sustaining medical treatment much more ethically problematic, if not outright impermissible, is unjustifiable. In several important and fundamentally descriptive ways, persons in these states are more alike than different.

Lawrence J. Nelson & Ronald E. Cranford, *Michael Martin and Robert Wendland: Beyond the Vegetative State*, 15 J Contemp Health L & Pol'y 427, 446-47 (1999).

By contrast, Adam Hildebrand argues that

> The medically invented phrase, "Persistent Vegetative State" has an inevitably pernicious effect on the way we look at those whose cognitive functions are drastically, and in most cases permanently and terminally, impaired. With the use of this phrase, we affix a label that places them not only outside of the human species but outside of the entire animal realm. It cannot but affect the moral outlook of those--attending physicians and others--who are called upon to treat patients wearing the badge of our disregard.
>
> If we ask "must we administer medically assisted hydration and nutrition as a treatment for a patient in a persistent vegetative state?" we are likely to reach a different conclusion than if we ask 'must we give food and water to a human being whose brain is severely impaired and who is totally dependent?' It is understandable that one might question the morality of supporting people to live out their lives with a profound neurological impairment. Who would want to live in a 'persistent vegetative state'? To be sure, no one would choose to live in such a condition. Yet dreadful conditions visit human beings all the time, through cancer, AIDS, heart disease and a host of other diseases that produce great suffering. While the desire to end or reduce suffering is a noble intention, one must not end suffering by killing the sufferer.

Adam J. Hildebrand, *Masked Intentions: The Masquerade of Killing Thoughts Used to Justify Dehydrating and Starving People in a "Persistent Vegetative State" and People with Other Profound Neurological Impairments*, 16 Issues L & Med 143 (2000).

While Hildebrand and Nelson & Cranford agree that PVS should not be distinguished from MCS, their arguments point in quite different directions. Nelson & Cranford urge that family members should have same power to terminate treatment for MCS as for PVS patients. Hildebrand believes that PVS patients should be treated the same way as MCS patients.

D. Treatment for Mental Illness: A Special Case?

Add at p. 537:

In 2005, a large, rigorous, government-financed study that compared drugs used to treat schizophrenia found that the new "atypical" antipsychotic drugs offered few, if any, benefits over older medicines. The study measured how long patients continued to take prescribed medications. After 18 months, 64% of the patients taking Zyprexa, one of the new drugs, had stopped, and at least 74% had quit each of the other medications. The most common reasons were ineffectiveness, lack of tolerance for the medicine, or side effects like sleepiness and weight gain or neurological symptoms like stiffness or tremors. Although prior studies had shown that the new medications posed a lower risk of tardive dyskinesia than the older ones, this study found that, at more modest doses, the older drug included in the comparison (perphenazine), while just as effective, was not significantly more likely to cause neurological symptoms. The researchers said that there was no reason to believe that modest doses of other older drugs would produce different results. The patients on Zyprexa were less likely to be hospitalized because their condition worsened than those taking the other drugs, the study found. But these patients also gained the most weight, adding an average of two pounds a month while on the drug, and their lipid levels increased more than those of people on the other drugs. *See* Benedict Carey, *Little Difference Found in Schizophrenia Drugs*, NY Times, Sept. 20, 2005.

State Medicaid programs are estimated to spend at least $3 billion per year on antipsychotic drugs, more than for any other drug class. Because the newer drugs cost three to ten times more than the older ones, several states — even before publication of the new research findings — had limited access to them. In response to the new research findings, one expert urged that they offered both opportunities and risks: "The opportunity is to lower the cost of these drugs," Dr. Goodman said. "The risk is that state Medicaid programs use this excuse to entirely deny some patients access to more effective and more expensive drugs which work for those patients." Carey, *supra*.

Add at p. 541

The evidence suggests that post-commitment noncompliance with prescribed medication regimes is common. A review of all published studies of noncompliance found, among ten reports that met a strict set of study inclusion criteria, a mean rate noncompliance rate of 41.2%; the five reports that met a stricter set of inclusion criteria had a mean nonadherence rate of 49.5%. In the 39 articles reviewed, factors most consistently associated with nonadherence included poor insight, negative attitude or subjective response toward medication, previous nonadherence, substance abuse, shorter illness duration, inadequate discharge planning or aftercare environment, and poorer therapeutic alliance. See J.P. Lacro et al., *Prevalence of and Risk Factors for Medication Nonadherence in patients with Schizophrenia: A Comprehensive Review of Recent Literature*, 63 J. Clin Psychiatry 892 (2002).

However, the efficacy of out-patient commitment remains unclear. In a recent review of all published research on outpatient commitment, Marvin S. Swartz & Jeffrey W. Swanson conclude that "current data suggest that, if OPC is effective, it can only be so when more intensive services are provided, obviating its use as an inexpensive remedy." *Involuntary Outpatient Commitment, Community Treatment Orders, and Assisted Outpatient Treatment: What's in the Data?*, 49 Can J Psychiatry 585 (2004). Swartz & Swanson found that involuntary outpatient commitment was most effective if sustained for 6 months or more and that it was only effective if combined with frequent services.

Add at p. 544 note 3:

Research reports suggest that approximately half of acutely ill inpatients with schizophrenia can pass standard tests for determining competence to consent to treatment. See T Grisso & Paul S. Applebaum, The MacArthur Treatment Competence Study, III: abilities of patients to consent to psychiatric and medical treatments. 19 Law Hum Behav 149 (1995); Bruce J. Cohen et al., *Willingness and Competence of Depressed and Schizophrenic Inpatients to Consent to Research*, 32 J Am Acad Psychiatry & L 134 (2004). But schizophrenics typically lack insight into their condition. Thus, without treatment, they are incapable of perceiving the need for treatment. See Robert C. Schwartz, *The Relationship Between Insight, Illness and Treatment Outcome in Schizophrenia*, 69 Psychiatric Q 1 (1998) (two different studies found that 90% of schizophrenics showed poor insight, 67% moderate to severe lack of insight). Researchers who correlated attitudes toward treatment with a number of variables found that insight, relationship with staff (especially the physician-prescriber), and the patient's admission experience were the most significant variables in determining a patient's attitude. A poor relationship with the prescriber, experience of coercion during admission, and low insight predicted a negative attitude toward treatment. See Jennifer

C. Day et al., *Attitudes Toward Antipsychotic Medication,* 62 Arch Gen Psychiatry 717 (2005).

SECTION 3: PATIENTS WITH FUTURE COMPETENCE: MAKING MEDICAL DECISIONS FOR CHILDREN

B. Parents' Rights and Children's Interests

Add at p. 564, note 1:

A survey of published opinions dealing with parent-physician disagreement over the appropriate medical treatment of a child found 50 opinions dealing with 66 children in 20 states. Overall, physicians prevailed at the trial level in 44 of the 50 disputes studied (88%). Physicians were more likely to prevail in religion-based disputes than in other cases (27 of 30). *See* Derry Ridgway, *Court-Mediated Disputes Between Physicians and Families over the Medical Care of children,* 158 Arch Pediatric Adolescent Med 891 (2004).

Add at p. 564, note 2:

In 2002, forty-eight states provided religion-based exemptions to vaccinations and sixteen provided exemptions for philosophical reasons. *See* Janna C. Merrick, *Spiritual Healing, Sick Kids and the Law: Inequities in the American Healthcare System*, 29 Am J L & Med 269 (2003). Janna Merrick reports that studies of infectious disease transmission suggest that "children who are exempted based on their parents' philosophical or religious preferences put others in the community at risk":

> A retrospective national study of measles for the years 1985 through 1992 showed that children ages five to nineteen years, who were exempted for religious or philosophical reasons, were thirty-five times more likely to contract measles than children who were vaccinated. A subsequent study of both measles and pertussis outbreaks in Colorado showed that day care and elementary age children who were exempted for religious or philosophical reasons were sixty-two times more likely to become infected with measles and sixteen times more likely to become infected with pertussis than children who were vaccinated. . . .
>
> Of the 179 cases of measles studied in Colorado, forty-five (twenty-five percent) were known to be among children exempted for religious or philosophical reasons. This figure does not include children who did not receive conventional medical care, were not

reported to health officials and, as a result, not included in the study. Thus, the actual number of cases among philosophical and religious exemptors may be higher. The rest of the cases were children who had been vaccinated or had been medically exempted from the vaccine. Of the vaccinated children who became infected, at least eleven percent contracted measles from someone with a religious or philosophical exemption. The authors point out that the source of infection was unknown in sixty-seven percent of the vaccinated children, and therefore the number of vaccinated children infected by someone with a philosophical or religious vaccination exemption is probably higher than eleven percent.

The situation is more problematic in communities with high numbers of religious exemptors. For example, a 1996 outbreak of measles in Washington County, Utah, a community with seven times the national average of exemptors, infected 107 individuals. The Colorado study found that for each one percent increase in religious or philosophical exemptors in a school, the risk of having a pertussis outbreak increased by twelve percent.

Thus, it is clear that spiritual exemptions from vaccinations create a burden for third parties. The burden is shouldered both by the exempted child who becomes ill from vaccine-preventable diseases and by the child's friends, classmates and members of the public-at-large who may then also become infected. . . . .

Merrick, *supra*, at 275-76. How might lawyers seeking to overturn a religious-accommodation law on constitutional grounds use the evidence cited by Merrick? What result should a court hearing such a case reach?

D. The Newborn

Add at p. 594 following **"I Am Not What You See"**

John M. Freeman,

On Learning Humility, A Thirty-Year Journey

34 HCR 13 (May-June, 2004)

[In 1969 I was] hired to direct the pediatric neurology division at Johns Hopkins. I was also to run the March of Dimes Birth Defects Clinic which primarily cared for children with spina bifida, a congenital malformation of the spine associated with varying degrees of paralysis of the legs, bladder, and bowels, and often associated with hydrocephalus (water on the brain). During the mid-1960s, newborns affected with spina bifida were sent home or to an institution, typically to die. Children who did not die had treatment begun when they were a year old. As surgical and anesthetic techniques improved, however, surgery for the newborn with spina bifida became increasingly feasible, and John Lorber, of Sheffield, England, showed that early closure of the back to avoid meningitis increased the child's chances of survival. When I began to work in the Birth Defects Clinic, early surgery was the norm but was not mandatory. As director of the clinic, it became my responsibility to elicit the parent's informed consent for the operation to repair the back. I needed to discuss the likelihood of the child's future ability to walk, with or without braces and crutches, and to explain the consequences and management of the probable incontinence of bowel and bladder and the likelihood of hydrocephalus and of mental retardation. . . .

. . . In 1971, . . . Lorber re-evaluated [] the results of his recommendations for early surgery for children with spina bifida and concluded that the early treatment of all children with spina bifida was a mistake. Half of the children he had treated early and vigorously had died anyway, and a substantial number of those who survived would be in wheelchairs or require bracing and crutches. He believed that they would be better off dead. He published criteria that could predict a child's future impairment and recommended "selection" and nontreatment of those who would be in wheelchairs or walk only with braces and crutches. He stated that such selection, at birth, would reduce the suffering of the children and their families, and reduce the resources needed for their care.

Lorber claimed that infants "selected" would die quickly, but . . . I knew that was not necessarily true. . . . Later . . ., I debated John Lorber in front of the American Academy of Pediatrics. He articulated the results of his study, stating that those not selected for treatment died quickly. What was not apparent to the audience, and initially not to me, was that in England, infants were fed on demand. If they were sedated with morphine and phenobarbital *and* fed on demand, they demanded less, and died more quickly. Infants in this country were fed every four hours and were patiently waiting to die without their physicians knowing the "trick."

Recently I was asked to write a review of the ethical issues involved in treating spina bifida. It had been years since I had worked with children who had that condition, and both the field and society had changed. Now, prenatal folic acid may prevent spina bifida, routine amniocentesis and ultra sound examination often detect a lesion early in pregnancy, and the abortion of an affected fetus is common. I wondered if these changes had affected perinatal decisionmaking. I went to the spina bifida groups' annual Christmas Party and spoke with two young women in their 20s who had been poster children for what we could do. I had always believed that if the child was given the proper medical care, if complications were prevented, if adequate education and psychological support were provided, these affected children could be given a good life. If they were dissatisfied with their lot, it was our fault for not having adequately met their needs. During their childhood and early adolescence, I had considered these two to be among my treatment successes. Although both of these young women have high paraplegia and are in wheelchairs, they are of good intelligence, have graduated from high school, and hold government jobs. One has had twenty-seven operations for shunt blockage and for hip, back, and kidney problems. The other had only one shunt but many other surgical procedures. Both live at home. When I asked about their lives they both complained about having few friends, no social life, little prospect for marriage, and little independence. I mentioned that I was writing an article about decisionmaking for infants with spina bifida. One said that although she was Catholic and did not believe in abortion, nevertheless, she wished she had not been born and would advise parents to terminate an affected fetus. The other agreed. I was shocked. I was reminded of Lorber's statement, which I had disputed in 1971, that "most [of his survivors] had a quality of life inconsistent with self-respect, earning capacity, happiness, and even marriage."

    I consider myself to be a moral, caring, dedicated, compassionate, paternalistic physician whose life's work has been with children and parents of children with disabilities. Over the course of my career I had became increasingly confident in the correctness of my decisions, and therefore grew even more paternalistic. My confidence may even have turned into arrogance as I found and articulated the flaws in Lorber's position. Now, with time and experience, and partly as a result of speaking to these young women, my arrogance has become doubt and ignorance, once again. I now do not know what to recommend to the family of a newborn with a severe birth defect, or how to counsel the family whose fetus has been diagnosed in utero. I no longer know what is "the right decision," or even the ethics underpinning a proper decision. My patients and parents have taught me that families have amazing abilities to cope. I am repeatedly struck by the families who rise to meet what I would have considered terrible, ongoing adversities. I am awed by those who continue to care lovingly for the profoundly disabled child who does not interact with them or with the environment, and who has constant seizures. I remain overwhelmed by the parent who is constantly demonstrating love, care, and compassion without the immediate positive feedbacks and rewards that I as a parent have come to expect.

Predicting the future for children with major abnormalities may be fraught with hazard; so also may be predicting the parental response to a handicapped child. I was taught this by three mothers, each referred to me for counseling late in their pregnancies. Each was carrying a fetus who, by ultrasound, had hydrocephalus. One child, when born, had hydranencephalaphy (no cortical mantle) and made almost no development. Stasia had seizures and died at three years of age. Her parents considered her "a gift" and wrote of their experience. The second at birth was found to have massive hydrocephalus with only a very thin cortical mantle. She was shunted and has become an "A" student in high school and a competitive swimmer. The third, similarly treated, made little developmental progress, had major complications, and a devastated, ultimately broken, family who came to curse me for advising them to carry the child to term. When seen in utero, I could not predict the three fetuses' medical outcomes, let alone their parents' future reactions.

Since these problems were detected only late in pregnancy, the only alternative was the currently banned "partial birth abortion." Would that have been better? For which of the children? How do you work to achieve the greatest good for the greatest number when "the good" is so unpredictable both for the children and for their families?

I realized the depths of the biases and prejudices that continue to underlie my personal ethics and my decisionmaking. As I tried to factor my perception of quality of life into my advice, I also realized how limited is my own view of other people's quality of life—how tolerant we must become of those with a different quality of life.

In reflecting on my career, I find that I have progressed from ignorance to paternalism through arrogance to a new humility. I have become more tolerant, perhaps more compassionate, less judgmental, somewhat wiser, more confused. I am still learning how deep my own biases run, and how little I really know about the lives of those with disabilities. I no longer know the ethically correct answer to the specific questions posed by the patients' problems. I have also learned, much to my continued disappointment, that ethical theories and ethicists are rarely helpful in decisionmaking at the bedside or for the individual.

But one lesson I believe I have learned is that decisionmaking should be a process, and the process for arriving at a decision is far more important than the decision arrived at. This process cannot be left solely to the family, or to relatives and friends, with their biases and prejudices, any more than it can be left solely to the physician. Physicians and families together must learn to work out a plan for the handicapped or potentially handicapped newborn—and likewise for the premature infant, for the person with late-stage Alzheimer's disease, for the critically ill, for individuals at both ends of life.

Add at p. 600, note 7:

Although the prospects for extremely low-birth-weight infants remain poor, they are improving. A recent examination of survival and outcome data for such births showed a significant increase in survival and a significant decrease in neurodevelopmental impairment. *See* Betty R. Vohr et al., *Neurodevelopmental Outcomes of Extremely Low Birth Weight Infants <32 Weeks' Gestation Between 1993 and 1998*, 116 Pediatrics 635 (2005).

SECTION 5. THE PARTICIPATION OF MENTALLY INCAPACITATED
PATIENTS IN MEDICAL RESEARCH

Add at p. 636

In 1998 the National Bioethics Advisory Commission recommended the institution of additional federal regulations aimed at protecting research subjects with mental disorders that could affect their decisional capacity. The Commission recommended that studies that subject such individuals to "greater than minimal risk" be required to utilize an independent evaluator who would assess the capacity of all prospective participants. Further, it recommended that research studies not offering the potential for "direct medical benefit" be required to obtain the approval of an independent federal review board. *See* Nat. Advisory Comm., Research Involving Persons with Mental Disorders that May Affect Decisionmaking Capacity (1998).

Noting the dearth of empirical research on whether patients with acute psychiatric illness are in fact more likely than others to consent to high-risk studies, Bruce Cohen and colleagues investigated the willingness and capacity of inpatients with major depressive disorder and schizophrenia to provide informed consent to participation in research. Of those who were approached to enter the study, 29% (6 of 21) of the schizophrenia patients, 91% (20 of 22) of the depressed patients, and 95% (20 of 21) of the community control subjects agreed to participate. Among those who entered, 100% of the community controls, 50% of the depression group, and 17% of the schizophrenia group decided that they would participate in one or both of the studies in which the research team solicited their participation. The depressed patients exhibited relatively high decision-making capacity and were able to distinguish levels of risk between studies. Their pattern of preferences did not differ from control subjects. However, they were six times more likely to decline to participate in the lower-risk study and 1.4 times more likely to decline the higher-risk study. Within the schizophrenia group, the five subjects who declined to participate in both studies were fairly evenly distributed among the full range of capacity scores. The two subjects with the most severe levels of psychosis (scores of 47 on the BPRS) also received the lowest scores on the three capacities. "Our finding that individuals with depression and schizophrenia were less likely to volunteer for research than were non-ill individuals suggests that the influence of their illness on their capacity for volunteerism may be predominantly in the negative direction." Bruce J. Cohen et al., *Willingness and Competence of Depressed and Schizophrenic Inpatients to Consent to Research*, 32 J Am Acad Psychiatry & L 134 (2004).

Chapter 5

THE BODY AS COMMODITY

SECTION 2. MY BODY, MY PROPERTY?

Add at p. 669

Problem

In 1987, a group of parents whose children had been born afflicted with Canavan Disease, a fatal, hereditary disorder, approached Dr. Matalon, a research physician, for assistance in discovering the genes responsible for Canavan Disease, so that tests could be developed to determine carriers and allow for prenatal testing.

After Dr. Matalon agreed to engage in research on Canavan Disease, the parents, in collaboration with the National Tay-Sachs and Allied Disease Association, Inc. ("NTSAD") located other Canavan families and convinced them to provide tissue (such as blood, urine, and autopsy samples), financial support, and aid in identifying the location of Canavan families internationally. The parents and NTSAD also created a confidential database with epidemiological, medical and other information about the families.

In 1990, Dr. Matalon became associated with Miami Children's Hospital Research Institute, Inc., (MCHRI) and in 1993, there was a breakthrough in Matalon's research. Using the blood and tissue samples, family pedigree information, contacts, and financial support provided by the parents and NTSAD, Matalon and his research team successfully isolated the gene responsible for Canavan Disease.

In 1994, Matalon and MCHRI submitted a patent application for the genetic sequence that Matalon had identified. This application was granted in 1997, and Dr. Matalon was listed as an inventor on the gene patent. Through patenting, Matalon and MCHRI acquired the ability to restrict any activity related to the Canavan Disease gene, including carrier and prenatal testing, gene therapy and other treatments for Canavan Disease, and research involving the gene and its mutations.

Although the Patent was issued in 1997, NTSAD and the Canavan parent group did not learn of it until a year later when MCHRI revealed its plan to limit Canavan Disease testing through restrictive licensing of the Patent and began to restrict public access through exclusive licensing agreements and royalty fees.

Thereafter, the Canavan parent group and NTSAD brought an action against Matalon and MCHRI alleging that they had provided Matalon with genetic information, samples and confidential information "with the understanding and expectations that such samples and information would be used for the specific purpose of researching Canavan disease and identifying mutations in which could lead to carrier detection within their families and benefit the population at large." They also claimed that it was their "understanding that any carrier and prenatal testing developed in connection with the research for which they were providing essential support would be provided on an affordable and accessible basis, and that Matalon's research would remain in the public domain to promote the discovery of more effective prevention techniques and treatments and, eventually, to effectuate a cure for Canavan disease," and that this understanding stemmed from their "experience in community testing for Tay-Sachs disease, another deadly genetic disease that occurs most frequently in families of Ashkenazi Jewish descent." The plaintiffs also alleged they were never informed that either Matalon or MCHRI intended to seek a patent on the research or that they intended to commercialize the fruits of the research and restrict access to Canavan Disease testing.

Based on these allegations, the plaintiffs sued Matalon and MCHRI for: (1) lack of informed consent; (2) breach of fiduciary duty; (3) unjust enrichment; and (4) conversion. Plaintiffs allege that the defendants have already earned more than $75,000 in royalties from the Canavan Disease gene patent, and that Dr. Matalon has personally profited by receiving a recent substantial federal grant to undertake further research related to the gene patent.

Under *Moore*, what arguments are available to the plaintiffs and defendants? Assuming that the plaintiffs' allegations are borne out by the evidence, who should win? *See* Greenberg v. Miami Children's Hospital, 264 F. Supp.2d 1064 (S.D. Fla. 2003), 121 ALR 5th 687.

SECTION 3. TRANSFERRING THE BODY

B. Transfers After Death

Add at p. 683 note 2:

Brotherton describes " the existence of a [protectible] interest" as a "matter of state law." But the Court says that "whether that interest rises to the level of a "legitimate claim of entitlement" protected by the due process clause is determined by federal law" and – most difficult for the legislative draftsperson – "[t]his determination does not rest on the label attached to a right granted by the state but rather on the substance of that right." The State could thus *minimize* the likelihood of successful *Brotherton*-type litigation by specifying the nature of family members' rights in a body and limitations on those rights; the relevant statute might, for example, grant the decedent's next-of-kin a right to determine whether to donate organs and how the body should be disposed of "*only* in accordance with state law and any written instructions by the decedent regarding the disposition of his organs and body." But the state could not ensure that a zealous federal judge might not find unlabelled substance somewhere within state tort-law precedents.

In *Newman v. Sathyavaglswaran*, 287 F3d 786 (9th Cir 2002), dissenting Judge Fernandez urged that the 9th Circuit Court of Appeals had done just that. Like *Brotherton*, *Newman* involved a section 1983 by surviving members based on a coroner's nonconsensual removal of the decedents corneas pursuant to a statute like the one upheld in *Powell*. After detailing the Roman and common law history of rights and duties in dead bodies, the majority held that,

> [b]ecause the property interests of next of kin to dead bodies are firmly entrenched in the "background principles of property law," based on values and understandings contained in our legal history dating from the Roman Empire, California may not be free to alter them with exceptions that lack "a firm basis in traditional property principles." "While the legislature may elect not to confer a property interest . . . it may not constitutionally authorize the deprivation of such an interest, once conferred, without appropriate procedural safeguards." With § 27491.47, California eliminated procedural safeguards but retained the interest.

To dissenting Judge Fernandez, on the other hand, the majority opinion transformed an "asthenic legal interest in a decedent's body, which California confers upon relatives and others," into "a puissant giant for federal constitutional purposes."

> California's statutory scheme . . . decidedly does not confer a property right upon anyone. Assuming that a decedent has not made his own arrangements for disposal of his own earthly remains, the state makes sure that somebody else will both do so and pay for it. To that end, California has provided that "[t]he right to control the disposition of the remains of a deceased person ... vests in, and the duty of disposition and the liability for the reasonable cost of disposition of the remains devolves upon," a list of individuals. Cal. Health & Safety Code § 7100(a). Thus, this so-called right is actually in the nature of a duty and expense designed to assure that the remains will not simply be left about, but will be quickly interred. And the state has created something like a table of intestate succession for the purpose of assuring that the right and duty land firmly on a defined group. . . . Is not it interesting that the holder of a power of attorney comes before the closest relatives, and equally interesting to see that the public administrator may wind up with the "right?" Or is it essentially a duty?
>
> I rather think that it is really a duty rather than a right. . . [T]hat hardly looks like the kind of interest that United States Constitution was designed to protect.

Id. at 800.

The problem is exacerbated by the fact that state courts may want to permit some section 1983 actions based on interference with the body. For example, in *Crocker v. Pleasant*, 727 So2d 1087 (1999), involving allegations that defendant police officials had failed to notify the decedent's family of his death for six months despite knowledge of their whereabouts, the trial and intermediate appellate courts found that the defendants' alleged actions would, if proven, "constitute outrageous conduct and tortious interference with the right of burial" and thus represented conduct "much more egregious than the claim made in *Powell*." But they nonetheless dismissed the complaint on authority of *Powell*.

Responding to the certified question, "Does . . . *Powell*. . . Preclude All Section 1983 Claims Grounded on Interference with an Interest in a Dead Body?", the Florida Supreme Court responded in the negative:

> Despite broad language used in the *Powell* opinion, our holding in that case was limited to an analysis of the constitutionality

of the cornea removal statute that addressed a public health issue. . . . Our rejection in *Powell* of a constitutional attack on a narrowly drawn statute regulating the disposition of the corneas of a deceased person does not necessarily translate into the broader conclusion that the right to possess a loved one's remains for the purposes of burial should never be accorded protected status under the Fourteenth Amendment, whether labeled a "quasi-property right" or a "legitimate claim of entitlement." Although we rejected the petitioners' constitutional claims in *Powell*, we explained that Florida recognizes a limited right to possession of the body for "burial, sepulture or other lawful disposition." This conclusion is consistent with the approach of other courts that have found that this right constitutes a legitimate claim of entitlement or a quasi-property interest. . . .

Florida law also contains a number of indicia, both in its statutes and case law, that recognize the rights of the next of kin in their dead relatives' remains. . . . Based upon these statutory rights . . . [and] case law. . ., we conclude that in Florida there is a legitimate claim of entitlement by the next of kin to possession of the remains of a decedent for burial or other lawful disposition. We also find that referring to the interest as a "legitimate claim of entitlement" most accurately describes the nature of the interest. Accordingly, *Powell* does not "preclude all section 1983 claims grounded on interference with an interest in a dead body," and therefore we answer the certified question in the negative.

Crocker v. Pleasant, 778 So2d 978, 985-87 (2001).

Add at p. 683

7. In 1998, the Icelandic Parliament enacted legislation authorizing "the creation and operation of a centralised database of non-personally identifiable health data" for use in producing "new or improved methods of achieving better health, prediction, diagnosis and treatment of disease." The Act provides for the recording of the encrypted medical records of all Icelandic citizens who do not opt out and the linking of this information to databases containing genealogical and genetic information.

The database was the brainchild of an Icelandic geneticist and Harvard professor, Kari Steffanson, who concluded that Iceland was an ideal place to study the genetic origins of various human illnesses. His conclusion was based on Iceland's small (275,000), homogeneous (almost all Icelanders come from Scandinavia) and readily traceable population (80% of all Icelanders who have ever lived can be placed on family trees) as well as its unusually old and detailed medical records. Steffanson formed a company, DeCODE, convinced the Icelandic government to establish the database at issue in the Guethsmondsdottir litigation, and further convinced the government to give DeCODE an exclusive license to use the data for twelve years in return for $200 million.

DeCODE has already proved the worth of the Icelandic database in studies of conditions caused by single defective genes, for example, rare hereditary conditions, including forms of dwarfism, epilepsy, and eye disorders. The company has also initiated projects in 25 common diseases including multiple sclerosis, psoriasis, preeclampsia, inflammatory bowel disease, aortic aneurism, alcoholism and obesity.

Under the arrangement between DeCODE and the Icelandic government, the database belongs to the national health system, but DeCODE has the exclusive right to commercialize the data for 12 years. DeCODE is a commercial enterprise, and it plans to market information obtained from the database to pharmaceutical companies, which would use it to develop diagnostic tests and drugs. It has already entered into an arrangement with Hoffman-LaRoche with respect to information about twelve diseases. In return, Hoffman-LaRoche agreed to pay DeCODE $200 million and give Icelanders free access to treatments developed through the partnership. *See Human Genetics: DeCODEing Iceland's DNA*, http://bioteach.ubc.ca/Bioinformatics/DeCODE/; Erika Check, *The Decode Database: Should a private company market a nation's genetic information?*, 1 Stan. J Int'l Rel (Spring, 1999), http://www.stanford.edu/group/sjir/1.2.08_check.html.

In 2000, the guardian of fifteen-year-old Ragnhildur Guethmundsdottir wrote to the Office of the Medical Director of Health requesting, pursuant to the Act's opt-out clause, that no medical, genealogical, or genetic information about Guethmundsdottir's deceased father be included in the database. The Director refused, noting that the Act contained no "provision for an individual to refuse to permit the transfer to the database of information about his/her deceased parents."

Guethmundsdottir filed suit against the Director, claiming that she had a personal interest in excluding her father's medical information from the database because inferences about her own health might be drawn from his health data. The trial court found that medical information contained in the database is not personally identifiable and held that Guethmundsdottir lacked standing to challenge the inclusion of her father's health information. The Icelandic Supreme Court reversed, holding that, "for reasons of personal privacy," Guethmundsdottir "has a personal interest in preventing the transfer of data from her father's medical records to the Health Sector Database, as it is possible to infer, from the data, information relating to her father's hereditary characteristics which could also apply to herself." The Court noted that Icelandic medical records contain a great deal of information "relating to some of the most intimately private affairs of the person concerned" and concluded that the Icelandic Constitution, which provides that "everyone shall enjoy freedom from interference with privacy, home, and family life," unequivocally applies "to information of this kind and . . . guarantees protection of privacy in this respect." Although the Court found that Guethmundsdottir had not shown that data encryption failed to protect her privacy interest, it also found that, because the Act did not specify which data must be encrypted, it did not adequately ensure her privacy. The court thus concluded that Guethmodsdottir had a right to prohibit the transfer of her father's medical records into the database.

One comment on the Guethmundsdottir litigation concludes that there are "[g]ood reasons . . . for . . . courts to follow Iceland's lead in recognizing relational interests in genetic information. . ," but urges that "privacy law may not be the most effective way to protect these interests in the United States":

> . . . The merits of property rights versus privacy rights are at issue in debates about how best to protect two entities closely related to genetic information - the body and its parts and personal information generally. However, genetic information differs from these other areas in its inherent propensity for revealing quantifiable, sensitive information about individuals who are not themselves the source of the information. Thus, whatever the conclusions of these analyses for these other areas, they do not necessarily hold for genetic information.
>
> Any legal framework able to protect privacy interests in genetic information must recognize all the stakeholders involved. Such a frame-work must also address complex questions that the Icelandic Supreme Court left unanswered, such as how far along the branches of one's family tree a relational interest in genetic information extends and how courts should adjudicate disagreements among relatives over the disposition of their shared information. A rich understanding of property rights as legally enforceable

relationships among persons may be better able than privacy rights - at least as they are currently understood - to accommodate the relational nature of genetic information. . . .

Current privacy law, by contrast, is a hodgepodge of constitutional, common law, and statutory protections. Unlike their Icelandic counterparts, U.S. constitutional privacy rights "are on weak ground," since privacy is not explicitly guaranteed by the Constitution "and therefore must be inferred or derived from other enumerated rights and from judicial interpretation of what the Founding Fathers meant or intended." Common law torts have been "particularly ineffective" in protecting privacy, since they often conflict with "constitutional protections of free speech and expression." The invasion of privacy tort is thus "a battle between First Amendment values and an inchoate, elastic privacy "right.'" Despite the best intentions of Samuel Warren and Louis Brandeis in creating a common law right to privacy that is separate from property rights, it is this very separation from the power of the property framework that has caused "the tort's eventual failure." State and federal statutes fare no better. Since no enforcement agencies exist, individuals must fund their own suits to recover damages. Moreover, statutory provisions vary considerably from state to state, permitting would-be privacy violators to forum-shop.

Recent Case, Guomundsdottir v. Iceland, No. 151/2003 (Nov. 27, 2003) (Ice.), 118 Harv L Rev 810, 812-15 (2004).

Is the Icelandic database case best analyzed from a property or privacy perspective? Under American constitutional and tort law, what arguments would be available to Guomundsdottir? Are those arguments meritorious?

SECTION 4. INCREASING THE SUPPLY OF ORGANS FOR TRANSPLANTATION

A. Transplantable Organs: The Imbalance Between Supply and Demand

By late September, 2005, more than 89,000 individuals were awaiting organs. Between January-June, 2005, 14,010 organs were transplanted. Despite lengthier waiting lists, the number of individuals who die while awaiting an organ has remained relatively constant; in 2004, there 234 7,168 such deaths. *See* United Network for Organ Sharing, Data, http://www.unos.org/.

In 1999-2000, the last period for which UNOS reports data on median waiting times, there was still a substantial gap between the median kidney-transplant waiting period for African-Americans (1784 days) and European-Americans (1256 days). *See* United Network for Organ Sharing, http://www.optn.org/latestData/rptStrat.asp.

Add at p. 714, note 7: Cohen's impressionistic research on kidney vendors in India has now been supplemented with a larger-scale cross-sectional survey of 305 individuals who had sold a kidney in Chennai, India, an average of 6 years before the survey. The survey was conducted in February, 2001. The researchers found that

> Ninety-six percent of participants sold their kidneys to pay off debts. The average amount received was $1070. Most of the money received was spent on debts, food, and clothing. Average family income declined by one third after nephrectomy ($P<.001$), and the number of participants living below the poverty line increased. Three fourths of participants were still in debt at the time of the survey. About 86% of participants reported a deterioration in their health status after nephrectomy. Seventy-nine percent would not recommend that others sell a kidney. . . .
>
> Almost all the participants sold their kidneys to pay off debts. Food and household expenses, rent, marriage expenses, and medical expenses were the most common sources of these debts. Forty-seven participants noted that their spouse had also sold a kidney. The other 221 married participants (159 female participants and 62 male participants) were asked why they sold rather than their spouse. The most common responses by female participants were that their husbands were the breadwinners (30%) or were ill (28%). The most common responses by male participants were that they sold voluntarily (52%) or that their wives were ill or pregnant (19%). . . .
>
> Increased time since nephrectomy was associated with a larger amount received from selling a kidney and a larger decline in economic status. The 47 participants who sold a kidney more than 10 years ago received $1603 compared with $975 for participants who sold within the last 10 years ($P<.001$). Participants who sold more than 10 years ago also reported a 56% decline in annual family income compared with a 29% decline among participants who sold more recently ($P<.001$). There was no relationship between time since nephrectomy and reasons for selling, how the money was spent, changes in health status, and advice for others.

Madhav Goyal et al., *Economic and Health Consequences of Selling a Kidney in India,* 288 JAMA 1589 (2002). Goyal et al. also report, like

Cohen, that the "majority of donors were women" and that, "[g]iven the often weak position of women in Indian society, the voluntary nature of some donations is questionable." Two participants in the survey said that "their husbands forced them to donate." And "[b]ecause the interviews were generally conducted with other family members present, other participants may have been reluctant to mention being forced to donate." *Id.*

Interpreting their findings, the researchers concluded that

[o]ur quantitative findings, along with those of previous qualitative studies, undercut 5 key assumptions made by supporters of the sale of kidneys. First, although paying people to donate may have increased the supply of organs for transplantation, the financial incentive did not supplement underlying altruistic motivations. Only 5% of participants said wanting to help a sick person was a major factor in their decision to sell. Second, selling a kidney did not help poor donors overcome poverty. Family income actually declined by one third, and most participants were still in debt and living below the poverty line at the time of the survey. Third, . . . most participants [79%] would not recommend that others sell a kidney, which suggests that potential donors would be unlikely to sell a kidney if they were better informed of the likely outcomes. Fourth, safeguards such as eliminating middlemen or having an authorization committee did not appear to be effective. Middlemen and clinics paid less than they promised, and the authorization committees did not ensure that donations were motivated by altruism alone. Fifth, nephrectomy was associated with a decline in health status. Previous qualitative reports suggest that a diminished ability to perform physical labor may explain the observed worsening of economic status. Persistent pain and decline in health status have not been reported in previous long-term follow-up of volunteer donors in developed countries.

. . . In developed countries such as the United States, our findings may give pause to efforts to provide financial incentives to encourage donation. In particular, our findings raise concerns about whether providing financial incentives may be viewed by the public as taking advantage of poor families. If perceptions about transplantation are adversely affected, such incentives may actually lead to fewer total donations.

Id.

Chapter 6
REPRODUCTION AND BIRTH

SECTION 1. MATERNAL-FETAL CONFLICT

Add at p. 743: Although Gilligan's study is old, more recent surveys of women seeking abortions suggests that little has changed. A recent profile of women obtaining abortions in Arkansas concluded that, "while public conversation about abortion is dominated by advocates with all-or-nothing positions -- treating the fetus as a complete person, with full rights, or as a nonentity, with none -- most patients at the clinic, like most Americans, found themselves on rockier ground, weighing religious, ethical, practical, sentimental and financial imperatives that were often in conflict." John Leland, *Under Din of Abortion Debate, An Experience Shared Quietly*, NY Times, Sept. 18, 2005, at A1.

Add at p. 755, note 7:

7.   *Abortion Incidence, Distribution, and Trends*: The U.S. legal induced abortion rate was 14 per 1,000 women aged 15 – 44 years in 1973, the year *Roe* was decided. The rate rose to 25 per 1,000 in 1980, remained stable, at 23 – 24 per 1,000 during the 1980s and early 1990s, and declined to 20 – 21 per 1,000 during 1994 – 1997, and declined further to 17 per 1,000 during 1997 – 1999 in the same 48 reporting areas. In 2000-01, the abortion rate was 16 per 1,000. See Lilo T. Strauss et al., *Abortion Surveillance – United States, 2001*, 53 MMWR 1 (Nov. 26, 2004), http://www.cdc.gov/mmwr/preview/mmwrhtml/ss5309a1.htm. The decline in the abortion rate has been steepest among teenagers. Researchers attribute the drop in teenage abortion to reduced rates of pregnancy resulting from better (for example, the three-month Depo-Provera injection) and contraception and increased abstinence. The lowest abortion rate is that of educated, financially secure women. For poor and low-income women, the abortion rate actually increased during the 1990's, despite the overall decline. Some experts attribute this increase to 1996 welfare reforms, which reduced public support for poor women who carry their fetuses to term. See John Leland, *Under Din of Abortion Debate, An Experience Shared Quietly*, NY Times, Sept. 18, 2005, at A1.

In 2001, the abortion rate of African-American women (29 per 1,000 women) was 3.0 times the rate for European-American women (10 per 1,000). 79% of women who obtained abortions in 2001 were known to be unmarried. The abortion ratio for unmarried women (572 per 1,000 live births) was 8.8 times that for married women (65 per 1,000). Stratified by age, abortion ratios were highest for adolescents aged <15 years (744 per 1,000 live births) and lowest for women aged 30 – 34 years (147 per 1,000). However, the highest abortion rate was among women aged 20 – 24 years (32 per 1,000 women); the lowest rates were for women at the extremes of reproductive age (1 per 1,000 adolescents aged 13 – 14 years and 2 per 1,000 women aged 40 – 44 years). See Strauss et al., *supra*.

Of all abortions for which gestational age was reported, 59% were performed at ≤8 weeks' gestation and 88% at <13 weeks. From 1992 (when detailed data regarding early abortions were first collected) through 2001, steady increases have occurred in the percentage of abortions performed at ≤ 6 weeks' gestation. A limited number of abortions were obtained at >15 weeks' gestation, including 4.3% at 16--20 weeks and 1.4% at ≥21 weeks. See Strauss et al., *supra*.

Add at p. 782, note 5:

For a detailed review of the literature and an analysis of Canadian law, see Daniel Sperling, *Maternal Brain Death*, 30 Am. J. L. and Med. 453 (2004).

Add at p. 795 note 4:

A recent report detailing the findings of a comparatively large and careful longitudinal study did find some cognitive effects from prenatal exposure to cocaine. Although prenatal exposure was not associated with lower full-scale, verbal, or performance IQ scores, it was associated with an increased risk for specific cognitive impairments and lower likelihood of IQ above the normative mean at 4 years. A better home environment was associated with IQ scores for cocaine-exposed children that are similar to scores in nonexposed children. See Lynn T. Singer et al., *Cognitive Outcomes of Preschool Children with with Prental Cocaine Exposure*, 294 JAMA 2448 (2004). Another recent study, which looked at the immediate effects of prenatal cocaine exposure, failed to find an increased incidence of abnormal anatomic outcomes, but did find that central and autonomic nervous system symptoms were more frequent in the exposed cohort and persisted in an adjusted analysis. These effects were usually transient; the researchers concluded that they "may be a true cocaine effect." Charles R. Bauer et al., *Acute Neonatal Effects of Cocaine Exposure During Pregnancy*, 159 Arch Pediatric & Adolescent Med 824 (2005).

Add at p. 798 Problem 6.2

For a thorough review of the literature, see Zita Lazzarini & Lorilyn Rosales, *Legal Issues Concerning Public Health Efforts To Reduce Perinatal HIV Transmission*, 3 Yale J. Health Pol'y L. & Ethics 67 (2002).

SECTION 2. CHOOSING OUR CHILDREN

Add at p. 807 note 1:

In 2004, 28 states, by judicial opinion, statute, or both, had either refused to recognize or limited a wrongful life action. Three states (California, New Jersey, and Washington) had allowed such a cause of action by judicial opinion, and one, Maine, arguably had done so by statute. See 24 Me. Rev. Stat. Ann. § 2931 (limiting damages for birth of healthy, unplanned child to wrongful pregnancy cases and establishing recoverable damages for birth of unhealthy child born as a result of professional negligence); Thibeault v. Larson, 666 A.2d 112 (Me. 1995). Twenty jurisdictions had not addressed the issue. See Willis v. Wu, 607 S.E.2d 63 (S.C. 2004).

Add at p. 813 note 9:

The purposeful creation of a deaf child is not simply a theoretical possibility:

> In 1996 and again in 2002, Sharon Duchesneau and Candy McCullough, a lesbian couple living in Maryland, both of whom are deaf, hoped to have a deaf child -- a child "whom they felt they could guide and nurture with more understanding than a child with normal hearing." Both times, they maximized their chances by using donor sperm from a friend with five generations of deafness in his family. Both times, the couple succeeded; their children were born deaf. . .

Note, *Regulating Preimplantation Genetic Diagnosis: The Pathologization Problem*, 118 Harv L Rev 2770, 2782 (2005). Duchesneau and McCullough described deafness as "simply 'a cultural difference' . . . [and urged that they] 'feel whole as deaf people.'" *Id.*

Add at p. 822, new note 4:

4.   A survey of prospective jurors, pregnant couples, and couples enrolling in an IVF program found few group differences in desires to select or manipulate various genetic traits. Respondents were asked to "Imagine that you have a magic wand and can control what your future child will be like. We want to know how you would use your magic wand to choose traits in your child." They were asked to state how likely they would be to choose or improve the following fourteen traits: not be susceptible to breast cancer, have a certain hair color, be very creative, have a good memory, have a good sense of humor, have key social skills, be skilled at activities (e.g. sports, music, art), be attractive, not be very short or very tall, not be homosexual, have a certain eye color, not be very heavy, increased IQ, and have normal hearing. They were also asked how important it would be to them for their child to have their genes and their partner's genes.

Across the sample, health traits were most likely to be chosen or improved and appearance traits were least likely. Traits relating to personality and abilities fell in between the health and appearance traits in reported likelihood of being chosen or improved. The researchers concluded that

> IVF couples we studied cared less than or only as much as others about their children having specific or enhanced traits. Desires to genetically engineer one's children were no stronger among our IVF couples than the rest of our study population. However, and perhaps more interesting from a scientific point of view given the arguments of those for and against the use of ART as an aid to the neuro or physiologic betterment of the human species, the IVF couples we studied were significantly more likely than other couples or individuals to care about making children who have a genetic link to the couple. The evidence for a preference among IVF parents for a genotypic link was manifest both in terms of the specific desires of IVF parents as well as in their general attitudes, whereas, by contrast, the differences among studied groups in terms of each group's likelihood to choose or improve individual traits were reduced to a statistically insignificant level when adjusting for age, education and race. Group differences in the importance of a genetic link remained after adjusting for demographics: those who became hose who became pregnant without IVF and jurors expressed no such strong interest.

Andrea Gurmankin et al., *Medical Study – Aspiring Parents, Genotypes, and Phenotypes: The Unexamined Myth of the Perfect Baby*, 68 Alb L Rev 1097, 1104-05 (2005).

SECTION 3. TECHNOLOGICAL CONCEPTION

A. The Status of the Preembryo

Replace *Davis v. Davis,* p. 826 with:

In re Marriage of Witten
Iowa Supreme Court (2003)
672 N.W.2d 768 (2003)

TERNUS, J.

The primary issue raised on appeal of the district court's decree in this dissolution action is whether the court properly determined the rights of Arthur (known as Trip) and Tamera Witten with respect to the parties' frozen human embryos stored at a medical facility. While we agree with Tamera that the informed consent signed by the parties at the request of the medical facility does not control the current dispute between the donors over the use or disposition of the embryos, we reject Tamera's request that she be allowed to use the embryos over Trip's objection. Therefore, we affirm the trial court's order that neither party may use or dispose of the embryos without the consent of the other party. . . .

I. *Background Facts and Proceedings.*

The appellee, Arthur (Trip) Witten, and the appellant, Tamera Witten, had been married for approximately seven and one-half years when Trip sought to have their marriage dissolved in April 2002. One of the contested issues at trial was control of the parties' frozen embryos. During the parties' marriage they had tried to become parents through the process of in vitro fertilization. Because Tamera was unable to conceive children naturally, they had eggs taken from Tamera artificially fertilized with Trip's sperm. Tamera then underwent several unsuccessful embryo transfers in an attempt to become pregnant. At the time of trial seventeen fertilized eggs remained in storage at the University of Nebraska Medical Center (UNMC).

Prior to commencing the process for in vitro fertilization, the parties signed informed consent documents prepared by the medical center. These documents included an "Embryo Storage Agreement," which was signed by Tamera and Trip as well as by a representative of UNMC. It provided in part:

> *Release of Embryos.* The Client Depositors [Trip and Tamera] understand and agree that containers of embryos stored pursuant to this agreement will be used for transfer, release or disposition only with the signed approval of both Client Depositors. UNMC will release the containers of embryos only to a licensed physician recipient of written authorization of the Client Depositors.

The agreement had one exception to the joint-approval requirement that governed the disposition of the embryos upon the death of one or both of the client depositors. Another provision of the contract provided for termination of UNMC's responsibility to store the embryos upon several contingencies: (1) the client depositors' written authorization to release the embryos or to destroy them; (2) the death of the client depositors; (3) the failure of the client depositors to pay the annual storage fee; or (4) the expiration of ten years from the date of the agreement.

At trial, Tamera asked that she be awarded "custody" of the embryos. She wanted to have the embryos implanted in her or a surrogate mother in an effort to bear a genetically linked child. She testified that upon a successful pregnancy she would afford Trip the opportunity to exercise parental rights or to have his rights terminated. She adamantly opposed any destruction of the embryos, and was also unwilling to donate the eggs to another couple.

Trip testified at the trial that while he did not want the embryos destroyed, he did not want Tamera to use them. He would not oppose donating the embryos for use by another couple. Trip asked the court to enter a permanent injunction prohibiting either party from transferring, releasing, or utilizing the embryos without the written consent of both parties.

The district court decided the dispute should be governed by the "embryo storage agreement" between the parties and UNMC, which required both parties' consent to any use or disposition of the embryos. Enforcing this agreement, the trial court enjoined both parties "from transferring, releasing or in any other way using or disposing of the embryos . . . without the written and signed approval and authorization" of the other party.

Tamera has appealed the trial court's order.... She claims the storage agreement is silent with respect to disposition or use of the embryos upon the parties' dissolution because there is no provision specifically addressing that contingency. Therefore, she argues, the court should have applied the "best interests" test of Iowa Code chapter 598 (2001) and, pursuant to that analysis, awarded custody of the embryos to her. She makes the alternative argument that she is entitled to the fertilized eggs due to her fundamental right to bear children. Finally, Tamera claims it would violate the public policy of this state if Trip were allowed to back out of his agreement to have children. She claims such an agreement is evidenced by his participation in the in vitro fertilization procedure....

III. *Disposition of Embryos.*

A. *Scope of storage agreement.* We first consider Tamera's contention that the storage agreement does not address the situation at hand. As noted earlier, the agreement had a specific provision governing control of the embryos if one or both parties died, but did not explicitly deal with the possibility of divorce. Nonetheless, we think the present predicament falls within the general provision governing "release of embryos," in which the parties agreed that the embryos would not be transferred, released, or discarded without "the signed approval" of both Tamera and Trip. This provision is certainly broad enough to encompass the decision-making protocol when the parties are unmarried as well as when they are married.

The only question, then, is whether such agreements are enforceable when one of the parties later changes his or her mind with respect to the proper disposition of the embryos. In reviewing the scarce case law from other jurisdictions on this point, we have found differing views of how the parties' rights should be determined. There is, however, abundant literature that has scrutinized the approaches taken to date. Some writers have suggested refinements of the analytical framework employed by the courts thus far; some have proposed an entirely new model of analysis. From these various sources, we have identified three primary approaches to resolving disputes over the disposition of frozen embryos, which we have identified as (1) the contractual approach, (2) the contemporaneous mutual consent model, and (3) the balancing test.

Tamera's argument that her right to bear children should override the parties' prior agreement as well as Trip's current opposition to her use of the embryos resembles the balancing test. As for Tamera's alternative argument, we have found no authority supporting a "best interests" analysis in determining the disposition of frozen embryos. Nonetheless, we will first consider whether chapter 598 requires application of that analysis under the circumstances presented by this case. Then, we will discuss and consider the three approaches suggested by decisions from other jurisdictions and the literature on this subject.

B. *"Best interests" test.* Iowa Code section 598.41 sets forth various standards governing a court's determination of the custody of the parties' children in a dissolution case, including the requirement that any custody award reflect "the best interest of the child." Tamera contends the embryos are children and their best interest demands placement with her. Trip argues the frozen embryos are not children and should not be considered as such for purposes of applying chapter 598 in dissolution actions.

In resolving this disagreement, we note initially that we are not called upon to determine the religious or philosophical status of the fertilized eggs. Rather, we are merely required to decide whether the embryos have the *legal* status of children under our dissolution-of-marriage statute.

Our first step is to consider the legislature's definition of "child" as that term is used in chapter 598. The term "minor child" is defined in section 598.1(6) as "any *person* under legal age." Iowa Code § 598.1(6) (emphasis added). Whether frozen embryos fall within this definition is an issue of first impression for this court.

While we have not considered the legal status of frozen embryos before, our court has had the opportunity to determine whether an unborn fetus is a "person" or a "child" in the context of other statutory provisions. In the *Weitl* and *McKillip* cases, this court considered whether an unborn fetus, viable in *Weitl* and nonviable in *McKillip*, was a "person" within the meaning of Iowa's survival statute. Noting in *McKillip* that we "expressed no opinion as to the existence of the fetus as a person in either the philosophical or actual sense," we held the word "person" as used in the statute meant "only those born alive."

We reached a seemingly inconsistent result in *Dunn,* in which . . . we were called upon to decide whether a parent could recover under the rule for damages resulting from the death of the plaintiff's unborn child in an automobile accident. No statutory definition of the term "minor child" guided our analysis. We also found little assistance in linguistic arguments, observing whether the term "minor child" included the unborn depended on which dictionary was consulted. *Id.* at 833. Consequently, "setting completely aside all the philosophical arguments about the status of the unborn," we based our decision "on the rule's purpose." Noting the purpose of the rule was to permit parents to recover "when they are deprived of the anticipated services, companionship, and society of a minor child," we concluded a parent's "deprivation [did] not necessarily relate to the child's birth." We held, therefore, that the parent's right of recovery should "not depend on the legal status of the child" and [that] recovery . . . was permissible even when the deceased "child" was an unborn fetus.

The common denominator in all three of our cases that consider the legal status of a fetus is our focus on the purpose of the law at issue and the legislative intent reflected by that purpose. That is the approach we follow in deciding the issue in this case. Therefore, rather than relying on our prior cases involving different statutes, we center our attention on the legislative intent with respect to the statute at issue here.

With this focus in mind, we conclude [that] . . . the principles developed under th[e child-custody] statute are simply not suited to the resolution of disputes over the control of frozen embryos. Such disputes do not involve maximizing physical and emotional contact between both parents and the child; they involve the more fundamental decision of whether the parties will be parents at all. Moreover, it would be premature to consider which parent can most effectively raise the child when the "child" is still frozen in a storage facility.

. . . [T]he issue here is who will have decision-making authority with respect to the fertilized eggs. Thus, the factors that are relevant in determining the custody of children in dissolution cases are simply not useful in determining how decisions will be made with respect to the disposition and use of a divorced couple's fertilized eggs. For these reasons, we conclude the legislature did not intend to include fertilized eggs or frozen embryos within the scope of section 598.41.

C. *Enforcement of storage agreement.* We now consider the appropriateness of the trial court's decision to allow Tamera and Trip's agreement with the medical center to control the current dispute between them. As we noted above, there are three methods of analysis that have been suggested to resolve disputes over frozen embryos. We will discuss them separately.

1. *Contractual approach.* The currently prevailing view – expressed in three states – is that contracts entered into at the time of in vitro fertilization are enforceable so long as they do not violate public policy. See *Kass*, 696 N.E.2d at 180 (stating agreements between donors "regarding disposition of pre-zygotes should generally be presumed valid and binding"); *Davis*, 842 S.W.2d at 597 (holding agreement regarding disposition of embryos "should be considered binding"); *In re Litowitz*, 146 Wn.2d 514, 48 P.3d 261, 271 (Wash. 2002) (enforcing parties' contract providing for disposition of preembryos after five years of storage). The New York Court of Appeals expressed the following rationale for this contractual approach:[2]

> [It is] particularly important that courts seek to honor the parties' expressions of choice, made before disputes erupt, with the parties' over-all direction always uppermost in the analysis. Knowing that advance agreements will be enforced underscores the seriousness and integrity of the consent process. Advance agreements as to disposition would have little purpose if they were enforceable only in the event the parties continued to agree. To the extent possible, it should be the progenitors--not the State and not the courts--who by their prior directive make this deeply personal life choice.

Kass, 696 N.E.2d at 180.

This approach has been criticized, however, because it "insufficiently protects the individual and societal interests at stake":

---

[2] Application of the contractual approach in *Kass* resulted in enforcement of the parties' agreement that the fertilized eggs would be donated for research should the parties be "unable to make a decision regarding the disposition of [the] stored, frozen pre-zygotes." In *Litowitz*, the court permitted execution of the parties' previous agreement that the preembryos would be "disposed of" after five years. The resolution of the divorcing couple's dispute was more complex in *Davis* because the parties did not have a contract addressing the disposition of any unused preembryos. Noting that a "prior agreement concerning disposition should be carried out," the court concluded in the absence of such an agreement, "the relative interests of the parties in using or not using the preembryos must be weighed." The court awarded the preembryos to the husband, concluding his interest in not becoming a parent outweighed his former wife's interest in donating the preembryos to another couple for implantation. The court noted the issue might be closer if the wife had wanted to use the preembryos herself; but in view of the fact she had "a reasonable possibility of achieving parenthood by means other than use of the preembryos in question," she would not have prevailed even under those circumstances.

First, decisions about the disposition of frozen embryos implicate rights central to individual identity. On matters of such fundamental personal importance, individuals are entitled to make decisions consistent with their contemporaneous wishes, values, and beliefs. Second, requiring couples to make binding decisions about the future use of their frozen embryos ignores the difficulty of predicting one's future response to life-altering events such as parenthood. Third, conditioning the provision of infertility treatment on the execution of binding disposition agreements is coercive and calls into question the authenticity of the couple's original choice. Finally, treating couples' decisions about the future use of their frozen embryos as binding contracts undermines important values about families, reproduction, and the strength of genetic ties.

Coleman, 84 Minn. L. Rev. at 88-89. . . . In response to such concerns, one commentator has suggested an alternative model requiring contemporaneous mutual consent. We now examine that approach.

2. *Contemporaneous mutual consent.* The contractual approach and the contemporaneous mutual consent model share an underlying premise: "decisions about the disposition of frozen embryos belong to the couple that created the embryo, with each partner entitled to an equal say in how the embryos should be disposed." Coleman, 84 Minn. L. Rev. at 81. Departing from this common starting point, the alternative framework asserts the important question is "at what time does the partners' consent matter?" *Id.* at 91. Proponents of the mutual-consent approach suggest that, with respect to "decisions about intensely emotional matters, where people act more on the basis of feeling and instinct than rational deliberation," it may "be impossible to make a knowing and intelligent decision to relinquish a right in advance of the time the right is to be exercised." *Id.* at 98; *see also* Sara D. Petersen, Comment, *Dealing With Cryopreserved Embryos Upon Divorce: A Contractual Approach Aimed at Preserving Party Expectations*, 50 UCLA L. Rev. 1065, 1090 & n.156 (2003) (stating "surveys of couples that have stored frozen embryos suggest that they may be prone to changing their minds while their embryos remain frozen" and citing a study that found "'of the 41 couples that had recorded both a pre-treatment and post-treatment decision about embryo disposition, only 12 (29%) kept the same disposition choice'"). One's erroneous prediction of how she or he will feel about the matter at some point in the future can have grave repercussions. "Like decisions about marriage or relinquishing a child for adoption, decisions about the use of one's reproductive capacity have lifelong

consequences for a person's identity and sense of self". . . . To accommodate these concerns, advocates of the mutual-consent model propose "no embryo should be used by either partner, donated to another patient, used in research, or destroyed without the [contemporaneous] mutual consent of the couple that created the embryo." *Id.* at 110. Under this alternate framework,

> advance instructions would not be treated as binding contracts. If either partner has a change of mind about disposition decisions made in advance, that person's current objection would take precedence over the prior consent. If one of the partners rescinds an advance disposition decision and the other does not, the mutual consent principle would not be satisfied and the previously agreed-upon disposition decision could not be carried out. . . .
>
> When the couple is unable to agree to any disposition decision, the most appropriate solution is to keep the embryos where they are – in frozen storage. Unlike the other possible disposition decisions – use by one partner, donation to another patient, donation to research, or destruction – keeping the embryos frozen is not final and irrevocable. By preserving the status quo, it makes it possible for the partners to reach an agreement at a later time.

Id. at 110-12. Although this model precludes one party's use of the embryos to have children over the objection of the other party, the outcome under the contractual approach and the balancing test would generally be the same. *See A.Z. v. B.Z.*, 431 Mass. 150, 725 N.E.2d 1051, 1057-58 (Mass. 2000) ("As a matter of public policy, . . . forced procreation is not an area amenable to judicial enforcement."); *J.B.*, 783 A.2d at 717 (evaluating relative interests of parties in disposition of embryos, concluding husband should not be able to use embryos over wife's objection); *Davis*, 842 S.W.2d at 604 ("Ordinarily, the party wishing to avoid procreation should prevail.")

    3. *Balancing test.* The New Jersey Supreme Court appears to have adopted an analysis regarding the disposition of frozen human embryos that incorporates the idea of contemporaneous decision-making, but not that of mutual consent. In *J.B.*, the New Jersey court rejected the *Kass* and *Davis* contractual approach, noting public policy concerns in "enforcement of a contract that would allow the implantation of preembryos at some future date in a case where one party has reconsidered his or her earlier acquiescence." The court stated:

> We believe that the better rule, and the one we adopt, is to enforce agreements entered into at the time in vitro fertilization is begun, *subject to the right of either party to change his or her mind about disposition up to the point of use or destruction of any stored preembryos.*

The court based its decision on "the public policy concerns that underlie limitations on contracts involving family relationships." *Id.*; *see also A.Z.*, 725 N.E.2d at 1057-58 (refusing, in light of the same public policy concerns, to enforce an agreement that allowed the wife, upon the parties' separation, to use the couple's preembryos for implantation).

The New Jersey court did not, however, adopt the requirement for mutual consent as a prerequisite for any use or disposition of the preembryos. Rather, that court stated that "if there is a disagreement between the parties as to disposition . . ., the interests of both parties must be evaluated" by the court. This balancing test was also the default analysis employed by the Tennessee Supreme Court in *Davis* where the parties had not executed a written agreement. *See Davis*, 842 S.W.2d at 604 (holding in the absence of a prior agreement concerning disposition, "the relative interests of the parties in using or not using the preembryos must be weighed" by the court).

The obvious problem with the balancing test model is its internal inconsistency. Public policy concerns similar to those that prompt courts to refrain from enforcement of contracts addressing reproductive choice demand even more strongly that we not substitute the courts as decision makers in this highly emotional and personal area. Nonetheless, that is exactly what happens under the decisional framework based on the balancing test because the court must weigh the relative interests of the parties in deciding the disposition of embryos when the parties cannot agree.

D. *Discussion.* With these alternative approaches in mind, we turn to the present case. Trip asks that the contractual provision requiring mutual consent be enforced; Tamera claims this agreement is against the public policy of Iowa because it allows Trip to back out of his prior agreement to become a parent. We first consider whether there is any merit to Tamera's public policy argument. . . .

"To strike down a contract on public policy grounds, we must conclude that "the preservation of the general public welfare . . . outweighs the weighty societal interest in the freedom of contract." In consideration of the delicate balancing required in this arena, we exercise the power to invalidate a contract on public policy grounds cautiously and only in cases free from doubt.

Tamera contends the contract at issue here violates public policy because it allows a person who has agreed to participate in an in vitro fertilization program to later change his mind about becoming a parent. While there is some question whether Trip's participation constitutes an implied agreement to become a father, we accept Tamera's assertion for purposes of the present discussion and proceed to consider whether there is any public policy against an agreement allowing a donor to abandon in vitro fertilization attempts when viable embryos remain. Tamera cites to no Iowa statute or prior case that articulates such a policy in the factual context we face here. While Iowa statutes clearly impose responsibilities on parents for the support and safekeeping of their children, such statutes, as we have already discussed in connection with chapter 598, do not contemplate the complex issues surrounding the disposition and use of frozen human embryos. The public policy evidenced by our law relates to the State's concern for the physical, emotional, and psychological well being of children who have been born, not fertilized eggs that have not even resulted in a pregnancy.

Nor can we say that the "morals of the times" are such that a party participating in an in vitro fertilization process has the duty to use or facilitate the use of each fertilized egg for purposes of pregnancy. To the contrary, courts that have considered one party's desire to use frozen embryos over the objection of the other progenitor have held that the objecting party's fundamental right not to procreate outweighs the other party's procreative rights, even in the face of a prior agreement allowing one party to use the embryos upon the parties' divorce. Thus, we find no public policy that requires the use of the frozen embryos over one party's objection.

That brings us to the more complex issue: are prior agreements regarding the future disposition of embryos enforceable when one of the donors is no longer comfortable with his or her prior decision? We first note our agreement with other courts considering such matters that the partners who created the embryos have the primary, and equal, decision-making authority with respect to the use or disposition of their embryos. We think, however, that it would be against the public policy of this state to enforce a prior agreement between the parties in this highly personal area of reproductive choice when one of the parties has changed his or her mind concerning the disposition or use of the embryos.

Our statutes and case law evidence an understanding that decisions involving marital and family relationships are emotional and subject to change. For example, Iowa law imposes a seventy-two hour waiting period after the birth of a child before the biological parents can release parental rights. In addition, although this court has not abolished claims for breach of promise to marry, only recovery of monetary damages is permitted; the court will not force a party to actually consummate the marriage. It has also long been recognized in this state that agreements for the purpose of bringing about a dissolution of marriage are contrary to public policy and therefore void.

This court has also expressed a general reluctance to become involved in intimate questions inherent in personal relationships. In *Miller*, we refused to enforce a contract between husband and wife that required, in part, each "to behave respectfully, and fairly treat the other." . . . Certainly reproductive decisions are likewise not proper matters of judicial inquiry and enforcement.

We have considered and rejected the arguments of some commentators that embryo disposition agreements are analogous to antenuptial agreements and divorce stipulations, which courts generally enforce. Whether embryos are viewed as having life or simply as having the potential for life, this characteristic or potential renders embryos fundamentally distinct from the chattels, real estate, and money that are the subjects of antenuptial agreements. . . .

We think judicial decisions and statutes in Iowa reflect respect for the right of individuals to make family and reproductive decisions based on their current views and values. They also reveal awareness that such decisions are highly emotional in nature and subject to a later change of heart. For this reason, we think judicial enforcement of an agreement between a couple regarding their future family and reproductive choices would be against the public policy of this state.

Our decision should not be construed, however, to mean that disposition agreements *between donors and fertility clinics* have no validity at all. We recognize a disposition or storage agreement serves an important purpose in defining and governing the relationship between the couple and the medical facility, ensuring that all parties understand their respective rights and obligations. . . . Within this context, the medical facility and the donors should be able to rely on the terms of the parties' contract.

In view of these competing needs, we reject the contractual approach and hold that agreements entered into at the time in vitro fertilization is commenced are enforceable and binding on the parties, "subject to the right of either party to change his or her mind about disposition up to the point of use or destruction of any stored embryo." *J.B.*, 783 A.2d at 719. This decisional model encourages prior agreements that can guide the actions of all parties, unless a later objection to any dispositional provision is asserted. It also recognizes that, *absent a change of heart by one of the partners*, an agreement governing disposition of embryos does not violate public policy. Only when one person makes known the agreement no longer reflects his or her current values or wishes is public policy implicated. Upon this occurrence, allowing either party to withdraw his or her agreement to a disposition that person no longer accepts acknowledges the public policy concerns inherent in enforcing prior decisions of a fundamentally personal nature. In fairness to the medical facility that is a party to the agreement, however, any change of intention must be communicated in writing to all parties in order to reopen the disposition issues covered by the agreement.

That brings us, then, to the dilemma presented when one or both partners change their minds and the parties cannot reach a mutual decision on disposition. We have already explained the grave public policy concerns we have with the balancing test, which simply substitutes the court as decision maker. A better principle to apply, we think, is the requirement of contemporaneous mutual consent. Under that model, no transfer, release, disposition, or use of the embryos can occur without the signed authorization of both donors. If a stalemate results, the status quo would be maintained. The practical effect will be that the embryos are stored indefinitely unless both parties can agree to destroy the fertilized eggs. Thus, any expense associated with maintaining the status quo should logically be borne by the person opposing destruction.

Turning to the present case, we find a situation in which one party no longer concurs in the parties' prior agreement with respect to the disposition of their frozen embryos, but the parties have been unable to reach a new agreement that is mutually satisfactory. Based on this fact, under the principles we have set forth today, we hold there can be no use or disposition of the Wittens' embryos unless Trip and

Tamera reach an agreement. Until then, the party or parties who oppose destruction shall be responsible for any storage fees. Therefore, we affirm the trial court's ruling enjoining both parties from transferring, releasing, or utilizing the embryos without the other's written consent.

Replace note 5, at p. 835:

5.   What, if any, purpose is served by a contract with an IVF facility if either party can void the contract at will? How would the *Davis, Kass, A.Z.* and *J.B.* courts have ruled in *Witten*? Is the *Witten* court's analysis of the merits of the various approaches persuasive?

B. Parental Rights and Obligations

Replace, at p. 854, *Johnson v. Calvert, Moschetta v. Moschetta, and Buzzanca v. Buzzanca* with:

K.M. v. E.G.

California Supreme Court (2005)

37 Cal. 4th 130; 117 P.3d 673; 33 Cal. Rptr. 3d 61

MORENO, J.

We granted review in this case, as well as in *Elisa B. v. Superior Court* (2005) 37 Cal.4th 108, and *Kristine H. v. Lisa R.* (2005) 37 Cal.4th 156, to consider the parental rights and obligations, if any, of a woman with regard to a child born to her partner in a lesbian relationship. . . .

Facts

On March 6, 2001, petitioner K.M. filed a petition to establish a parental relationship with twin five-year-old girls born to respondent E.G., her former lesbian partner. K.M. alleged that she "is the biological parent of the minor children" because "[s]he donated her egg to respondent, the gestational mother of the children." E.G. moved to dismiss the petition on the grounds that, although K.M. and E.G. "were lesbian partners who lived together until this action was filed," K.M. "explicitly donated her ovum under a clear written agreement by which she relinquished any claim to offspring born of her donation."

On April 18, 2001, K.M. filed a motion for custody of and visitation with the twins. A hearing was held at which E.G. testified that she first considered raising a child before she met K.M., at a time when she did not have a partner. She met K.M. in October 1992 and they became romantically involved in June 1993. E.G. told K.M. that she planned to adopt a baby as a single mother. E.G. applied for adoption in November 1993. K.M. and E.G. began living together in March 1994 and registered as domestic partners in San Francisco.

E.G. visited several fertility clinics in March 1993 to inquire about artificial insemination and she attempted artificial insemination, without success, on 13 occasions from July 1993 through November 1994. K.M. accompanied her to most of these appointments. K.M. testified that she and E.G. planned to raise the child together, while E.G. insisted that, although K.M. was very supportive, E.G. made it clear that her intention was to become "a single parent."

In December 1994, E.G. consulted with Dr. Mary Martin at the fertility practice of the University of California at San Francisco Medical Center (UCSF). E.G.'s first attempts at in vitro fertilization failed because she was unable to produce sufficient ova. In January 1995, Dr. Martin suggested using K.M.'s ova. E.G. then asked K.M. to donate her ova, explaining that she would accept the ova only if K.M. "would really be a donor" and E.G. would "be the mother of any child," adding that she would not even consider permitting K.M. to adopt the child "for at least five years until [she] felt the relationship was stable and would endure." E.G. told K.M. that she "had seen too many lesbian relationships end quickly, and [she] did not want to be in a custody battle." E.G. and K.M. agreed they would not tell anyone that K.M. was the ova donor.

K.M. acknowledged that she agreed not to disclose to anyone that she was the ova donor, but insisted that she only agreed to provide her ova because she and E.G. had agreed to raise the child together. K.M. and E.G. selected the sperm donor together. K.M. denied that E.G. had said she wanted to be a single parent and insisted that she would not have donated her ova had she known E.G. intended to be the sole parent.

On March 8, 1995, K.M. signed a four-page form on UCSF letterhead entitled "Consent Form for Ovum Donor (Known)." The form states that K.M. agrees "to have eggs taken from my ovaries, in order that they may be donated to another woman." After explaining the medical procedures involved, the form states on the third page: "It is understood that I waive any right and relinquish any claim to the donated eggs or any pregnancy or offspring that might result from them. I agree that the recipient may regard the donated eggs and any offspring resulting therefrom as her own children." The following appears on page 4 of the form, above K.M.'s signature and the signature of a witness: "I specifically disclaim and waive any right in or any child that may be [**8] conceived as a result of the use of any ovum or egg of mine, and I agree not to attempt to discover the identity of the recipient thereof." E.G. signed a form entitled "Consent Form for Ovum Recipient" that stated, in part: "I acknowledge that the child or children produced by the IVF procedure is and shall be my own legitimate child or children and the heir or heirs of my body with all rights and privileges accompanying such status."

E.G. testified she received these two forms in a letter from UCSF dated February 2, 1995, and discussed the consent forms with K.M. during February and March. E.G. stated she would not have accepted K.M.'s ova if K.M. had not signed the consent form, because E.G. wanted to have a child on her own and believed the consent form "protected" her in this regard.

K.M. testified to the contrary that she first saw the ovum donation consent form 10 minutes before she signed it on March 8, 1995. K.M. admitted reading the form, but thought parts of the form were "odd" and did not pertain to her, such as the part stating that the donor promised not to discover the identity of the recipient. She did not intend to relinquish her rights and only signed the form so that "we could have children." Despite having signed the form, K.M. "thought [she] was going to be a parent."

Ova were withdrawn from K.M. on April 11, 1995, and embryos were implanted in E.G. on April 13, 1995. K.M. and E.G. told K.M.'s father about the resulting pregnancy by announcing that he was going to be a grandfather. The twins were born on December 7, 1995. The twins' birth certificates listed E.G. as their mother and did not reflect a father's name. As they had agreed, neither E.G. nor K.M. told anyone K.M. had donated the ova, including their friends, family and the twins' pediatrician. Soon after the twins were born, E.G. asked K.M. to marry her, and on Christmas Day, the couple exchanged rings.

Within a month of their birth, E.G. added the twins to her health insurance policy, named them as her beneficiary for all employment benefits, and increased her life insurance with the twins as the beneficiary. K.M. did not do the same.

E.G. referred to her mother, as well as K.M.'s parents, as the twins' grandparents and referred to K.M.'s sister and brother as the twins' aunt and uncle, and K.M.'s nieces as their cousins. Two school forms listed both K.M. and respondent as the twins' parents. The children's nanny testified that both K.M. and E.G. "were the babies' mother."

The relationship between K.M. and E.G. ended in March 2001 and K.M. filed the present action. In September 2001, E.G. and the twins moved to Massachusetts to live with E.G.'s mother.

The superior court granted the motion to dismiss finding, in a statement of decision, "that [K.M.]. . . knowingly, voluntarily and intelligently executed the ovum donor form, thereby acknowledging her understanding that, by the donation of her ova, she was relinquishing and waiving all rights to claim legal parentage of any children who might result from the *in vitro* fertilization and implantation of her ova in a recipient (in this case, a known recipient, her domestic partner [E.G.]). . . . [K.M.]'s testimony on the subject of her execution of the ovum donor form was contradictory and not always credible."

> . . . By voluntarily signing the ovum donation form, [K.M.] was donating genetic material. Her position was analogous to that of a sperm donor, who is treated as a legal stranger to a child if he donates sperm through a licensed physician and surgeon under Family Code section 7613[, subdivision] (b). The Court finds no reason to treat ovum donors as having greater claims to parentage than sperm donors. . . .
>
> [K.M.]'s claim to 'presumed' parenthood rests upon her contention that she has met the criteria of Family Code section 7611[, subdivision] (d). [K.M.] . . . has failed to establish either that she received the twins into her home or that she held them out 'as [her] natural child[ren.]' Although [K.M.] *treated* the twins in all regards as though they were her own (and there can be no question but that they are fully bonded to her as such), the children were *received* into the parties' home as [E.G.]'s children and, up until late 1999, both parties scrupulously held confidential [petitioner]'s 'natural,' i.e., in this case, her genetic relationship to the children. . . .

The Court of Appeal affirmed the judgment. . . . We granted review.

Discussion

K.M. asserts that she is a parent of the twins because she supplied the ova that were fertilized in vitro and implanted in her lesbian partner, resulting in the birth of the twins. As we will explain, we agree that K.M. is a parent of the twins because she supplied the ova that produced the children, and Family Code section 7613 (b) (hereafter section 7613(b)), which provides that a man is not a father if he provides semen to a physician to inseminate a woman who is not his wife, does not apply because K.M. supplied her ova to impregnate her lesbian partner in order to produce children who would be raised in their joint home.

The determination of parentage is governed by the Uniform Parentage Act (UPA). . . .

In *Johnson v. Calvert* (1993), we determined that a wife whose ovum was fertilized in vitro by her husband's sperm and implanted in a surrogate mother was the "natural mother" of the child thus produced. We noted that the UPA states that provisions applicable to determining a father and child relationship shall be used to determine a mother and child relationship "insofar as practicable." We relied, therefore, on the provisions in the UPA regarding presumptions of paternity and concluded that "genetic consanguinity" could be the basis for a finding of maternity just as it is for paternity. Under this authority, K.M.'s genetic relationship to the children in the present case constitutes "evidence of a mother and child relationship as contemplated by the Act.

The Court of Appeal in the present case concluded, however, that K.M. was not a parent of the twins, despite her genetic relationship to them, because she had the same status as a sperm donor. Section 7613(b) states: "The donor of semen provided to a licensed physician and surgeon for use in artificial insemination of a woman other than the donor's wife is treated in law as if he were not the natural father of a child thereby conceived." In *Johnson*, we considered the predecessor statute to section 7613(b). . . . We did not discuss whether this statute applied to a woman who provides ova used to impregnate another woman, but we observed that "in a true 'egg donation' situation, where a woman gestates and gives birth to a child formed from the egg of another woman with the intent to raise the child as her own, the birth mother is the natural mother under California law." We held that the statute did not apply under the circumstances in *Johnson*, because the husband and wife in *Johnson* did not intend to "donate" their sperm and ova to the surrogate mother, but rather "intended to procreate a child genetically related to them by the only available means."

The circumstances of the present case are not identical to those in *Johnson*, but they are similar in a crucial respect; both the couple in *Johnson* and the couple in the present case intended to produce a child that would be raised in their own home. In *Johnson*, it was clear that the married couple did not intend to "donate" their semen and ova to the surrogate mother, but rather permitted their semen and ova to be used to impregnate the surrogate mother in order to produce a child to be raised by them. In the present case, K.M. contends that she did not intend to donate her ova, but rather provided her ova so that E. G. could give birth to a child to be raised jointly by K.M. and E.G. E.G. hotly contests this, asserting that K.M. donated her ova to E.G., agreeing that E.G. would be the sole parent. It is undisputed, however, that the couple lived together and that they both intended to bring the child into their joint home. Thus, even accepting as true E.G.'s version of the facts (which the superior court did), the present case, like *Johnson*, does not present a "true 'egg donation'" situation. K.M. did not intend to simply donate her ova to E.G., but rather provided her ova to her lesbian partner with whom she was living so that E.G. could give birth to a child that would be raised in their joint home. Even if we assume that the provisions of section 7613(b) apply to women who donate ova, the statute does not apply under the circumstances of the present case. . . .

Although the predecessor to section 7613 was based upon the Model UPA, the California Legislature made one significant change; it expanded the reach of the provision to apply to both married and unmarried women. . . .

This . . . was purposeful. . . . California intended to expand the protection of the model act to include unmarried women so that unmarried women could avail themselves of artificial insemination. But there is nothing to indicate that California intended to expand the reach of this provision so far that it would apply if a man provided semen to be used to impregnate his unmarried partner in order to produce a child that would be raised in their joint home. It would be surprising, to say the least, to conclude that the Legislature intended such a result. The Colorado Supreme Court considered a related issue and reached a similar conclusion.

In *In Interest of R.C.*, the Colorado Supreme Court addressed a Colorado statute identical to section 7613(b), which applied to both married and unmarried women. At issue were the parental rights, if any, of a man who provided semen to a physician that was used to impregnate an unmarried friend of the man. The man claimed that the woman had promised that he would be treated as the child's father. The court recognized that the Model UPA addressed only the artificial insemination of a woman married to someone other than the semen donor, adding that the parental rights of a semen donor are "least clearly understood when the semen donor is known and the recipient is unmarried." The court concluded that the statute did not apply when a man donated semen to an unmarried woman with the understanding that he would be the father of the resulting child: "[W]e conclude that the General Assembly neither considered nor intended to affect the rights of known donors who gave their semen to unmarried women for use in artificial insemination with the agreement that the donor would be the father of any child so conceived. [The statute] simply does not apply in that circumstance."

. . . We are faced with an even more compelling situation, because K.M. and E.G. were more than "friends" when K.M. provided her ova, through a physician, to be used to impregnate E.G.; they lived together and were registered domestic partners. Although the parties dispute whether both women were intended to be parents of the resulting child, it is undisputed that they intended that the resulting child would be raised in their joint home. Neither the Model UPA, nor section 7613(b) was intended to apply under such circumstances.

As noted *ante*, K.M.'s genetic relationship with the twins constitutes evidence of a mother and child relationship under the UPA and, as explained *ante*, section 7613(b) does not apply to exclude K.M. as a parent of the twins. The circumstance that E.G. gave birth to the twins also constitutes evidence of a mother and child relationship. Thus, both K.M. and E.G. are mothers of the twins under the UPA.

It is true we said in *Johnson* that "for any child California law recognizes only one natural mother." But as we explain in the companion case of *Elisa B. v. Superior Court*, this statement in *Johnson* must be understood in light of the issue presented in that case; "our decision in *Johnson* does not preclude a child from having two parents both of whom are women ... ."

Justice Werdegar's dissent argues that we should determine whether K.M. is a parent using the "intent test" we developed in *Johnson v. Calvert*. In *Johnson*, an embryo created using the sperm and egg of a married couple was implanted in a surrogate mother. It was undisputed that the husband was the father of the resulting child, but the wife and the surrogate both claimed to be the mother. We recognized that both women "have adduced evidence of a mother and child relationship" under the UPA – the wife because she is genetically related to the child and the surrogate because she gave birth to the child--but we rejected the suggestion that, under the circumstances of that case, the child could have two mothers, leaving the child with three parents. In order to determine which woman was the child's sole mother under the UPA, we looked to their respective intents: "Because two women each have presented acceptable proof of maternity, we do not believe this case can be decided without enquiring into the parties' intentions ... ."

As the dissent acknowledges, a child can have two mothers. Thus, this case differs from *Johnson* in that both K.M. and E.G. can be the children's mothers. Unlike in *Johnson*, their parental claims are not mutually exclusive. K.M. acknowledges that E.G. is the twins' mother. K.M. does not claim to be the twins' mother *instead of* E.G., but *in addition to* E.G., so we need not consider their intent in order to decide between them. Rather, the parentage of the twins is determined by application of the UPA. E.G. is the twins' mother because she gave birth to them and K.M. also is the twins' mother because she provided the ova from which they were produced.

Justice Werdegar's dissent claims that we are "changing the law" by creating a "new rule" for determining whether a woman who supplies an ovum is the mother of the resulting child. We are not. Nothing in *Johnson* suggests that the intent test applies in cases not involving surrogacy agreements, and the dissent agrees that the linchpin of the decision in *Johnson* – that a child cannot have two mothers – does not apply here. We simply hold that section 7613(b), which creates an exception to the usual rules governing parentage that applies when a man donates semen to inseminate a woman who is not his wife, does not apply under the circumstances of this case in which K.M. supplied ova to impregnate her lesbian partner in order to produce children who would be raised in their joint home. Because the exception provided in section 7613(b) does not apply, K.M.'s parentage is determined by the usual provisions of the UPA. As noted above, under the UPA, K.M.'s genetic relationship to the twins constitutes "evidence of a mother and child relationship."

It would be unwise to expand application of the *Johnson* intent test as suggested by Justice Werdegar's dissent beyond the circumstances presented in *Johnson*. Usually, whether there is evidence of a parent and child relationship under the UPA does not depend upon the intent of the parent. For example, a man who engages in sexual intercourse with a woman who assures him, falsely, that she is incapable of conceiving children is the father of a resulting child, despite his lack of intent to become a father.

Justice Werdegar's dissent states that predictability in this area is important, but relying upon a later judicial determination of the intent of the parties, as the dissent suggests, would not provide such predictability. The present case is a good example. Justice Werdegar's dissent concludes that K.M. did not intend to become a parent, because the superior court "found on the basis of conflicting evidence that she did not," noting that "[w]e must defer to the trial court's findings on this point because substantial evidence supports them." Had the superior court reached the opposite conclusion, however, the dissent presumably again would defer to the trial court's findings and reach the opposite conclusion that K.M. is a parent of the twins. Rather than provide predictability, therefore, using the intent test would rest the determination of parentage upon a later judicial determination of intent made years after the birth of the child. . . .

The superior court in the present case found that K.M. signed a waiver form, thereby "relinquishing and waiving all rights to claim legal parentage of any children who might result." But such a waiver does not affect our determination of parentage. Section 7632 provides: "Regardless of its terms, an agreement between an alleged or presumed father and the mother or child does not bar an action under this chapter." (See *In re Marriage of Buzzanca*, *supra*, 61 Cal.App.4th 1410, 1426 ["It is well established that parents cannot, by agreement, limit or abrogate a child's right to support.") A woman who supplies ova to be used to impregnate her lesbian partner, with the understanding that the resulting child will be raised in their joint home, cannot waive her responsibility to support that child. Nor can such a purported waiver effectively cause that woman to relinquish her parental rights.

In light of our conclusion that section 7613(b) does not apply and that K.M. is the twins' parent (together with E.G.), based upon K.M.'s genetic relationship to the twins, we need not, and do not, consider whether K.M. is presumed to be a parent of the twins under section 7611, subdivision (d), which provides that a man is presumed to be a child's father if "[h]e receives the child into his home and openly holds out the child as his natural child."

The judgment of the Court of Appeal is reversed.

KENNARD, J., Dissenting.

. . . .

I recognize that California law does not expressly address the maternal status of ova donors. But, . . .[a]s the trial court here explained: K.M.'s "position was analogous to that of a sperm donor, who is treated as a legal stranger to the child if he donates sperm through a licensed physician and surgeon." Like the trial court, I see "no reason to treat ovum donors as having greater claims to parentage than sperm donors."

The analogy between sperm and ova donors is not new. Indeed, in *Johnson*, this court signalled its view that an ova donor would not be treated as the child's mother. *Johnson* held that "in a true 'egg donation' situation, where a woman gestates and gives birth to a child formed from the egg of another women with the intent to raise the child as her own, the birth mother is the natural mother under California law." Nearly two years after that decision, E.G. in this case undertook in vitro fertilization with ova from K.M.

In the 12 years since this court's decision in *Johnson*, an unknown number of Californians have made procreative choices in reliance on it. For example, in the companion case of *Kristine H. v. Lisa R.*, a lesbian couple obtained a prebirth stipulated judgment declaring them to be 'the joint *intended legal parents*' of the child born to one of them, language they presumably used in order to bring themselves within *Johnson* where the preconception intent to become a parent is the determinative inquiry. We do know that prebirth judgments of parentage on behalf of the nonbiologically related partner of a child's biological parent have been entered in this state, and that such judgments were touted to same-sex couples as less expensive and time-consuming than second parent adoption. How will today's majority holding affect the validity of the various procreative choices made in reliance on *Johnson*? The majority's decision offers no answers.

The majority's desire to give the twins a second parent is understandable and laudable. To achieve that worthy goal, however, the majority must rewrite a statute and disregard the intentions that the parties expressed when the twins were conceived. . . . Relying on the plain meaning of the statutory language, and the trial court's findings that both K.M. and E.G. intended that E.G. would be the only parent of any children resulting from the artificial insemination, I would affirm the judgment of the Court of Appeal, which in turn affirmed the trial court, rejecting K.M.'s claim to parentage of the twins born to E.G.

WERDEGAR, J., Dissenting.

. . . .

I find the majority's reasons for not applying the *Johnson* intent test unpersuasive. The majority criticizes the test as basing "the determination of parentage upon a later judicial determination of intent made years after the birth of the child." But the task of determining the intent of persons who have undertaken assisted reproduction is not fundamentally different than the task of determining intent in the context of disputes involving contract, tort or criminal law, something courts have done satisfactorily for centuries. The expectation that courts will in most cases accurately decide factual issues such as intent is one of the fundamental premises of our judicial system. Indeed, the majority itself expresses willingness to continue applying the *Johnson* intent test to determine whether gestational surrogacy agreements are enforceable. This position leaves no plausible basis for refusing to apply the same test to determine whether ovum donation agreements are enforceable. Ovum donation and gestational surrogacy agreements are two sides of the same coin; each involves an ovum provider, a gestator, and an agreement about who will become the parent or parents of any resulting offspring. Indeed, when two women divide in this way the genetic and gestational components of motherhood, only an examination of their intent permits us to determine whether we are dealing with an ovum donation agreement, a gestational surrogacy agreement, or neither. If courts can perform one of these tasks acceptably, they can also perform the other.

No more persuasive is the majority's suggestion that to respect the formally expressed intent of the parties to an ovum donation agreement is prohibited by the rule that parental obligations may not be waived by contract. We expressly rejected a similar argument directed against a gestational surrogacy agreement in *Johnson*. Certainly parental obligations may not be waived by contract. But *Johnson*'s intent test does not *enforce* ovum donation and gestational surrogacy agreements; it merely directs courts to consider such documents, along with all other relevant evidence, in determining preconception intent.

As a final reason for rejecting the intent test, the majority suggests that to apply the test outside the context of *Johnson* might shield from the obligations of fatherhood, contrary to existing law, a man who, lacking the intent to become a father, "engages in sexual intercourse with a woman who assures him, falsely, that she is incapable of conceiving children. . . ." But no one, to my knowledge, proposes to apply the intent test to determine the parentage of children conceived through ordinary sexual reproduction. This court adopted the intent test to resolve cases of assisted reproduction in which disputes over motherhood arise because one woman has provided the ova and another has gestated them. Both *Johnson*, and the case before us belong to that category. Although the majority may be correct in asserting that "[u]sually, whether there is evidence of a parent and child relationship under the UPA does not depend upon the intent of the parent", we adopted the intent test precisely because the UPA does not expressly resolve conflicting claims to motherhood arising from ovum transplants. The majority's speculation about men who engage in sexual activity despite mental reservations about fatherhood is irrelevant.

The new rule the majority substitutes for the intent test entails serious problems. First, the rule inappropriately confers rights and imposes disabilities on persons because of their sexual orientation. In a standard ovum donation agreement, such as the agreement between K.M. and E.G., the donor confirms her intention to assist another woman to become a parent without the donor becoming a parent herself. The majority's rule vitiates such agreements when its conditions are satisfied – conditions that include the fact the parties to the agreement are lesbian. Although the majority denies that its rule depends on sexual orientation, the opinion speaks for itself. The majority has chosen to use the term "lesbian" no less than six times in articulating its holding. Moreover, the majority prevents future courts from applying its holding automatically to persons other than lesbians by stating that it "decide[s] only the case before us, which involves a lesbian couple who registered as domestic partners." I see no rational basis – and the majority articulates none – for permitting the enforceability of an ovum donation agreement to depend on the sexual orientation of the parties. Indeed, lacking a rational basis, the rule may well violate equal protection. See *Romer v. Evans* (1996) 517 U.S. 620, 631-636 Why should a lesbian not have the same right as other women to donate ova without becoming a mother, or to accept a donation of ova without accepting the donor as a coparent, even if the donor and recipient live together and both plan to help raise the child?

. . . To make the determination of natural parentage rest in part on the intent to *raise* a child [also] injects into that determination a best interests factor – something we have previously refused to do. I realize the court in *Johnson* wrote that "she who intended to procreate the child – that is, she who intended to bring about the birth of a child that she intended to raise as her own – is the natural mother under California law." But the phrase "*raise as her own*" in that context did not refer simply to providing childcare; instead, it meant that the woman in question intended to be a *parent* – to raise a child of *her own*. In no sense did the *Johnson* court base its decision of parentage on the question of who would provide childcare. By analogy, Family Code section 7611, subdivision (d), which creates the presumption that a man who "receives [a] child into his home and openly holds out the child as his natural child" is not satisfied simply because a man receives the child into his home; to become a presumed father he must also hold out the child *as his natural child*.

Perhaps the most serious problem with the majority's new rule is that it threatens to destabilize ovum donation and gestational surrogacy agreements. One important function of *Johnson*'s intent test was to permit persons who made use of reproductive technology to create, before conception, settled and enforceable expectations about who would and would not become parents. *Johnson*, thus gave E.G. a right at the time she conceived to expect that she alone would be the parent of her children – a right the majority now retrospectively abrogates. . . . We cannot recognize K.M. as a parent without diminishing E.G.'s existing parental rights. In light of the majority's abrogation of *Johnson* and apparent willingness to ignore preconception manifestations of intent, at least in some cases, women who wish to donate ova without becoming mothers, serve as gestational surrogates without becoming mothers, or accept ovum donations without also accepting the donor as a coparent would be well advised to proceed with the most extreme caution. While the majority purports to limit its holding to cohabiting lesbians, and possibly only to those cohabiting lesbians who are also domestic partners, these limitations, as I have explained, rest on questionable legal grounds and may well not stand the test of time. . . .

. . . We expressly eschewed a best interests approach in *Johnson*, explaining that it "raises the repugnant specter of governmental interference in matters implicating our most fundamental notions of privacy, and confuses concepts of parentage and custody." This case, in which the majority compels E.G. to accept K.M. as an unintended parent to E.G.'s children, in part because of E.G.'s and K.M.'s sexual orientation and the character of their private relationship, shows that *Johnson*'s warning was prescient. Only legislation defining parentage in the context of assisted reproduction is likely to restore predictability and prevent further lapses into the disorder of ad hoc adjudication.

Replace notes 2-5, at p. 866-67 with:

2. In one companion case to *K.M.*, *Elisa B. v. Superior Court*, 37 Cal. 4th 108, 117 P.3d 660 (2005), the California Supreme Court held that a same-sex cohabitant who had treated her partner's twins, one of whom had Down's Syndrome, as her own, was legally obligated to support the twins despite the absence of a biological or adoptive relationship or any written support agreement.

The trial court concluded that the cohabitant was obligated to support the twins under the doctrine of equitable estoppel, a doctrine which "expressing the law's distate for inconsistent actions and positions – like consenting to an act which brings a child into existence and then turning around and disclaiming any responsibility." *Buzzanca v. Buzzanca*, 61 Cal App 4th 1410, 72 Cal Prtr 2d 280 (Ca. Ct. App. 1998). In *Elisa B.*, the biological mother "agreed to have children with Respondent, and relied on her promise to raise and support her children. She would not have agreed to impregnation but for this agreement and understanding. . . . . The need for the application of this doctrine is underscored by the fact that the decision of Respondent to create a family and desert them has caused the remaining family members to seek county assistance. . . . The child was deprived of the right to have a traditional father to take care of the financial needs of this child. Respondent chose to step in those shoes and assume the role and responsibility of the 'other' parent. This should be her responsibility and not the responsibility of the taxpayer." *Id.* at 115.

The California Supreme Court relied on the same interpretation of Cal. Fam. Code that it utilized in *K.G.* instead of the estoppel doctrine. Its decision was unanimous.

In the other companion case to *K.G.*, the California Supreme Court relied on the estoppel doctrine instead of the statute; this decision, too, was unanimous. *Kristine H v. Lisa R.*, 37 Cal. 4th 156,

117 P.3d 690 (2005), involved a same-sex couple who had stipulated to the parentage of the child that they planned to raise together during the biological mother's pregnancy. The couple separated two years after the child's birth and the nonparent sought to vacate the judgment. The California Supreme Court held that, in light of the fact that "stipulated to the issuance of a judgment, and enjoyed the benefits of that judgment for nearly two years, it would be unfair both to Lisa and the child to permit Kristine to challenge the validity of that judgment. To permit her to attack the validity of the judgment she sought and to which she stipulated would "trifle with the courts." *Id.* at 166.

3. Under *K.G., Kristine H.,* and *Elisa B.*, what result in:

a. a "traditional" surrogacy case, in which a husband and wife contract with a woman to bear "their" child through artificial insemination with the husband's sperm, when the woman seeks to retain custody of the child after its birth? *See Moschetta v. Moschetta,* 25 Cal App 4th 1218, 30 Cal Rptr 2d 893 (1994).

b. a gestational surrogacy case, in which a husband and wife contract with a woman to bear "their" child, using a preembryo created from husband's sperm and wife's ova, when the woman seeks to retain custody of the child after its birth?

c. a gestational surrogacy case, in which a husband and wife contract with a woman to bear "their" child, using a preembryo created from donated sperm and donated ova, when the husband seeks to avoid the responsibilities of parentage after the child's birth?   d a gestational surrogacy case, in which a husband and wife contract with a woman to bear "their" child, using a preembryo created from donated sperm and donated ova, when the husband seeks to avoid the responsibilities of parenthood after the child's birth? *See Buzzanca v. Buzzanca,*

61 Cal App 4th 1410, 72 Cal Rptr 2d 280.

e. a case in which husband and wife utilize what they believe to be a donated preembryo and IVF to produce "their" child and it later develops that the preembryo was misappropriated by the fertility clinic? *See* Alice M. Noble-Allgire, *Switched at the Fertility Clinic: Determining Maternal Rights When a Child is Born from Stolen or Misdelivered Genetic Material,* 64 Mo L Rev 417 (1999).

Add at p. 881.

In Europe in 2000, IVF and ICSI produced deliveries of twins in 24% of cases, triplets in 2.0%, and quadruplets in 0.04%. In the United States in 1998, the respective rates were 31.7%, 6.2%, and 0.2%. Belgium has restricted the number of embryos that can be transferred into healthy younger women to one, and Sweden provides insurance incentives for single-embryo transfers. *See* John A. Robertson, *Reproductive Technology in Germany and the United States: An Essay in Comparative Law and Bioethics*, 43 Colum. J. Transnat'l L. 189 (2004).

Chapter 7
AUTONOMY IN A BUREAUCRATIC WORLD

SECTION 1. ALLOCATING MEDICAL RESOURCES: WHO SHOULD DECIDE? WHAT CRITERIA SHOULD WE USE?

C. The Allocation Problem in Microcosm: The Case of Organ Transplants

Replace Adult Liver Transplantation Policy, at p. 913 with:

3.6 ALLOCATION OF LIVERS.

Unless otherwise approved . . . the allocation of livers according to the following system is mandatory. For the purpose of enabling physicians to apply their consensus medical judgement for the benefit of liver transplant candidates as a group, each candidate will be assigned a status code or probability of candidate death derived from a mortality risk score corresponding to the degree of medical urgency as described in Policy 3.6.4 below. Mortality risk scores shall be determined by the prognostic factors specified in Tables 1 and 2 and calculated in accordance with the Model for End-Stage Liver Disease (MELD) Scoring System. . . . Candidates will be stratified within MELD . . . score by blood type similarity as described in Policy 3.6.2. No individual or property rights are conferred by this system of liver allocation.

Livers will be offered to candidates with an assigned Status of 1A and 1B in descending point sequence with the candidate having the highest number of points receiving the highest priority before being offered for patients listed in other categories within distribution areas as noted below. Following Status 1, livers will be offered to candidates based upon their probability of candidate death derived from assigned MELD . . . scores, as applicable, in descending point sequence with the candidate having the highest probability ranking receiving the highest priority before being offered to candidates having lower probability rankings.

At each level of distribution, adult livers (i.e., greater than or equal to 18 years old) will be allocated in the following sequence (adult donor liver allocation algorithm):

Local

1. Status 1A candidates in descending point order

Regional

2. Status 1A candidates in descending point

Local

3. Status 1B candidates in descending order.

Regional

4. Status 1B candidates in descending point order

Local

5. Candidates with MELD/PELD Scores >=15 in descending order of mortality risk scores (probability of candidate death)

Regional

6. Candidates with MELD/PELD Scores >=15 in descending order of mortality risk scores (probability of candidate death)

Local

7. Candidates with MELD/PELD Scores < 15 in descending order of mortality risk scores (probability of candidate death)

Regional

8. Candidates with MELD/PELD Scores < 15 in descending order of mortality risk scores (probability of candidate death).

National

9. Status 1A candidates in descending point order

10. Status 1B candidates in descending point order

11. All other candidates in descending order of mortality risk scores (probability of candidate death)

3.6.2 Blood Type Similarity Stratification/Points.

For Status 1A and 1B transplant candidates, patients with the same ABO type as the liver donor shall receive 10 points. Candidates with compatible but not identical ABO types shall receive 5 points, and candidates with incompatible types shall receive 0 points. . . . Within each MELD . . . score, donor livers shall be offered to transplant candidates who are ABO-identical with the donor first, then to candidates who are ABO-compatible, followed by candidates who are ABO-incompatible with the donor.

3.6.3 Time Waiting.

Transplant candidates on the UNOS patient waiting list shall accrue waiting time within Status 1A or 1B or any assigned MELD . . . score; however, waiting time accrued while listed at a lower MELD score will not be counted toward liver allocation if the patient is upgraded to a higher MELD score. Stratification of patients within a particular MELD score shall be based on total waiting time currently and previously accrued at that score on the same waiting list registration added to waiting time accrued at any higher MELD score. For example, if there are 2 persons with a MELD score of 30 who were both of identical blood types with the donor, the patient with the longest accrued waiting time in MELD score 30 or higher would receive the first offer. Waiting time will not be accrued by patients awaiting a liver transplant while they are registered on the UNOS Patient Waiting List as inactive.

Patients in Status 1A or 1B will receive waiting time points based on their waiting time in that Status. Ten points will be accrued by the patient waiting for the longest period for a liver transplant and proportionately fewer points will be accrued by those patients with shorter tenure. For example, if there were 75 persons of O blood type waiting who were of a size compatible with a blood group O donor, the person waiting the longest would accrue 10 points (75/75 x 10). A person whose rank order was 60 would accrue 2 points. ((75-60)/75 x 10 = 2).

3.6.4 Degree of Medical Urgency.

Each candidate is assigned a status code or mortality risk score (probability of candidate death) which corresponds to how medically urgent it is that the patient receive a transplant.

3.6.4.1 Adult Candidate Status.

Medical urgency is assigned to an adult liver transplant candidate (greater than or equal to 18 years of age) based on either the criteria defined below for Status 1A, or the candidate's mortality risk score as determined by the prognostic factors specified in Table 1 and calculated in accordance with the MELD Scoring System. A candidate who does not have a MELD score that, in the judgment of the candidate's transplant physician, appropriately reflects the patient's medical urgency, may nevertheless be assigned a higher MELD score upon application by his/her transplant physician(s) and justification to the applicable Regional Review Board that the candidate is considered, by consensus medical judgment, using accepted medical criteria, to have an urgency and potential for benefit comparable to that of other candidates having the higher MELD score. The justification must include a rationale for incorporating the exceptional case as part of MELD calculation. . . .

Insert on page 994 after the first two lines.

SECTION 2. THE PATIENT IN THE BUREAUCRACY

B. Medical Ethics in the Age of Bureaucracy

1. Stating the Problem: Conflicts of Interest

AETNA HEALTH, INC. v. DAVILA
124 S Ct 2488 (2004)

Justice THOMAS delivered the opinion of the Court.

In these consolidated cases, two individuals sued their respective health maintenance organizations (HMOs) for alleged failures to exercise ordinary care in the handling of coverage decisions, in violation of a duty imposed by the Texas Health Care Liability Act (THCLA).

I

A

Respondent Juan Davila is a participant, and respondent Ruby Calad is a beneficiary, in ERISA-regulated employee benefit plans. Their respective plan sponsors had entered into agreements with petitioners, Aetna Health Inc. and CIGNA Healthcare of Texas, Inc., to administer the plans. Under Davila's plan, for instance, Aetna reviews requests for coverage and pays providers, such as doctors, hospitals, and nursing homes, which perform covered services for members; under Calad's plan sponsor's agreement, CIGNA is responsible for plan benefits and coverage decisions.

Respondents both suffered injuries allegedly arising from Aetna's and CIGNA's decisions not to provide coverage for certain treatment and services recommended by respondents' treating physicians. Davila's treating physician prescribed Vioxx to remedy

Davila's arthritis pain, but Aetna refused to pay for it. Davila did not appeal or contest this decision, nor did he purchase Vioxx with his own resources and seek reimbursement. Instead, Davila began taking Naprosyn, from which he allegedly suffered a severe reaction that required extensive treatment and hospitalization. Calad underwent surgery, and although her treating physician recommended an extended hospital stay, a CIGNA discharge nurse determined that Calad did not meet the plan's criteria for a continued hospital stay. CIGNA consequently denied coverage for the extended hospital stay. Calad experienced postsurgery complications forcing her to return to the hospital. She alleges that these complications would not have occurred had CIGNA approved coverage for a longer hospital stay.

Respondents brought separate suits in Texas state court against petitioners. Invoking THCLA § 88.002(a), respondents argued that petitioners' refusal to cover the requested services violated their "duty to exercise ordinary care when making health care treatment decisions," and that these refusals "proximately caused" their injuries. Petitioners removed the cases to Federal District Courts, arguing that respondents' causes of action fit within the scope of, and were therefore completely pre-empted by, ERISA § 502(a). The respective District Courts agreed, and declined to remand the cases to state court. Because respondents refused to amend their complaints to bring explicit ERISA claims, the District Courts dismissed the complaints with prejudice.

B

Both Davila and Calad appealed the refusals to remand to state court.... The Court of Appeals recognized that state causes of action that "duplicat[e] or fal[l] within the scope of an ERISA § 502(a) remedy" are completely pre-empted and hence removable to federal court. After examining the causes of action available under § 502(a), the Court of Appeals determined that respondents' claims could possibly fall under only two: § 502(a)(1)(B), which provides a cause of action for the recovery of wrongfully denied benefits, and § 502(a)(2), which allows suit against a plan fiduciary for breaches of fiduciary duty to the plan.

Analyzing § 502(a)(2) first, the Court of Appeals concluded that, under *Pegram v. Herdrich*, 530 U.S. 211 (2000), the decisions for which petitioners were being sued were "mixed eligibility and treatment decisions" and hence were not fiduciary in nature. The Court of Appeals next determined that respondents' claims did not fall within §

502(a)(1)(B)'s scope. It found significant that respondents "assert tort claims," while § 502(a)(1)(B) "creates a cause of action for breach of contract," and also that respondents "are not seeking reimbursement for benefits denied them," but rather request "tort damages" arising from "an external, statutorily imposed duty of 'ordinary care.'" From *Rush Prudential HMO, Inc. v. Moran,* 536 U.S. 355 (2002), the Court of Appeals derived the principle that complete pre-emption is limited to situations in which "States ... duplicate the causes of action listed in ERISA § 502(a)," and concluded that "[b]ecause the THCLA does not provide an action for collecting benefits," it fell outside the scope of § 502(a)(1)(B).

II . . . .

B

Congress enacted ERISA to "protect ... the interests of participants in employee benefit plans and their beneficiaries" by setting out substantive regulatory requirements for employee benefit plans and to "provid[e] for appropriate remedies, sanctions, and ready access to the Federal courts." 29 U.S.C. § 1001(b). The purpose of ERISA is to provide a uniform regulatory regime over employee benefit plans. To this end, ERISA includes expansive pre-emption provisions which are intended to ensure that employee benefit plan regulation would be "exclusively a federal concern."

ERISA's "comprehensive legislative scheme" includes "an integrated system of procedures for enforcement." This integrated enforcement mechanism, ERISA § 502(a), is a distinctive feature of ERISA, and essential to accomplish Congress' purpose of creating a comprehensive statute for the regulation of employee benefit plans. As the Court said in *Pilot Life Ins. Co. v. Dedeaux,* 481 U.S. 41 (1987):

> "[T]he detailed provisions of § 502(a) set forth a comprehensive civil enforcement scheme that represents a careful balancing of the need for prompt and fair claims settlement procedures against the public interest in encouraging the formation of employee benefit plans. The policy choices reflected in the inclusion of certain remedies and the exclusion of others under the federal scheme would be completely undermined if ERISA-plan participants and beneficiaries were free to obtain remedies under state law that Congress rejected in ERISA. 'The six carefully

integrated civil enforcement provisions found in § 502(a) of the statute as finally enacted ... provide strong evidence that Congress did *not* intend to authorize other remedies that it simply forgot to incorporate expressly.'"

Therefore, any state-law cause of action that duplicates, supplements, or supplants the ERISA civil enforcement remedy conflicts with the clear congressional intent to make the ERISA remedy exclusive and is therefore pre-empted.

The pre-emptive force of ERISA § 502(a) is still stronger. In *Metropolitan Life Ins. Co. v. Taylor,* 481 U.S. 58, 65-66 (1987), the Court determined that the similarity of the language used in the Labor Management Relations Act, 1947 (LMRA), and ERISA, combined with the "clear intention" of Congress "to make § 502(a)(1)(B) suits brought by participants or beneficiaries federal questions for the purposes of federal court jurisdiction in like manner as § 301 of the LMRA," established that ERISA § 502(a)(1)(B)'s pre-emptive force mirrored the pre-emptive force of LMRA § 301. Since LMRA § 301 converts state causes of action into federal ones for purposes of determining the propriety of removal, so too does ERISA § 502(a)(1)(B). Thus, the ERISA civil enforcement mechanism is one of those provisions with such "extraordinary pre-emptive power" that it "converts an ordinary state common law complaint into one stating a federal claim for purposes of the well-pleaded complaint rule." Hence, "causes of action within the scope of the civil enforcement provisions of § 502(a) [are] removable to federal court."

III

A

ERISA § 502(a)(1)(B) provides:

"A civil action may be brought--(1) by a participant or beneficiary--... (B) to recover benefits due to him under the terms of his plan, to enforce his rights under the terms of the plan, or to clarify his rights to future benefits under the terms of the plan."

This provision is relatively straightforward. If a participant or beneficiary believes that benefits promised to him under the terms of the plan are not provided, he can bring suit seeking provision of those benefits. A participant or beneficiary can also bring suit generically to "enforce his rights" under the plan, or to clarify any of his rights to future benefits. Any dispute over the precise terms of the plan is resolved by a court under a *de novo* review standard, unless the terms of the plan "giv[e] the administrator or fiduciary discretionary authority to determine eligibility for benefits or to construe the terms of the plan." *Firestone Tire & Rubber Co. v. Bruch,* 489 U.S. 101, 115 (1989).

It follows that if an individual brings suit complaining of a denial of coverage for medical care, where the individual is entitled to such coverage only because of the terms of an ERISA-regulated employee benefit plan, and where no legal duty (state or federal) independent of ERISA or the plan terms is violated, then the suit falls "within the scope of" ERISA § 502(a)(1)(B). In other words, if an individual, at some point in time, could have brought his claim under ERISA § 502(a)(1)(B), and where there is no other independent legal duty that is implicated by a defendant's actions, then the individual's cause of action is completely pre-empted by ERISA § 502(a)(1)(B).

To determine whether respondents' causes of action fall "within the scope" of ERISA § 502(a)(1)(B), we must examine respondents' complaints, the statute on which their claims are based (the THCLA), and the various plan documents. Davila alleges that Aetna provides health coverage under his employer's health benefits plan. Davila also alleges that after his primary care physician prescribed Vioxx, Aetna refused to pay for it. The only action complained of was Aetna's refusal to approve payment for Davila's Vioxx prescription. Further, the only relationship Aetna had with Davila was its partial administration of Davila's employer's benefit plan.

Similarly, Calad alleges that she receives, as her husband's beneficiary under an ERISA-regulated benefit plan, health coverage from CIGNA. She alleges that she was informed by CIGNA, upon admittance into a hospital for major surgery, that she would be authorized to stay for only one day. She also alleges that CIGNA, acting through a discharge nurse, refused to authorize more than a single day despite the advice and recommendation of her treating physician. Calad contests only CIGNA's decision to refuse coverage for her hospital stay. And, as in Davila's case, the only connection between Calad and CIGNA is CIGNA's administration of portions of Calad's ERISA-regulated benefit plan.

It is clear, then, that respondents complain only about denials of coverage promised under the terms of ERISA-regulated employee benefit plans. Upon the denial of benefits, respondents could have paid for the treatment themselves and then sought reimbursement through a § 502(a)(1)(B) action, or sought a preliminary injunction.

Respondents contend, however, that the complained-of actions violate legal duties that arise independently of ERISA or the terms of the employee benefit plans at issue in these cases. Both respondents brought suit specifically under the THCLA, alleging that petitioners "controlled, influenced, participated in and made decisions which affected the quality of the diagnosis, care, and treatment provided" in a manner that violated "the duty of ordinary care set forth in §§ 88.001 and 88.002." Respondents contend that this duty of ordinary care is an independent legal duty. They analogize to this Court's decisions interpreting LMRA § 301 with particular focus on *Caterpillar Inc. v. Williams,* 482 U.S. 386 (1987) (suit for breach of individual employment contract, even if defendant's action also constituted a breach of an entirely separate collective bargaining agreement, not pre-empted by LMRA § 301). Because this duty of ordinary care arises independently of any duty imposed by ERISA or the plan terms, the argument goes, any civil action to enforce this duty is not within the scope of the ERISA civil enforcement mechanism.

The duties imposed by the THCLA in the context of these cases, however, do not arise independently of ERISA or the plan terms. The THCLA does impose a duty on managed care entities to "exercise ordinary care when making health care treatment decisions," and makes them liable for damages proximately caused by failures to abide by that duty. However, if a managed care entity correctly concluded that, under the terms of the relevant plan, a particular treatment was not covered, the managed care entity's denial of coverage would not be a proximate cause of any injuries arising from the denial. Rather, the failure of the plan itself to cover the requested treatment would be the proximate cause. More significantly, the THCLA clearly states that "[t]he standards in Subsections (a) and (b) create no obligation on the part of the health insurance carrier, health maintenance organization, or other managed care entity to provide to an insured or enrollee treatment which is not covered by the health care plan of the entity." Hence, a managed care entity could not be subject to liability under the THCLA if it denied coverage for any treatment not covered by the health care plan that it was administering.

Thus, interpretation of the terms of respondents' benefit plans forms an essential part of their THCLA claim, and THCLA liability would exist here only because of petitioners' administration of ERISA-regulated benefit plans. Petitioners' potential liability under the THCLA in these cases, then, derives entirely from the particular rights and obligations established by the benefit plans. So, unlike the state-law claims in *Caterpillar, supra,* respondents' THCLA causes of action are not entirely independent of the federally regulated contract itself.

Hence, respondents bring suit only to rectify a wrongful denial of benefits promised under ERISA-regulated plans, and do not attempt to remedy any violation of a legal duty independent of ERISA. We hold that respondents' state causes of action fall "within the scope of" ERISA § 502(a)(1)(B), *Metropolitan Life,* 481 U.S., at 66 and are therefore completely pre-empted by ERISA § 502 and removable to federal district court.

B

The Court of Appeals came to a contrary conclusion for several reasons, all of them erroneous. First, the Court of Appeals found significant that respondents "assert a tort claim for tort damages" rather than "a contract claim for contract damages," and that respondents "are not seeking reimbursement for benefits denied them." But, distinguishing between pre-empted and non-pre-empted claims based on the particular label affixed to them would "elevate form over substance and allow parties to evade" the pre-emptive scope of ERISA simply "by relabeling their contract claims as claims for tortious breach of contract." Nor can the mere fact that the state cause of action attempts to authorize remedies beyond those authorized by ERISA § 502(a) put the cause of action outside the scope of the ERISA civil enforcement mechanism. In *Pilot Life, Metropolitan Life,* and *Ingersoll-Rand,* the plaintiffs all brought state claims that were labeled either tort or tort-like. And, in all these cases, the plaintiffs' claims were pre-empted. The limited remedies available under ERISA are an inherent part of the "careful balancing" between ensuring fair and prompt enforcement of rights under a plan and the encouragement of the creation of such plans.

Second, the Court of Appeals believed that "the wording of [respondents'] plans is immaterial" to their claims, as "they invoke an external, statutorily imposed duty of 'ordinary care.'" But as we have already discussed, the wording of the plans is certainly material to their state causes of action, and the duty of "ordinary care" that the

THCLA creates is not external to their rights under their respective plans.

Ultimately, the Court of Appeals rested its decision on one line from *Rush Prudential.* There, we described our holding in *Ingersoll-Rand* as follows: "[W]hile state law duplicated the elements of a claim available under ERISA, it converted the remedy from an equitable one under § 1132(a)(3) (available exclusively in federal district courts) into a legal one for money damages (available in a state tribunal)." The point of this sentence was to describe why the state cause of action in *Ingersoll-Rand* was pre-empted by ERISA § 502(a): It was pre-empted because it attempted to convert an equitable remedy into a legal remedy. Nowhere in *Rush Prudential* did we suggest that the pre-emptive force of ERISA § 502(a) is limited to the situation in which a state cause of action precisely duplicates a cause of action under ERISA § 502(a).

Nor would it be consistent with our precedent to conclude that only strictly duplicative state causes of action are pre-empted. Frequently, in order to receive exemplary damages on a state claim, a plaintiff must prove facts beyond the bare minimum necessary to establish entitlement to an award. Cf. *Allis-Chalmers* (bad-faith refusal to honor a claim needed to be proved in order to recover exemplary damages). In order to recover for mental anguish, for instance, the plaintiffs in *Ingersoll-Rand* and *Metropolitan Life* would presumably have had to prove the existence of mental anguish; there is no such element in an ordinary suit brought under ERISA § 502(a)(1)(B). This did not save these state causes of action from pre-emption. Congress' intent to make the ERISA civil enforcement mechanism exclusive would be undermined if state causes of action that supplement the ERISA § 502(a) remedies were permitted, even if the elements of the state cause of action did not precisely duplicate the elements of an ERISA claim.

C

Respondents also argue--for the first time in their brief to this Court--that the THCLA is a law that regulates insurance, and hence that ERISA § 514(b)(2)(A) saves their causes of action from pre-emption (and thereby from complete pre-emption). This argument is unavailing. The existence of a comprehensive remedial scheme can demonstrate an "overpowering federal policy" that determines the interpretation of a statutory provision designed to save state law from being pre-empted. ERISA's civil enforcement provision is one such example.

As this Court stated in *Pilot Life,* "our understanding of [§ 514(b)(2)(A)] must be informed by the legislative intent concerning the civil enforcement provisions provided by ERISA § 502(a). The Court concluded that "[t]he policy choices reflected in the inclusion of certain remedies and the exclusion of others under the federal scheme would be completely undermined if ERISA-plan participants and beneficiaries were free to obtain remedies under state law that Congress rejected in ERISA." The Court then held, based on

> "the common-sense understanding of the saving clause, the McCarran-Ferguson Act factors defining the business of insurance, and, *most importantly,* the clear expression of congressional intent that ERISA's civil enforcement scheme be exclusive, ... that [the plaintiff's] state law suit asserting improper processing of a claim for benefits under an ERISA-regulated plan is not saved by § 514(b)(2)(A)."

Pilot Life's reasoning applies here with full force. Allowing respondents to proceed with their state-law suits would "pose an obstacle to the purposes and objectives of Congress." As this Court has recognized in both *Rush Prudential* and *Pilot Life,* ERISA § 514(b)(2)(A) must be interpreted in light of the congressional intent to create an exclusive federal remedy in ERISA § 502(a). Under ordinary principles of conflict pre-emption, then, even a state law that can arguably be characterized as "regulating insurance" will be pre-empted if it provides a separate vehicle to assert a claim for benefits outside of, or in addition to, ERISA's remedial scheme.

IV

Respondents, their *amici,* and some Courts of Appeals have relied heavily upon *Pegram v. Herdrich,* 530 U.S. 211 (2000), in arguing that ERISA does not pre-empt or completely pre-empt state suits such as respondents'. They contend that *Pegram* makes it clear that causes of action such as respondents' do not "relate to [an] employee benefit plan," ERISA § 514(a) and hence are not pre-empted.

Pegram cannot be read so broadly. In *Pegram,* the plaintiff sued her physician-owned-and-operated HMO (which provided medical coverage through plaintiff's employer pursuant to an

ERISA-regulated benefit plan) and her treating physician, both for medical malpractice and for a breach of an ERISA fiduciary duty. The plaintiff's treating physician was also the person charged with administering plaintiff's benefits; it was she who decided whether certain treatments were covered. We reasoned that the physician's "eligibility decision and the treatment decision were inextricably mixed." We concluded that "Congress did not intend [the defendant HMO] or any other HMO to be treated as a fiduciary to the extent that it makes mixed eligibility decisions acting through its physicians."

A benefit determination under ERISA, though, is generally a fiduciary act. "At common law, fiduciary duties characteristically attach to decisions about managing assets and distributing property to beneficiaries." *Pegram*. Hence, a benefit determination is part and parcel of the ordinary fiduciary responsibilities connected to the administration of a plan. See *Varity Corp. v. Howe,* 516 U.S. 489, 512 (1996) (relevant plan fiduciaries owe a "fiduciary duty with respect to the interpretation of plan documents and the payment of claims"). The fact that a benefits determination is infused with medical judgments does not alter this result.

Pegram itself recognized this principle. *Pegram,* in highlighting its conclusion that "mixed eligibility decisions" were not fiduciary in nature, contrasted the operation of "[t]raditional trustees administer[ing] a medical trust" and "physicians through whom HMOs act." A traditional medical trust is administered by "paying out money to buy medical care, whereas physicians making mixed eligibility decisions consume the money as well." And, significantly, the Court stated that "[p]rivate trustees do not make treatment judgments." But a trustee managing a medical trust undoubtedly must make administrative decisions that require the exercise of medical judgment. Petitioners are not the employers of respondents' treating physicians and are therefore in a somewhat analogous position to that of a trustee for a traditional medical trust.

ERISA itself and its implementing regulations confirm this interpretation. ERISA defines a fiduciary as any person "to the extent ... he has any discretionary authority or discretionary responsibility in the administration of [an employee benefit] plan." § 3(21)(A)(iii). When administering employee benefit plans, HMOs must make discretionary decisions regarding eligibility for plan benefits, and, in this regard, must be treated as plan fiduciaries. Also, ERISA § 503, which specifies minimum requirements for a plan's claim procedure, requires plans to "afford a reasonable opportunity to any participant whose claim for benefits has been denied for a full and fair review by the appropriate named fiduciary of the decision denying the claim." This strongly suggests that the ultimate decisionmaker in a plan regarding an award of benefits must be a fiduciary and must be acting as a fiduciary when determining a participant's or beneficiary's claim. The relevant regulations also establish extensive requirements to ensure full and fair review of benefit denials. See 29 CFR § 2560.503-1 (2004). These regulations, on their face, apply equally to health benefit plans and other plans, and do not draw distinctions between medical and nonmedical benefits determinations. Indeed, the regulations strongly imply that benefits determinations involving medical judgments are, just as much as any other benefits determinations, actions by plan fiduciaries. See, e.g., § 2560.503-1(h)(3)(iii). Classifying any entity with discretionary authority over benefits determinations as anything but a plan fiduciary would thus conflict with ERISA's statutory and regulatory scheme.

Since administrators making benefits determinations, even determinations based extensively on medical judgments, are ordinarily acting as plan fiduciaries, it was essential to *Pegram*'s conclusion that the decisions challenged there were truly "mixed eligibility and treatment decisions," *i.e.,* medical necessity decisions made by the plaintiff's treating physician *qua* treating physician and *qua* benefits administrator. Put another way, the reasoning of *Pegram* "only make[s] sense where the underlying negligence also plausibly constitutes medical maltreatment by a party who can be deemed to be a treating physician or such a physician's employer." *Cicio v. Does,* 321 F.3d 83, 109 (C.A.2 2003) (Calabresi, J., dissenting in part). Here, however, petitioners are neither respondents' treating physicians nor the employers of respondents' treating physicians. Petitioners' coverage decisions, then, are pure eligibility decisions, and *Pegram* is not implicated.

V

We hold that respondents' causes of action, brought to remedy only the denial of benefits under ERISA-regulated benefit plans, fall within the scope of, and are completely pre-empted by, ERISA § 502(a)(1)(B), and thus removable to federal district court. The judgment of the Court of Appeals is reversed, and the cases are remanded for further proceedings consistent with this opinion.

Justice GINSBURG, with whom Justice BREYER joins, concurring.

The Court today holds that the claims respondents asserted under Texas law are totally preempted by § 502(a). That decision is consistent with our governing case law on ERISA's preemptive scope. I therefore join the Court's opinion. But, with greater enthusiasm, . . . I also join "the rising judicial chorus urging that Congress and [this] Court revisit what is an unjust and increasingly tangled ERISA regime."

Because the Court has coupled an encompassing interpretation of ERISA's preemptive force with a cramped construction of the "equitable relief" allowable under § 502(a)(3), a "regulatory vacuum" exists: "[V]irtually all state law remedies are preempted but very few federal substitutes are provided."

1054. Insert after the end of the first paragraph.

But let us return to the problem that got us here, the question whether there is any effective governmental approach to the problem posed by physicians and MCOs with conflicts of interests. A recent study of conflicts of interests suggests the recalcitrance of the problem. Daylian M. Cain et al, *The Dirt on Coming Clean: Perverse Effects of Disclosing Conflicts of Interest*, 34 J Legal Studies 1 (2005).

> First, estimating the impact of a conflict of interest on an advice giver is an extraordinarily difficult problem that requires both economic and psychological insight. . . . [O]ne would want to know the extent to which the advisor embraces professional norms or is instead corrupt. One would also want to know how tempting the advisor finds the incentives for providing biased advice, and one would want to have an accurate mental model of how such incentives can bias advice. However, prior research suggests that most people have an incorrect understanding of the psychological mechanisms that transform conflicts of interest into biased advice. While most people think conflicts of interest are a problem of overt corruption, that is, that professionals consciously and intentionally misrepresent the advice they give so as to secure personal gain, considerable research suggests that bias is more frequently the result of motivational processes that are unintentional and unconscious . . . .
>
> Second, there is at least suggestive evidence that people tend to be naturally trusting and credulous toward their own advisors. . . . [F]or example, research shows that while many people are ready to acknowledge that doctors might generally be affected by conflicts of interest, few can imagine that their own doctors would be affected . . . . Indeed, . . . disclosure could sometimes increase rather than decrease trust, especially if the person with the conflict of interest . . . issues the disclosure. Research suggests that when managers

offer negative financial disclosures about future earnings, they are . . . more credible agents, at least in the short term. . . .

Third, even when estimators realize that they should make some adjustment for the conflict of interest that is disclosed, such adjustments are likely to be insufficient. As a rule, people have trouble unlearning, ignoring, or suppressing the use of knowledge (such as biased advice) even if they are aware that it is inaccurate . . . . Research on anchoring, for example, shows that quantitative judgments are often drawn toward numbers (the anchors) that happen to be mentally available. This effect holds even when those anchors are known to be irrelevant. . . . or even manipulative . . . . Research on the "curse of knowledge" . . . shows that people's judgments are influenced even by information they know they should ignore. And research on what has been called the "failure of evidentiary discreditation" shows that when the evidence on which beliefs were revised is totally discredited, those beliefs do not revert to their original states but show a persistent effect of the discredited evidence . . . Furthermore, attempts to willfully suppress undesired thoughts can lead to ironic rebound effects, in some cases even increasing the spontaneous use of undesired knowledge . . . .

Logically, it is not clear how self-interested advisors should respond to disclosure of their conflict of interest. On one hand, disclosure might deter advisors from giving biased advice by increasing their concern that estimators (now thought to be alerted by disclosure) will completely discount extreme advice or attribute corrupt motives to advice that seems even remotely questionable. On the other hand, advisors might be tempted to provide even more biased advice, exaggerating their advice in order to counteract the diminished weight that they expect estimators to place on it . . . .

In an "admittedly stylized experiment," Cain et al found that disclosure "benefited the providers of information but not its recipients." They speculated that disclosure can "fail because it (1) gives advisors strategic reason and moral license to further exaggerate their advice and (2) it may not lead to sufficient discounting to counteract this effect." In sum,

The general conclusion that disclosure is most likely to help the sophisticated estimator is somewhat dismaying, since unsophisticated estimators are exactly the ones who are most likely to need protection from exploitation. . . . The paradigmatic example of the person who disclosure is unlikely to help is the medical patient who deals with only a small number of doctors, does so infrequently, lacks expertise in medicine, and enters the patient-doctor relationship trusting the doctor.